3167/75

ESSENTIALS OF
MODERN GERMAN GRAMMAR

ESSENTIALS OF
MODERN GERMAN GRAMMAR

REVISED EDITION

BY

J. A. CORBETT B.A. Ph.D.

FORMER EDUCATION OFFICER BOROUGH OF LUTON
FORMERLY SENIOR MODERN LANGUAGE MASTER
THE COUNTY SCHOOL FOR BOYS BROMLEY

HARRAP   LONDON

First published in Great Britain 1935
by GEORGE G. HARRAP & CO. LTD
182-184 High Holborn, London WC1V 7AX

Revised edition 1948

Reprinted: 1952; 1956; 1958; 1960;
1962; 1965; 1968; 1973

ISBN 0 245 55940 X

Printed in Great Britain by
Redwood Press Limited
Trowbridge, Wiltshire

PREFACE

In writing this book I have had in mind the requirements of those who have already had some grounding in German. Experience in the teaching of the upper forms of schools and of university classes has shown me that, however well trained in the early stages a student may be, there is a need for the study of a certain nucleus of grammatical knowledge. I have tried to present this without the use of involved terminology, and I have been concerned more with the language as used to-day than with rules and usages which, in practice, have been discarded.

A particular feature of the book is the treatment of prepositions. I have found that many English students make mistakes for lack of a list which they could learn or refer to when the question arises as to the case governed by a preposition in a definite context.

Lack of time and overcrowding of classes in schools too often militate against the success of the best methods of teaching German. Accordingly, it is not surprising that students often reach the sixth form or even the university without acquiring an ability to use the right preposition in the right place. In translation they tend to use the German preposition which seems cognate with or parallel to the English, and show a resigned bewilderment when it is revealed to them that, although we speak of "belief *in* God," the German will say **Glauben an Gott.**

Anyone who wishes to obtain some mastery of the German language should make the necessary effort and learn the examples of the prepositions in actual use. For those who require information more quickly there is an index.

My thanks are due and are gladly given to Miss G. Craig Houston, M.A., lecturer in charge of German in the Durham Colleges, Durham University, for help with the section on prepositions; to Fräulein Käthe Kröncke, assistant in the High School for Girls, Bromley; and to Dr Gunther Wilmsen and Studienrat Otto Eichele, assistants in the County School for Boys, Bromley, for advice during the revision of examples.

J. A. C.

NOTE TO THE REVISED EDITION

THIS revised edition includes additional points which experience has shown to be necessary. Quotations from National Socialist newspapers have been replaced by less tendentious examples. Section numbers have been placed at the top of each page for easier reference.

Since this Grammar was originally published I have been urged to produce a book of Exercises. This need has, I think, been met, at least so far as Fifth and first-year Sixth form work is concerned, by the publication in 1937 by George G. Harrap and Co., Ltd., of *Classified Revision Exercises in German*, compiled by Otto Eichele and myself in collaboration.

For a number of useful suggestions for the revised edition of this Grammar, I am again indebted to Miss G. Craig Houston, M.A., now Reader in German at Westfield College. Furthermore, I must take this opportunity of thanking Dr R. J. M. Jaffé for his careful checking of the text and his valuable help on several points of German usage.

J. A. C.

1947.

CONTENTS

I. ORTHOGRAPHY

1. The German Alphabet.

(a) *German Type*

German Letters	Name (Phonetic Spelling)	German Letters	Name (Phonetic Spelling)
a 𝔄, a	['aː]	n 𝔑, n	['ɛn]
b 𝔅, b	[beː]	o 𝔒, o	['oː]
c ℭ, c	[tseː]	p 𝔓, p	[peː]
d 𝔇, d	[deː]	q 𝔔, q	[kuː]
e 𝔈, e	['eː]	r 𝔑, r	['ɛr]
f 𝔉, f	['ɛf]	s 𝔖, ſ, s	['ɛs]
g 𝔊, g	[geː]	t 𝔗, t	[teː]
h 𝔥, h	[haː]	u 𝔘, u	['uː]
i 𝔍, i	['iː]	v 𝔙, v	[fau]
j 𝔍, j	[jɔt]	w 𝔚, w	[veː]
k 𝔎, k	[kaː]	x 𝔛, x	['iks]
l 𝔏, l	['ɛl]	y 𝔜, y	['ypsilon]
m 𝔐, m	['ɛm]	z 𝔷, ʒ	[tsɛt]

(b) *German Script*

Capitals

Small letters

Compound Consonants:

ch (ch)	sch (sch)	th (th)
ck (ck)	tz (tz)	ß (ss, sz)

2. German Type.

Both German and Roman types are used in German printed matter. Most scientific periodicals and many newspapers are printed in Roman type.

Note.—(i) That in German type ch, ck, tz, and ß are ligatured (die Ligatur); t and z will not be ligatured, when the letters belong to different components of the word, thus in entzünden and Eiszeit there is no ligature.

(ii) To emphasize words in German the letters are spaced (der Sperrdruck). Compare italics in English.

> Sie konnte nur e i n e n Mann lieben.
> She could love only *one* man.

> Er hat nur englische Bücher gern
> He only likes *English* books.

3. German Script.

Both forms of handwriting are in use in Germany. Note the sign ‿ over the small *u*. It distinguishes u from similar letters. It is incorrect to write ˘ over u in Roman script; some Germans do so. The sign is the remnant of an old 'o'; Middle High German 'buoch' became Modern German Buch.

4. Small s in German print and script.

(*a*) The long ſ and *f* are used at the beginning and in the middle of words: ſolch, deſſen, *folch, deſſen*. Compare the long s in old English printing and handwriting.

(*b*) The other form s and *s*, is used at the end of words, *e.g.*, das Wachs. Notice also its use in a compound word such as der Hochzeitsgaſt, s being the last letter of the component Hochzeits.

Note.—Rule (*b*) does not apply to :

(i) Dresden, etc.
(ii) Nouns of foreign origin ending in ‑ismus, *e.g.*, Fanatismus.

5. Use of ſſ and ß (ss and sz).

(*a*) German type and German script use respectively ſſ and *ſſ* between vowels if the preceding vowel is short in pronunciation, *e.g.*, überdrüſſig.

(*b*) ß and *ß* are used (i) at the end of words: das Schloß;

(ii) after a long syllable: die Straßenbahn; (iii) in compound words: die Gießkanne; (iv) after a short syllable if it is not immediately followed by a vowel: wußte.

(*c*) When German is printed in Roman type a form ß (= sz) is sometimes used to represent ß. In Latin type and Latin script sz and often ss are used for the printed ß and the written *ß* In German script and German type the distinction must be observed.

6. Modification of Vowels (Umlaut, *i.e.*, changed sound).

(*a*) The vowels a, o, u, and the diphthong au are modified in certain words by the use of the sign ˝; thus, ä, ö, ü, äu. This sign is derived from the German script small e (*m*); its effect on the vowel is that of combining an e with it.

(*b*) e is used instead of the ˝ to modify vowels

  (i) In certain proper names, *e.g.*, Goethe.

  (ii) Very often after capital letters in German type and sometimes in Roman type; *e.g.*, Eine der Ueberraschungen.

  (iii) In some old printing and imitations thereof.

N.B.—In writing German use always the ˝ sign except in such proper names as modify the vowel by an e.

(*c*) Umlaut was caused by the presence of an i or j in a following syllable. In rendering the sound of the vowel the speech organs tended to approximate to the position they would take up for the pronunciation of the i or j; thus the sound of the vowel was modified. The i or j which originally caused this modification may have weakened to e or disappeared in Modern German.

Old High German	*Modern German*
tagalik	täglich
hohiro	höher

(*d*) This explains why many diminutives are modified:

       Bach, diminutive Bächlein.

(The ending =lein is the modern form of the older =lin.)

7. Capital Letters.

(*a*) Capitals are used—

  (i) To begin sentences.

  (ii) With all nouns and parts of speech used as nouns if they

can be preceded by an article, adjective, or some modifying word;
for example:

> das Schluchzen, sobbing (from schluchzen, to sob).
> der Bekannte, acquaintance.
> Sie wollten etwas Großes leisten und alles Bisherige in
> den Schatten stellen.

But: Alt und jung lief aus den Häusern.

(iii) With adjectives and possessives in titles.

> Seine Majestät.
> Das Königliche Museum.

(iv) With Sie (you) in all its cases and wherever it occurs, also
with the corresponding possessive adjective Ihr.

(v) With adjectives formed from the names of places.

> Eine Berliner Zeitung.   (But see also 90, Note.)

(*b*) In the writing of letters capitals are used with Du in all
its cases and wherever it occurs, also with the corresponding
possessive adjectives.

(*c*) Use small i with ich (I) unless it begins a sentence or unless
it is used as a noun.

(*d*) Use small letters with certain adverbial expressions containing nouns, because these expressions have come to be considered as speech units in themselves.

> Er ist zugrunde gegangen.
> Das kam mir eben zustatten.
> Er ist nicht imstande zu arbeiten.

8. Spelling.

(*a*) It should be noted that many words borrowed from French
have usually a Germanized spelling nowadays. This spelling is
often an attempt to give in German form the nearest approach
to the pronunciation of the original French word. Thus:

German	*French*
Frisör	friseur
Soße	sauce
Drogen	drogues

Die Fotos comes possibly from English 'photos.'
In Schiller we even find Mussje for Monsieur, but this would
hardly be correct in Modern German.

(*b*) tȟ is written in

(i) Proper names, *e.g.*, die Themſe, the Thames; Lothringen, Lorraine; also in der Thron (throne) and its compounds.

(ii) Words of Greek origin, *e.g.*, die Bibliothek, the library; die Theologie, theology.

The ȟ that used to be written after the t in words like tun, Tür, Tat, Träne is now obsolete.

(*c*) f has replaced pȟ in some words: Weſtfalen, Westphalia; der Elefant, the elephant; der Efeu, the ivy; *but* die Philoſophie, philosophy.

(*d*) k or z, according to the sound required, have replaced c in most German words (except of course when it occurs in ch, ck, or ſch). Thus: Lektion, lesson; Akzent, accent; kritiſieren, to criticize.

(*e*) When the first of the constituents of a compound word ends in two consonants which are the same as that beginning the next constituent, one consonant is omitted. Thus: Die ſchnellaufenden Maſchinen (ſchnell + laufenden), the speeding machines; Schiffahrt (Schiff + Fahrt), navigation.

N.B.—(i) This omitted consonant is restored if the word has to be divided (9, 2 (*d*)).

(ii) The consonant is not omitted if the compound is made with the use of hyphens (10, 4(*c*)); as in Schnell=Laſtwagen=Verkehr, express lorry traffic.

9. Division of Syllables.

1. A single consonant between two syllables is taken over to the second syllable. Thus Vater, weben are divided into Va=ter, we=ben.

Exceptions:

(i) Intereſſe is divided Inter=eſſe.

(ii) Compounds of dar= and wor= + prepositions are divided dar=auf, wor=in. (But da=rauf and wo=rin are also found.)

2. Two or more consonants together.

(*a*) ch, pȟ, tȟ, z, ſch, and ſt (except as provided for below) represent single sounds, and for purposes of syllable separation are treated as single consonants; accordingly they are not separated. Hence Groſchen is divided Gro=ſchen; Kaſten, Ka=ſten.

(*b*) (i) When two or more consonants occur together (except ch, pȟ, tȟ, z, ſch, and ſt) the last one is carried over to the next line. So ſilbern is divided ſil=bern.

(ii) But this must not violate the normal separation of compounds into the constituent parts. Umſchweiſe is divided into Um=ſchweiſe because it is compounded of um and ſchweiſe. Similarly we must divide ḫerein=brach, Ḫäus=chen, Ḫaus=tür.

(*c*) In foreign words b, p, d, t, g, ḟ, followed by l or r, are carried over to the beginning of the line. Natrium (sodium) is divided Na=trium; Ḫygrometer, Ḫy=grometer.

(*d*) In compounds which omit a consonant (8 (*e*)) this omitted consonant is restored when the word is separated at the point whence the consonant was taken. Thus, Schiffahrt is divided Schiff=fahrt.

(*e*) ck is separated into k=k. Ḟackel becomes Ḟak=kel.

10.   PUNCTUATION

    das Komma, the comma.
    das Semikolon, or der Strichpunkt, the semicolon.
    das Kolon, or der Doppelpunkt, the colon.
    der Punkt, the full-stop.
    das Ḟragezeichen, the question mark.
    das Ausruſungszeichen, the exclamation mark.
    die Anſührungszeichen, or⎱ the inverted commas.
    die Gänseſüßchen,   ⎰
    die Klammer *pl.* Klammern, the brackets, parenthesis.
    der Gedankenſtrich, the dash.
    der Bindeſtrich, the hyphen.
    der Apoſtroph, or   ⎱ the apostrophe.
    das Auslaſſungszeichen,⎰

In Roman type the hyphen is a single (-), in German type generally a double (=) stroke.

The following signs of punctuation call for special remark:

1. The **comma** is used in German:

(*a*) Where English has a decimal point.

      23,482 is read as dreiundzwanzig, Komma, vier, acht, zwei,

and is printed in English as 23·482.

(*b*) To separate marks from pfennigs, and metres from centimetres.

      RM 10,15—zehn Reichsmark ſünſzehn (Pſennig).
      10,15m—zehn Meter ſünſzehn (Zentimeter).

(*c*) To separate dependent clauses and main clauses.

> Als wir nach dem Arzt fragten, sagte das Mädchen, er sei nicht zu Hause.
> Wir fanden das Buch, das wir gesucht hatten.
> Er würde kommen, wenn er Zeit hätte.

(*d*) Before an infinitive phrase if it consists of more than merely zu + the infinitive.

> Er legte sich auf das Bett, um sich etwas auszuruhen.
> Wir hatten keine Lust, so früh zu schwimmen.

(*But* Wir hatten keine Lust zu schwimmen.)

(*e*) The comma before und.

(i) The general tendency is not to use the comma before und when it links together main clauses.

> Herr Grünlich goß sich Rotwein ins Glas, erhob die Kristall= glocke und ging zum Käse über (Thomas Mann).

Compare the English:

> Mr Grünlich poured some claret into his glass, lifted the glass cover of the cheese-dish, and began with the cheese.

(ii) No comma should be used before the und in a sequence of more than two adjectives or nouns.

> Er sah sein Ende nicht mehr als eine feine, theoretische und unbeträchtliche Notwendigkeit.
> Urahne, Großmutter, Mutter und Kind
> In dumpfer Stube zusammen sind.

Compare the punctuation in:

> He was easy-going, good-natured, and even generous when it cost him little.

(iii) Where two adjectives precede and qualify a noun they are not usually separated by a comma.

> Um die mächtigen gotischen Ecken und Winkel der Kirche pfiff der Wind.
> Ein berühmter preußischer General.

(iv) Always use a comma before und zwar.

> Sie haben nur ein Kind, und zwar einen Sohn.

2. The **Colon.**

(*a*) After a verb of saying or a similar introductory verb, a colon is used before words in inverted commas.

> „Du haſt mir auch das Gras abgenagt,“ ſagte der Wolf.
> Aber das Lämmlein erwiderte : „Wie habe ich das gekonnt?“

(*b*) A colon is used before enumerations.

> Die Jahreszeiten ſind : der Frühling, der Sommer, der Herbſt und der Winter.

3. An **exclamation mark** is placed :

(i) At the end of an imperative clause in the first and second person.

> Stehen Sie auf ! Stand up !

(ii) Very often after the introductory words of a letter.

> Sehr geehrter Herr ! Dear Sir,

(iii) After short public notices (to arrest the reader's **attention**).

> Achtung ! Caution !

4. The **hyphen** is used :

(*a*) To represent that part of two or more compound **nouns** which is common to these nouns.

Armaturen= und Autofabrik.
Factory for armatures and motor-cars.

Wortableitung und =zuſammenſetzung.
Formation of words by derivation and composition.

(*b*) In compounds containing a proper noun.

England will zum Macdonald=Plan zurück.
England wants to return to the Macdonald plan.

If the compound is well established by frequent use the **hyphen** may be omitted, as in Bismarckheringe, Wagnerkappe.

(*c*) In compounds which would be too long or confusing if written as a single **word.**

Betriebswirtſchafts=Wiſſenſchaft.
Science of business management.

Bei dem erſten Schlag des Neun=Uhr=Läutens.
At the first stroke of the nine-o'clock bell.

(*d*) In compounds the formation of which brings together the same vowel, as Tee=erſatz, Allee=eingang.

(*e*) In German addresses which contain the name of a large town and that of a district within that town:

Berlin=Tempelhof.

5. **Quotation marks** are used as in English, but the beginning mark is printed and written on the line, not above it.

„Da haben Sie recht,"   "You are right there," said the
erwiderte der Konſul.   consul.

6. The **apostrophe** indicates that a vowel or syllable which is normally part of the word has been omitted.

Na, komm 'rein, erkält' dich nicht ! If written in full this would be: Na, komm herein, erkälte dich nicht !

(*a*) Some strong verbs have two forms for the Imperative second person singular (**168**, Note (iv)).

ſinne !   or ſinn !
komme ! or komm !

If the second of these forms is used (and it is now the more usual) there is no need for an apostrophe.

(*b*) No apostrophe is required with the accepted contractions of preposition + definite article,

e.g., im   for in dem
aufs for auf das (33).

(*c*) No apostrophe is required in modern German before the =s of the Genitive Singular.

Goethes Leben.   Goethe's life,

except when the genitive singular of a proper noun ending in =s, =ts, =tz, =z is used. In this case an apostrophe is placed after the name in printing and a genitive =s is not added.

Kopernikus' Lehre hat unſer   Copernicus's theory changed
Weltbild verändert.   our conception of the world.

7. The **full-stop**, besides its ordinary use as in English, is used after all abbreviations except:

RM (= Reichsmark), m (= Meter),

km (= Kilometer) and other abbreviations of metric measurements.

A full stop is not used after titles of books and headings, as these are not considered to be sentences.

11.   ABBREVIATIONS

German Abbreviation	Word(s) which it represents	Corresponding English Abbreviation
u.	und	&
ufw. (occasionally u.f.w.)	und fo weiter	etc.
3.B	zum Beifpiel	e.g.
d.i.	das ift	i.e.
a.a.O.	am angeführten Ort	ibid.
f.	fiehe	v.
S.	Seite	p.
vgl.	vergleiche	cf.
Nr. or No.	Nummer	no. (= number)
Str.	Straße	St. (= street)
vor Chr. Geb.	vor Chrifti Geburt	B.C.
nach Chr. Geb.	nach Chrifti Geburt	A.D.
Gebr.	Gebrüder	Bros.

(only used in the name of a shop or firm)

A.G.	Aktien=Gefellfchaft	Co.
G.m.b.H.	Gefellfchaft mit befchränkter Haftung	Co. Ltd.

		Translated into English
v.	von	of
d.h.	das heißt	that is to say
u. dergl.	und dergleichen	and so forth
i.J.	im Jahre	in the year
geb.	geborene	née
bzw.	beziehungsweife	respectively
ca. (pronounced zirka)	circa (Latin)	about
Pf.	Pfennig	pfennig

II. NUMBER, GENDER, CASE

12. Number.

German has two numbers:

die Einzahl or der Singular	Singular
die Mehrzahl or der Plural	Plural

13. Gender.

German has three genders (60 to 65):

das männliche Geschlecht	Masculine
das weibliche Geschlecht	Feminine
das sächliche Geschlecht	Neuter

14. Cases.

German has four cases:

der Nominativ	Nominative
der Akkusativ	Accusative
der Genitiv	Genitive
der Dativ	Dative

15. THE NOMINATIVE CASE

(*a*) The subject of a finite verb is in the **Nominative**.

Der Mann gab dem Kind den Bleistift.	The man gave the pencil to the child.

NOTE.—In a few odd phrases an Accusative preceded by a preposition may be found as subject to a finite verb:

Gegen vierzig Leute waren da. Sie hatten die Waren ins Wasser geworfen. Für zweihundert Pfund lagen im Hafen.	About forty people were there. They had thrown the goods into the water. As much as £200 worth lay in the harbour.

(*b*) The Nominative is used as a form of direct address, corresponding to the Latin Vocative case.

Ja, mein lieber Karl, das werden wir tun.	Yes, my dear Charles, we'll do that.

(*c*) It is used as the predicate to sein (to be), werden (to become), bleiben (to remain), heißen (to be called), dünken (to seem), scheinen (to seem), erscheinen (to appear).

Lessing war der Sohn eines Geistlichen.	Lessing was a clergyman's son.

16.   THE ACCUSATIVE CASE

(*a*) The direct object of a transitive verb is in the **Accusative**.

Der Mann gab dem Kind den
  Bleistift.

The man gave the pencil to the
  child.

NOTE.—With these verbs what is the direct object in English is
rendered by a prepositional phrase in German :

Er klatschte in die Hände.	He clapped his hands.
Ich schnitt mich (*or* mir) in den Finger.	I cut my finger.
Er knirschte mit den Zähnen.	He gnashed his teeth.
Er nickte mit dem Kopf.	He nodded (his head).
Er winkte mit der Hand.	He waved (his hand).
Er zuckte mit den Schultern.	He shrugged his shoulders.
Der Hund wedelte mit dem Schwanz.	The dog wagged its tail.
Er warf uns mit Schneebällen.	He threw snowballs at us.

(*b*) The **Cognate Accusative**. This is found (in certain fixed
expressions) with verbs which are really intransitive.

Ein faules Leben leben (usually führen).	To live a lazy life.
Einen edlen Tod sterben.	To die a noble death.
Einen langen Weg gehen.	To go a long way.
Rad fahren (also radfahren).	To cycle.
Schlittschuh laufen.	To skate.
Ski laufen.	To ski.
Gefahr laufen.	To run a risk.
Spießruten laufen.	To run the gauntlet.

(*c*) The Accusative is used after these prepositions : durch, für,
gegen, bis, ohne, um, wider, ausgenommen (**220**) ;

and in some cases after : an, auf, hinter, in, neben, über, unter,
vor, zwischen (**221** to **234**).

(*d*) The **Absolute Accusative**. This resembles the Latin Abla-
tive Absolute and is the same as the French Absolute Accusative.

Er kam herein, den Hut in
  der Hand.

He entered with his hat in his
  hand.

Compare the French : Il entra, le chapeau à la main.

German is not so strict as French in adherence to this Absolute
Accusative to describe attendant circumstances. Mit + a Dative
may describe attendant circumstances.

| Mit Tränen in den Augen kam er langsam zurück. | With tears in his eyes he came slowly back. |

Gottfried Keller even has an example of both constructions in the same sentence:

| Der Pfarrer immer voran mit einer Entenflinte über dem Rücken oder ein mächtiges spanisches Rohr in der Hand . . . | The parson (was) always in front with a fowling-piece across his back or a large Spanish cane in his hand. |

17.   THE GENITIVE CASE

1. **Dependent on Nouns.**

(*a*) Genitive of **possession.** The Genitive is used to indicate the person or thing owning some other person or thing.

| Der Hut dieses Mannes. | This man's hat. |

(*b*) The Genitive is used to indicate **association with** or **descent from.**

| Die Folgen dieser Tat. | The consequences of this deed. |
| Die Kinder dieser Witwe. | This widow's children. |

(*c*) An **Objective Genitive** can be used with nouns formed from transitive verbs.

| Die Erziehung der Kinder. | The education of (the) children. |
| Die Verfolgung der Heiligen. | The persecution of the saints. |

(*d*) The **Descriptive Genitive.**

| Ein Abteil erster Klasse. | A first-class compartment. |

18. 2. The Genitive may be used **predicatively** after the verb sein in these phrases:

| Ich bin nicht dieser Meinung. | I am not of this opinion. |
| Er war willens zu gehen. | He intended to go. |

19. 3. The **Adverbial Genitive.** In the early history of the language the use of the Genitive to form adverbial phrases was quite common. Nowadays the Adverbial Genitive seems to be restricted to certain expressions.

(*a*) Adverbial phrases of **place.**

> eingangs, at the beginning.
> beiderseits, on both sides.
> seinerseits, on his part.

(Both these words are from die Seite; the s is by analogy.)

> unterwegs, on the way.
> halbwegs, half-way.

Darum, wenn ihr alle dieses Weges geht, werft einen Blick zu ihm hinauf.	So when you all go along this way look up at him.

(*b*) Adverbial phrases of **time**.

(i) Habitual time :

> morgens, des Morgens, in the morning.

(*Cf.* Eng. : He often does it of a morning.)

> mittags, at midday, at noon.

(Zu Mittag would mean at noon on some single occasion.)

des Tags (usually am Tage or tagsüber), in the daytime.
vormittags, des Vormittags, in the forenoon.
nachmittags, des Nachmittags, in the afternoon.
abends, des Abends, in the evening.
nachts, des Nachts (also in der Nacht), in the night-time, at night.

(*Cf.* Eng. : I can't sleep o' nights.)

NOTE.—Nacht is feminine, but this adverbial genitive in s is by analogy with the masculine des Tags.

(ii) Indefinite time :

> eines Tages, one day.
> eines Nachts, one night.
> tags darauf, the day after this.
> tags zuvor, the day before.

(iii) Definite time :

anfangs (or am Anfang), at the beginning.
letzten Endes (or am Ende), finally, when all has been said.

(*c*) Adverbial phrases of **manner**.

Sie fuhren dritter Klasse.	They travelled third class.
Allen Ernstes.	In all seriousness.

Also several adverbs in =weise (gen. of die Weise, the manner), *e.g.*, glücklicherweise, in a happy manner, happily.

(*d*) Adverbial phrases of **degree**.

derart (gen. of die Art, the way, manner), so, to such an extent
teils, partly.

Several adverbs in =maßen (an old weak gen. sing. of diu maʒiu, measure; Mod. German, das Maß), and =teils (gen. of der or das Teil, the part), as

gewissermaßen, to a certain extent, as it were.
größtenteils, for the most part.

(*e*) Note also:

meines Wissens, to my knowledge, as far as I know, as I know well enough.
meines Erachtens, in my opinion.
keineswegs, by no means.
stehenden Fußes, forthwith, straightway.
jedenfalls, in any case.
nötigenfalls (from adj. nötig + gen. of der Fall, the case), if necessary.

20. 4. The **Partitive Genitive.**

(*a*) In elevated style and in poetry the Genitive is still found in a partitive sense (*i.e.*, having the meaning 'some of,' 'a portion of'). Compare Genesis iv. 4: And Abel, he also brought of the firstlings of his flock and of the fat thereof.

Schiller has:

Es schenkte der Böhme des   The Bohemian poured out some
perlenden Weins.   of the sparkling wine.

NOTE.—In Modern German this partitive is more usually rendered by von + Dative.

Sie gaben mir von ihrem Fleisch. They gave me (some of) their meat.

(*b*) Note the use of the Genitive in =es with adjectives used as nouns after etwas, nichts, viel.

Nichts Wichtiges.   Nothing important.

(*Cf.* French: Rien d'important.)

This =es with adjectives used as nouns after etwas, etc., is no longer considered as a Genitive. Because =es is also the ending for the neuter nom. and acc. sing., the Wichtiges and similar formations have come to be regarded as neuter nom. and acc. sing. in apposition to the nichts, etwas, or viel. Accordingly if we were to decline etwas Gutes according to modern usage, we should have:

Nom. etwas Gutes.
Acc. etwas Gutes.

Gen. etwas Guten (the -en form of the gen. ad. declension being used to distinguish the Genitive from the Nominative and Accusative).

Dat. etwas Gutem.

21. 5. The **Genitive with Verbs.**

In earlier German it was quite common to find many verbs governing the Genitive which now have an Accusative or a prepositional construction.

Vergißmeinnicht. Forget-me-not.
Freut euch des Lebens ! Take pleasure in life, enjoy life.

The number of such verbs is now much restricted (**174**).

22. 6. Certain **prepositions** govern the Genitive.

The commonest are: anstatt, während, wegen, um . . . willen, trotz, ungeachtet (**216, 217**).

NOTE.—In Middle High German the Genitive was quite frequently used in exclamations. This construction may still be found.

O des eifersüchtigen Künstlers ! Oh! the jealous artist.
(Lessing: *Emilia Galotti.*)

THE DATIVE CASE

23. 1. The indirect object of a verb is in the **Dative** case.

Bringen Sie ihm seinen Hut ! Bring him his hat !
Er sagte mir seine Meinung. He told me his opinion.

24. 2. Certain **prepositions** govern the Dative.

These are: aus, außer, bei, entgegen, gegenüber, mit, nach, seit, von, zu (**218, 219**).

The Dative is used in some instances after: an, auf, hinter, in, neben, über, unter, vor, zwischen (**221** to **234**).

25. 3. The **Dative with Verbs.**

A number of German verbs govern the Dative, whereas the corresponding verbs in English may have their direct object in the Accusative (**172**).

Er folgte seinem Vater. He followed his father.

NOTE.—Occasionally in South Germany a Dative with the verb sein indicates possession.

Das Haus ist mir. The house belongs to me.

This would seem to be an imitation of the common French and Latin constructions. It has hardly found much use elsewhere in Germany.

26. 4. The Dative used **adverbially.**

(*a*) Adverbs of **place.**

 (i) **heim,** home (poet. for **nach Hause**).
   daheim, at home (poet. for **zu Hause**).
   allenthalben (an old dat. plur.), on all sides.

(ii) Sometimes in giving addresses the Dative without any preposition is used.

> **Coleridge wohnte damals Weenderlandstraße.** At that time Coleridge was living in Weenderlandstrasse.

(*b*) Adverbs of **time.** A few old ones remain:

> **bisweilen,** sometimes.
> **einstweilen,** for the time being.
> **zuweilen,** at times, now and then.
> **jeweilen** (obsolete), from time to time.

In these, **=weilen** is the dat. plur. of **die Weile,** 'while,' 'period.'

27. 5. The **Ethic Dative.**

The Ethic Dative is used to vivify a statement or to denote that the person has an interest more than normal in what he is saying. A good example in English is Casca's speech describing what he saw from the edge of the crowd which surrounded Cæsar when Antony offered him the coronet.

> "He plucked *me* ope his doublet and offered them his throat to cut."

Er war mir grausam gegen die Kinder.	(My belief is) he was cruel to the children.
Geht mir, nichts weiter da= von ! (Schiller).	Be off, I tell you, no more of that!

28. 6. The Dative indicating **ownership.**

The Dative is often used to make clear the ownership of a part of the body or a piece of clothing. This may be imitation of the French:

> Je lui ai lavé le visage, I washed his face.

Ich wasche mir die Hände.	I wash my hands.
Vom vielen Arbeiten raucht ihm der Kopf.	His head is swimming with so much work.
Ich wollte ihm die Schuhe putzen	I wanted to clean his shoes.

29. 7. Dative of Advantage.

With certain verbs the Dative is used for the person who gains by the action implied by the verb.

Jdj möchte mir ein Haus bauen.	I should like to build myself a house.
Dir scheint der Stern des Glückes.	The star of fortune is shining for you.
Das spart uns Zeit.	That saves time for us.

30. 8. Dative of Disadvantage.

Likewise the Dative is used to indicate the person who loses by the action implied by the verb.

Er hat mir diese schöne Gelegenheit geraubt.	He has robbed me of this fine opportunity.
Dem Laien wird der Antrieb zum eigenen Musizieren mehr und mehr genommen.	More and more is the amateur robbed of the impulse to make his own music.
Der Landmann ... seinen Kohl dem frechen Wilde baut (Goethe, *Ilmenau*).	The peasant cultivates his cabbages, and saucy game animals browse thereon.

APPOSITION

31. A noun which explains or develops the meaning of a previous noun is said to be **in apposition**. It is usually near the noun referred to (therefore the name apposition).

(*a*) In German the noun in apposition should be in the same case as that to which it refers.

> Kaiserin Zitta, die ebenso kluge wie energische Mutter Otto von Habsburgs, des Prätendenten der beiden Kronen Oesterreichs und Ungarns, war dieser Tage in Rom, um die Verlobung Ottos mit der jüngsten Tochter des italienischen Königspaares, der beinahe neunzehnjährigen Prinzessin Maria, durchzusetzen.

> In der Folgezeit wandte er sich wieder mehr seiner Lebensaufgabe, der Bakterienforschung, zu.

(*b*) Note the appositional construction with proper names after the following nouns:

die Stadt Hamburg, the town of Hamburg.
die Universität Heidelberg, the University of Heidelberg.

der Monat Juni, the month of June.

die Insel Man, the Isle of Man.

das alte Königreich Bayern, the old kingdom of Bavaria.

die Provinz Hannover, the province of Hanover.

(c) After nouns of measurement or type the noun describing the thing measured is usually in apposition.

ein Stück Brot, a piece of bread.

ein Pfund Kaffee, a pound of coffee.

diese Art Fisch, this type of fish.

Das Gericht verurteilte den Angeklagten zu zwei Jahren einer Woche Gefängnis.	The court condemned the accused to imprisonment for two years and one week.

Note.—If the noun of measurement is in the genitive, there is no apposition; the noun representing the thing measured is then in the nominative.

Der Besitz eines Pfundes Zucker.   The possession of a pound of sugar.

(d) If the noun representing the thing measured is qualified, the tendency is not to have apposition but to use the genitive:

Ein Glas roten Weins.   A glass of red wine.

III. DEFINITE AND INDEFINITE ARTICLES

32.   THE DEFINITE ARTICLE

	Masc.	Fem.	Neut.	Plur., all Genders	
Nom.	der	die	das	die	the
Acc.	den	die	das	die	the
Gen.	des	der	des	der	of the
Dat.	dem	der	dem	den	to the, for the

33. Contractions of **Preposition** + **Definite Article**.

(a) Masculine and Neuter: preposition + dem and das.

an dem	may be contracted to		am
an das	,,	,,	ans
auf das	,,	,,	aufs
bei dem	,,	,,	beim
durch das	,,	,,	durchs
für das	,,	,,	fürs

in dem	may be contracted to		im
in das	,,	,,	ins
von dem	,,	,,	vom
zu dem	,,	,,	zum

(Conversational German allows further contractions, such as aufm = auf dem.)

(*b*) Feminine: preposition + der.
The only contraction is zur for zu der.

(*c*) These contractions must be used in certain fixed phrases. Such are:

> zur Schule gehen, to go to school, to attend school.
> > (No particular school is thought of.)
>
> jemanden ins Auge fassen, to look at someone.
> im Gebrauch sein, to be in use.
> im guten Glauben, in good faith.
> im Gegenteil, on the contrary.
> im allgemeinen, as a general rule.
> zum Beispiel, for example, *e.g.*
> Er hat mich zum besten.   He is pulling my leg.

34. The Definite Article is used in German when it is not found in the corresponding English:

(*a*) With parts of the body (or clothing).

Er zuckte die Achseln (or mit den Achseln).	He shrugged his shoulders.
Er hatte ein Buch in der Hand.	He had a book in his hand.

NOTE.—English usage is to have the possessive adjective in these instances. If there is in the German mind any possibility of doubt as to whose body or article of clothing is referred to, the dative of the corresponding personal pronoun is added. (*Cf.* the French construction.)

Johann schneidet sich das Haar.	John cuts his hair (*i.e.*, his own hair).
(Jean se coupe les cheveux.)	
Johann schneidet ihm das Haar.	John cuts his hair (*i.e.*, that of someone else).
(Jean lui coupe les cheveux.)	

(*b*) With names of seasons.

Im Sommer geht die Sonne früh auf.	In summer the sun rises early.

(c) With names of months.

Die Konferenz wird im Au= | The conference will take place
guſt ſtattfinden. | in August.

NOTE.—The definite article may be omitted with names of months after Ende, Anfang, Mitte:

(am) Ende Juli, at the end of July.

(d) With names of days, parts of days, meals.

Die Beerdigung findet am | The funeral will take place on
Dienstag, dem 31. Oktober | Tuesday the 31st of October.
ſtatt.

Ich wurde zum Mittageſſen | I was invited to lunch.
eingeladen.

(e) With abstract nouns.

Der Tod kam als ein Segen. | Death came as a blessing.

NOTE.—The article may disappear in exclamations and proverbial expressions.

Übung macht den Meiſter.   Practice makes perfect.

(f) With most feminine and masculine names of countries, mountains, lakes, and streets.

Er wurde in der Schweiz | He was brought up in Switzer-
erzogen. | land.

Freiburg im Breisgau.

(See **64** (d) for gender of geographical names.)

Der Bodenſee. | Lake Constance.
Er arbeitet in der Bismarck= | He works in Bismarckstrasse.
ſtraße.
Der Veſuv. | Vesuvius.

(g) With proper names when qualified by an adjective.

der alte Fritz, old Freddy
das moderne Frankreich, modern France

NOTE.—This is not so when the name so qualified is used as a form of address; thus, beginning a letter to a friend:

Lieber Franz !   Dear Frank,

(h) Occasionally with names of persons or relationships; this is peculiar to South German.

Darum fragte das Kind: „Wem gehört dieſes?“   Die

Mutter erwiberte: „Mama!" „Unb das anbre?" fuhr bas Kind fort. „Dem Papa."

Wen haft du als Sprach= lehrer? Den Braun.	Who is your language master? Old Brown.

(*i*) With names of well-known writers to indicate (one of) their works.

In biesem Schrank habe ich den Schiller.	I have Schiller's works in this case.

(*j*) To distinguish cases and avoid ambiguity.

Den Alexis hielt Karl für einen Verräter.	Charles considered Alexis to be a traitor.

(*k*) Very often with nouns used in a general sense.

Der Mensch ist nie zufrieden.	Man is never satisfied.

We are not referring to any particular man; ber Mensch means 'man' or 'men' taken in a general sense.

35. Remember that the Definite Article had originally **demonstrative** force. It can still be used as a Demonstrative Adjective. When so used it receives voice stress, and the vowel in ben, bem, ber is long (**117**).

zu ber Zeit, at that time.

36. Special uses of the Definite Article.

(*a*)
Es koftet 50 Pf. bas Meter	It costs 6d. a yard.
Zwanzig Mark die Tonne.	Twenty marks a ton.
Dreimal die Woche.	Three times a week.

(*b*) The English Indefinite Article with the meaning 'any,' 'every,' is rendered by the German Definite Article:

Der Blinde entwickelt anbere Sinne.	A blind man develops other senses.

(*c*) Notice the use of the Definite Article in the following phrases when English uses the Indefinite:

im Nu, in a trice, in a moment.
in ber Lage fein, to be in a position (to do something).
im Galopp, at a gallop.
im Trab, at a trot.
zur Abwechselung, for a change.

(*d*) The Definite Article is omitted whenever a genitive precedes the noun on which it depends:

> Schmidts Freund, *i.e.*, der Freund Schmidts.
> Das ist eines Mannes Arbeit, *i.e.*, Das ist die Arbeit eines Mannes.

Das Buch, dessen Einband	The book, the binding of which
. . .	. . .

(*e*) Notice that in the following expressions the German Definite Article is omitted contrary to English usage:

(i) ersterer (erstere, ersteres), the former
letzterer (letztere, letzteres), the latter

Wir sahen Käthe und Klara; letztere ist sehr krank.	We saw Käthe and Klara; the latter is very ill.

(The Demonstratives dieser and jener are also used to contrast 'the former' and 'the latter.') (**118** (ii).)

NOTE.—In the genitive the Definite Article will have to be used to make the case clear.

Braun und Schmidt waren hier. So? Des letzteren Buch habe ich noch nicht gelesen.	Braun and Schmidt were here. Were they? I have not read the latter's book.

(ii) When erst is used as a pronoun after als (as):

Sie haben mich mit dem schönen Geschenk überrascht, das als erstes vor unsrer Abreise ankam.	You surprised me with the fine present, which, being the first, arrived before we left.

(iii) Folgendes:

Er hat mir folgendes mitgeteilt.	He has told me the following.

(iv) Whenever nach or gegen precede names of points of the compass:

Nach Süden nun sich lenken die Vöglein allzumal.	Now, all together, the little birds wing their way towards the south.
Schottland liegt gegen Norden.	Scotland lies to the north.

(v) Often after alle (**49** (*h*) (i)) and beide (**49** (*i*)).

Alle Lieder.	All the songs.
Beide Töchter.	Both (the) daughters. The two daughters.

37.   THE INDEFINITE ARTICLE

	Masc.	*Fem.*	*Neut.*	
Nom.	ein	eine	ein	a (an)
Acc.	einen	eine	ein	a (an)
Gen.	eines	einer	eines	of a (an)
Dat.	einem	einer	einem	to, for, a (an)

Words declined like the Indefinite Article are :

(*a*) fein, feine, fein.

(*b*) the Possessive Adjectives (**115**).

There is no plural to the Indefinite Article, but words which are declined like it are declined in the plural as follows :

Nom.	feine
Acc.	feine
Gen.	feiner
Dat.	feinen

Er hat keinen Vater.	He has no father.
Meine Frau und meine Kinder.	My wife and my children.
In Ihrem Hause.	In your house.

38. The Indefinite Article is also used as a **numeral adjective** (one). This use may be indicated by spaced printing.

In dem Sack war nur e i n Goldstück.	There was only *one* piece of gold in the bag.

39. Omission of the Indefinite Article.

The Indefinite Article is omitted in German where it would be used in English :

(*a*) After sein (to be), werden (to become), bleiben (to stay), if the noun indicates profession, trade, nationality, or rank.

Sein Vater war Arzt.	His father was a doctor.
Er will Soldat werden.	He wants to become a soldier.
Shakespeare war Eng= länder.	Shakespeare was an English- man.

NOTE.—The Indefinite Article is usually found after these verbs if the noun is qualified.

Er ist ein berühmter Arzt.	He is a famous doctor.
Goethe war ein Schriftsteller, dessen W e r t h e r viel Auf= sehen erregte.	Goethe was a writer whose *Werther* caused a great stir.

(b) After als in the sense of 'as,' 'in the capacity of.'

Er zeichnete sich als Kritiker aus.	He distinguished himself as a critic.

(c) Before hundert and tausend.

Hundert Pferde liefen herum.	A hundred horses were running round.

But: eine Million; eine Milliarde (1,000,000,000).

(d) In the following idiomatic construction: Preposition + adjective + noun where English would use the Indefinite Article after the preposition.

This construction is used:

(i) When the prepositional phrase is truly adjectival and refers to a singular noun introduced by ein.

Eine Kirche mit gewölbtem Dach.	A church with a vaulted roof. (*i.e.*, a vaulted-roofed church)
Ein Buch mit blauem Einband.	A book with a blue binding.

(ii) When the prepositional phrase is in the singular and is used in a synecdochical sense (referring to the part when the whole is meant).

Und hinein mit bedächtigem Schritt Ein Löwe tritt.	And with cautious step (*i.e.*, steps) a lion enters.
Daraus rennt Mit wildem Sprunge Ein Tiger hervor.	With a wild leap (*i.e.*, leaps) a tiger races out.

(iii) In poetry:

Und sittsam bracht' auf reinlichem Altar
Dianens Priesterin ihr Opfer dar.
And, as was seemly, Diana's priestess offered up her sacrifice on an unblemished altar.

(e) In idioms such as:

Aufsehen machen	to cause *a* stir
Gefahr laufen	to run *a* risk
Kopfweh haben	to have *a* headache
in Ohnmacht fallen	to fall into *a* faint

40. The **Partitive Idea.** ' Some,' ' any.'

(*a*) As **adjectives** *some, any* may be rendered :

(i) By **etwas** + singular noun.

> **Etwas Zucker.** Some sugar.
> **Ist etwas Milch übrig?** Is there any milk left?

(ii) By **einig** + singular abstract noun.

> **Nach einiger Zeit.** After some time.

(iii) By **einige** + plural noun.

> **Einige Leute sagen.** Some people say.

(iv) Rarely by the Genitive. See **20** (*a*).

(v) By the noun alone.

> **In ihrem Korb waren Äpfel.** In her basket there were some apples.

N.B.—' Not any ' is **kein.**

> **Sie hat kein Fleisch.** She has not any meat.

41. (*b*) As **Pronouns** they may be rendered :

(i) By **welch.**

> **Er hat mir welchen (welches) geliehen.** He has lent me some.
> **Und wenn es welche gegeben hätte.** And if there had been any.

(ii) By **einig.**

> **Einige waren schon gestorben.** Some had already died.

IV. PERSONAL PRONOUNS

42. Personal Pronouns of the **Third Person.**

	Masc.	*Fem.*	*Neut.*	*Plur., all Genders*
Nom.	er	sie	es	sie
Acc.	ihn	sie	es	sie
Gen.	seiner (sein)	ihrer (ihr)	seiner (sein)	ihrer (ihr)
Dat.	ihm	ihr	ihm	ihnen

(*a*) The short forms of the genitive, given above in round brackets, are used in poetry, a few fixed expressions, and in rhetorical style.

> **O ! gedenke sein !** Oh ! think of him !

(*b*) An old neuter genitive es is now only found in certain expressions :

Ich bin es satt.	I am 'fed up' with it.
Ich bin es müde.	I am tired of it.
Ich bin es zufrieden.	I am satisfied with it.
Es nimmt mich Wunder.	I am astonished (*lit.* Wonderment takes me on account of it).

This es was mistaken for an Accusative, and these expressions are sometimes found governing a noun or pronoun in the Accusative.

(*c*) Note the use of es to represent an idea that has been previously expressed.

Ist er traurig? Ja, er ist (e)s.	Is he sad? Yes, he is.

(*Cf.* French: *Est-il triste? Oui, il l'est.*)

(*d*) The anticipative es.

Es may be used as the grammatical subject of a verb when the idea which is really the subject follows.

Es hat sich kein König um mich bekümmert (Goethe).	No king has concerned himself about me.

The 'sense subject' of hat sich . . . bekümmert is kein König : the es is merely a grammatical subject to the verb.

This es is used even with a plural verb; the verb is put in the plural to agree with the 'sense subject.'

Es waren nur drei Leute da, die es wußten.	There were only three people there who knew it.

(waren because of the plural drei Leute.)

NOTE.—This anticipative es must stand before its verb in German ; if any other word comes before the verb the es is no longer used.

Es ist etwas Milch übrig geblieben.	There is some milk left.
Ist etwas Milch übrig geblieben?	Is there any milk left?
Heute ist etwas Milch übrig geblieben.	To-day there is some milk left.
Nach den Erfahrungen in der Schlacht von Tannenberg war anzunehmen, daß der Großfürst nicht in die Falle gehen würde.	After the experiences of the battle of Tannenberg it could be assumed that the Grand Duke would not walk into the trap.

But the es with the expression es gibt 'there is' (see 171 (*g*)) is not so omitted.

In der Welt gab es etwas Derartiges nicht zum zweiten Male.	Nothing like that occurred a second time in this world.

(*e*) Note:

> 3ch bin es. Du biſt es.   It is I.   It is thou (you).
> Er iſt es.   Sind Sie es?   It is he. Is it you?

In this construction the pronoun ich, du, er, etc., receives voice stress.

(*f*) Es (also das and dies) can be used with the verb ſein in the plural somewhat as French uses *ce sont* (*là*).

> Es ſind meine Vettern.   They are my cousins.
> (Ce sont mes cousins.)
> Das ſind ſeine Häuſer.   Those are his houses.
> (Ce sont là ses maisons.)
> Das waren ſo ſeine liebſten   These were his dearest thoughts
>   Gedanken.

This es construction should only be used where the idea of identification is implied or expressed. Thus a teacher might point to a pile of exercise books and say:

> Was ſind das?   What are those?

The correct answer would be:

> Das (or Es) ſind Hefte.   They are exercise books
> (*i.e.*, the pupil has now identified them as such).

But :   Wie ſind die Hefte?   What are the books like?
         Sie ſind braun.   They are brown

(because we are now describing, not identifying them).

(*g*) **The Adverbial Compound.** When the third person pronouns referring to *things* are governed by a preposition, there is a special compound form made up of

> da= + preposition (dar= if the prep. begins with a vowel).

Thus: damit, with it, with them, therewith.
      daraus, out of it, out of them.

With reference to *persons* the ordinary pronoun is used:

> Seine Eltern kamen auch;   His parents came too; the
>   mit ihnen war die Tante.   aunt was with them.

Note.—(i) This adverbial compound is possible with : an, auf, aus, bei, durch, für, gegen, hinter, in, mit, nach, neben, ob, über, unter, um, von, vor, wider, zu, zwiſchen.

(ii) darnach is found as well as danach.

(iii) Note the compounds **deshalb, deswegen,** on account of it (them). (**Halber** and **wegen** take the genitive.)

(iv) The adverbial compound representing

in + Accusative is **darein;**
in + Dative is **darin.**

Er warf sich darein	He threw himself in(to it).
(*i.e.,* in das Wasser).	

(More often **hinein,** or **herein,** is used.)

Er schwimmt darin	He is swimming in it.
(*i.e.,* in dem Wasser).	

(v) There is an increasing tendency to use the ordinary preposition + accusative or dative pronoun even with reference to things; *e.g.,* from an article on **Eine Hofburg: Friedrich Wilhelm III hatte viele Pläne mit ihr** (*i.e.,* with it, with the Hofburg).

43. First Person Pronouns.

	Singular	Plural
Nom.	ich	wir
Acc.	mich	uns
Gen.	meiner (mein)	uns(e)rer (unser)
Dat.	mir	uns

NOTE.—The plural may be used as in English for the editorial 'we' and the Royal 'we,' etc., in proclamations.

44. Second Person Pronouns.

(*a*) The familiar form.

	Singular	Plural
Nom.	du	ihr
Acc.	dich	euch
Gen.	deiner (dein)	euer (eurer, euerer)
Dat.	dir	euch

(*b*) The polite form.

	Singular and Plural
Nom.	Sie
Acc.	Sie
Gen.	Ihrer
Dat.	Ihnen

This form is the plural of the third person pronouns written with a capital letter.

45. Forms of Address.

(*a*) The familiar form, bu, etc., is used :

(i) Where intimacy exists between members of the same family, of the same form or class in school, between close friends.

Note.—(i) The verb buţen, to address someone as 'thou.' (*Cf.* French: *tutoyer*.)

(ii) Jd ftehe mit ihm auf bu und bu.	I'm on intimate terms with him.
(iii) Jd trug ihm das Du an.	I suggested he should 'thee and thou' me.

(ii) In poetic language.

(iii) In prayer and the language of the Church service.

(iv) To address the readers in books and newspapers.

> Wenn Du Frieden und Wiederaufbau fördern willft, dann gib Deine Stimme unferm Parteifandidaten !

(v) Where there is no need or no desire to observe the formality of the polite form (*e.g.*, in a polemic or in addressing little children).

(vi) In addressing animals.

> Karlo, feţ bid ! Karlo, sit down!

(*b*) Otherwise the polite form, Sie, etc., is used in ordinary dealings with people.

(*c*) A historical consideration of the pronouns used as forms of address :

(i) Original form: singular bu, plural ihr.

(ii) About the ninth century a form of address, singular Jhr, plural Jhr, was evolved from the plural of Majesty (**43**). This was gradually applied to all persons of some standing.

(iii) In the fifteenth century important personages were often addressed, as it were, indirectly, by using some noun as:

> Euer Gnaden. Your Grace.

The use of this noun in the plural involved the use of a plural verb; later this plural verb became obligatory in this form of address whether the noun used was plural or not.

Ew. Excellenz werden wohl ge= ftatten . . .	Your Excellency will, I suppose, allow . . .

(Ew. is an accepted printed and written abbreviation for Euer.)

Because of this plural verb and because of the plural noun which had preceded it, Euer was sometimes replaced by Jhre, or Seine ;

perhaps subconsciously it was felt that the noun needed a possessive adjective to correspond to it. So there were these forms:

> Ihre Majestät
> Seine Majestät } Your Majesty.
> Euer Majestät

Another archaic form Ihro Majestät was evolved.

(iv) In the sixteenth century this use of the third person was extended to people of lesser standing who had only the title Herr or Frau.

> Der Herr wird sich vielleicht   Perhaps you will sit down.
> setzen.

Then the nouns Herr and Frau were replaced by the pronouns Er and Sie, usually written with capitals. This usage fell on evil days, and in the eighteenth century it was used by superior to inferior.

Thus Frederick the Great to a subaltern:

> Hüte Er sich, dem König zu   Take care not to meet the King!
> begegnen!

(v) The modern polite form arose from the replacing of the noun in such forms as Euer Gnaden by a pronoun Sie, which was, of course, still followed by a plural verb.

(vi) In modern German there is a parallel with the form of address used in (iii) above, whereby a singular noun is followed by a plural verb. This is usually found when the speaker is exercising a rather studied politeness.

> Der Herr Doktor werden   You will come in, won't you,
> doch eintreten.   doctor?

46. Students of German literature should not forget that these various forms of address were, and in some cases still are, often coexistent. Consider the following from Schiller's *Kabale und Liebe*:

Miller to his wife: Willst du dein Maul halten?

Frau Miller to Wurm: Aber — wie der Herr Sekretäre selber die Einsicht werden haben.

Wurm to the President: Ihro Excellenz verzeihen!

President to Wurm: Wurm, besinne Er sich, daß ich hartnäckig glaube.

Luise to her father: Ich versteh' ihn, Vater.

Luise to her mother: Bleib sie doch, Mutter!

Ferdinand to his father: Sie sind heute sehr gnädig, mein Vater.

President to Ferdinand (his son): Du empfängst dein Glück von der zweiten Hand.

Ferdinand to Miller: Sei er ganz getrost, lieber Miller.

Add to this

Stauffacher to Pfeifer (*Wilhelm Tell*): Ihr seid mein Gast zu Schwytz.

47. The genitive plural of Personal Pronouns often precedes the word on which it depends; this is so when the word is one expressing number:

unser einer (rather heroic for: einer von uns), one of us.

(Also unsereiner in sense of: a person like us.)

Damit diese Unterweisung gelang, mußte ihrer die Hälfte das Leben lassen.	For the success of this order half of them had to lose their lives.

NOTE.—wir beide, both of us.
wir alle (etc.), all of us.

48. Declension of an adjective dependent on a personal pronoun.

Nom.	ich (du)	armer
Acc.	mich (dich)	armen
Gen.	meiner (deiner)	armen
Dat.	mir (dir)	armen or armem
Nom.	wir, ihr, Sie	armen (rarely *N.* arme
Acc.	uns, euch, Sie	armen *A.* arme)
Gen.	unserer, ihrer, Ihrer	armen
Dat.	uns, euch, Ihnen	armen

Wir Deutsche or wir Deutschen.	We Germans.
Ihr dunklen Drähte (F. von Saar.)	Ye gloomy wires.
Euch edlen Gästen entbiete ich meinen Gruß!	I welcome you, honourable guests!

V. INDEFINITE PRONOUNS AND ADJECTIVES

49. The **Indefinite Pronouns** are:

man, one, they, people	keiner, nobody, no one
einer, one	etwas, something
jedermann, every one	nichts, nothing
niemand, nobody, no one	beide(s), both
jemand, somebody, anybody	

The following are also used **adjectivally** :

all, all
ein anderer⎫
eine andere ⎬another
ein anderes⎭
der (die, das) andere, the other
die anderen, the others
beide, both
einige, some, a few
etliche, a few, several

ein paar (invariable), a few
jeder, =e, =es, each, every
mancher, =e, =es, many (a)
mehrere, several
verschiedene, various, several, diverse
viel(e), much, many
wenige, few
ein wenig, a little, some, a bit

NOTE.—'Some' and 'any' (adj. and pron.) are treated in 40.

(*a*) man, one, people, they, you (in a general sense). *Cf.* French *on.*

(i) This pronoun takes a third person singular verb.

(ii) man has no oblique forms; it borrows from einer; thus:

> *Nom.* man
> *Acc.* einen
> *Gen.* eines
> *Dat.* einem

But the reflexive form is, of course, sich.

Man muß seinen Nächsten wie sich selbst lieben.	One must love one's neighbour as oneself.

(iii) einer may be used in the nominative instead of man, and the pronoun er may be used instead of repeating einer.

Es mag vielleicht kümmerlich sein, was einer technisch leistet: wenn er helfen kann, die künstlerische Gestalt erstehen zu lassen, wird es für ihn das größte Glück bedeuten.	Technically one's performance may be wretched : if one can help to animate the artistic form, that will mean the greatest happiness for one.

(iv) The possessive adjective corresponding to man is sein.

Man sollte seinen Vater ehren.	One ought to honour one's father.

(*b*) jeder.

(i) Adjective.

Jede Stadt hat ihre eignen Probleme.	Every town has its own problems.

(ii) Pronoun.

Jeder von uns bekam einen Brief.	Each one of us received a letter.

(c) **jedermann**, *every one, everybody*, is declined:

Nom.	jedermann
Acc.	jedermann
Gen.	jedermanns
Dat.	jedermann

(d) **jemand**, *some one, somebody*, and **niemand**, *no one, nobody*, have both inflected and uninflected forms for the accusative and dative.

Nom.	jemand	niemand
Acc.	jemanden or jemand	niemanden or niemand
Gen.	jemandes	niemands
Dat.	jemandem or jemand	niemandem or niemand

Note.—'Some one else, no one else' are usually rendered by **jemand anders**, **niemand anders**, but **anders** may take adjective inflections.

Wir achten auf niemand(en) anders (or anderen).	We pay attention to no one else.

The genitive is rare and is best replaced by **eines andern** and **keines andern**.

Eines andern Buch.	Some one else's book.
Keines andern Buch.	No one else's book.

(e) **kein** and **keiner**. The adjective **kein** is declined like the indefinite article; the pronoun **keiner** like the pronoun **einer**:

	Masc.	*Fem.*	*Neut.*	*Plural*
Nom.	keiner	keine	keines	keine
Acc.	keinen	keine	keines	keine
Gen.	keines	keiner	keines	keiner
Dat.	keinem	keiner	keinem	keinen

Note.—(i) **keiner** is less vague than **niemand**; it usually means 'no person within some restricted area or group.'

Keiner von uns hat ihn gesehen.	None of us has seen him.

(ii) 'Neither' (pronoun) is rendered by **keiner** (=e, =es) **von beiden**.

Was ist der Plural von Baum? Baume oder Baumen? Keins von beiden !	What is the plural of Baum? Baume or Baumen? Neither.

('Neither . . . nor' is weder . . . noch.)

(*f*) etwas, *something*, and nichts, *nothing*, have no inflected forms.

(i) etwas Schönes, something beautiful. See **20** (*b*).

(ii) etwas is sometimes abbreviated to was.

Er hat keinem Menschen was gesagt.	He hasn't said anything to anyone.

(iii) etwas can be used adverbially, *somewhat*.

Er ist etwas spät gekommen.	He came somewhat late.

(iv) 'Not anything' is nichts (*Not* nicht etwas).

Seit Monaten hatten wir nichts von ihm erfahren.	We had not heard anything of him for months.

Similarly :

> not any children, keine Kinder
> not anybody, niemand

(*g*) 'Some . . . others.'

(i) If 'others' means 'all the others' which are not covered by the 'some,'

then 'some . . . others' is rendered by die einen . . . die anderen.

Die einen behaupteten, er sei ermordet worden, die anderen, er habe sich erschossen.	Some maintained that he was murdered, others that he had shot himself.

(*I.e.*, all the persons concerned held one or other of these opinions.)

(ii) If 'others' means 'some others,' then we must use einige . . andere.

Einige wollten Karl wählen, andere zogen den Pfarrer vor, Georg und sein Bruder waren aber fest entschlossen, daß keiner von beiden die Stelle haben sollte.	Some wanted to elect Karl, others preferred the parson, but George and his brother had definitely made up their minds that neither should **have** the post.

(h) 'All'; aller, alle, alles, *all, every,*

(i) is adjectival and pronominal.

> alles Fleiſch, all the meat.
> alle dieſe Leute, all these people.
> aller Soldaten, of all the soldiers.
> alles dies, or dies alles, all this; (all dies also occurs).
> alle Tage, every day.
> alle drei Jahre, every three years.
> alles ift vorüber, all is over.

(ii) all before the definite article or a possessive adjective is not declined in the singular.

All das Geld.	All the money.
Mit all meinem Gelde.	With all my money.

NOTE.—In such constructions all is usually replaced in Modern German by ganz:

Mit meinem ganzen Geld.	With all my money.
Das ganze Haus litt unter dieſem Fluch.	All the house (The whole house) suffered from this curse.

(iii) 'All the' standing before a plural noun is usually rendered by alle (*A.* alle, *G.* aller, *D.* allen), but all die is also found (*not* alle die).

Alle Fenſter ſtanden offen.	All the windows were open.
Fritz war mit allen Schiffern befreundet.	Fritz was friends with all the sailors.
Von all den Kindern war mir das jüngſte am liebſten.	Of all the children, I liked the youngest best.
Alle drei ſtanden da.	All (the) three (The whole three of them) stood there.

(iv) In the singular all may be declined like an ordinary adjective when it is not preceded by an article.

Aller Anfang iſt ſchwer.	Every beginning is hard.

(v) alle (invariable) is used predicatively in the sense of 'all gone.'

Das Brot iſt alle.	The bread is all gone.
Es muß alle werden.	It must be eaten up.

(vi) **alles** is sometimes found with the meaning 'everybody.'

Die Straßen wimmelten von Männern, Frauen und Kindern; alles lief dem Musikanten nach.	The streets swarmed with men, women, and children; everybody was running after the musician.

(*i*) **beide, beides,** *both, the two.*

(i) Note carefully the form used and the order of words in the following:

Beide Männer, or die beiden Männer, both the men, both men.
Die Namen der beiden Männer, or die Namen beider Männer, the names of the two men, of both the men.

In German a possessive adjective used with **beiden** always precedes it.

Meine beiden Brüder.	Both my brothers.
Die Karriere unsrer beiden Kinder.	The career of both our children.

(ii) **As a Pronoun.**

Dann gingen beide in den Garten.	Then both (of them) (the two of them) went into the garden.

Contrary to English usage German may use a singular form, as in:

Welches ist richtig — der Teil oder das Teil? Beides ist richtig.	Which is it correct to say— der Teil or das Teil? Both are correct.

(*j*) **irgend** gives additional indefiniteness. It is placed before:

(i) **ein, eine, ein** to make an indefinite adjective meaning 'any (whatsoever).'

Haben Sie irgendeine Ahnung von seinen Plänen?	Have you any idea whatever of his plans?

(ii) **einer, eine, eines** to make a corresponding indefinite pronoun:

Haben Sie eine Flasche Tinte? Welche Marke, mein Herr? Ach, irgend eine.	Have you a bottle of ink? What make, sir? Oh, any will do.

(iii) jemand, or wer, to make an indefinite pronoun meaning 'anybody.'

Das kann irgend jemand.	Anyone can do that.

(iv) etwas, 'anything at all.'

Wissen Sie irgend etwas darüber?	Do you know anything at all about it?

Some common adverbs:

> irgendwie, anyhow, somehow
> irgendwo, somewhere or other
> irgendwoher, from anywhere
> irgendwohin, anywhere (when motion is implied)
> irgendwomit, with whatever (you like)

(*k*) Note die meisten, *most people*.

Die meisten glauben ihm nicht.	Most people don't believe him.

(*l*) The Indefinite Adjective mancher is declined like dieser; in manch ein, which is found in older style and in poetry, the manch is invariable.

Mancher tapfere Soldat *or* Manch (ein) tapferer Sol= dat.	Many a brave soldier.

(*m*) viel, wenig. In the singular viel and wenig are usually uninflected in Modern German unless they follow the definite article.

Ich hab' nicht viel Zeit.	I haven't much time.
Er hatte wenig Hoffnung.	He had not much hope.
But: Die viele Zeit, die ich da verbrachte, blieb nicht ohne Erfolg.	The great deal of time which I spent there was not wasted.

An adjective after uninflected viel or wenig is declined like an adjective when no article precedes it.

Es lag noch viel gekochter Salm auf dem Teller.	There was still a lot of boiled salmon on the dish.

For the declension of an adjective after viele or wenige (plural), see **87**, Note (ii).

VI. INTERROGATIVE PRONOUNS AND ADJECTIVES

50. Interrogative Pronouns.

Of Persons	*Of Things*
Nom. wer, who?	was, what?
Acc. wen, whom?	was, what?
Gen. wessen, whose, of whom?	wes (see (*f*) below).
Dat. wem, to or for whom?	(see (*e*) and (*h*) below).

Note.—Lovers of the whimsical will enjoy Christian Morgenstern's Der Werwolf.

(*a*) The old personal genitive was wes, as in

Wes ist das Bild und die Überschrift? (Matt. xxii. 20.)	Whose is this image and superscription?

(*b*) In the declension of wer anders (who else), the anders is not usually inflected.

(*c*) Wer is occasionally used as an indefinite pronoun with the meaning of 'somebody.'

(*d*) There is no special plural form for the Interrogative Pronouns; wer and was govern a third person singular verb, but they may govern the third person plural if the verb is sein.

> Was sind das?   What are those? (42 (*f*).)

(*e*) Wem as a Dative of was is found, but only as the object of verbs which govern the Dative.

Wem anders als der mitteldeutschen Gruppe gehört diese Mundart an?	To what else but the Middle German group does this dialect belong?

(*f*) Wes as the Genitive of was is only used with verbs which govern the Genitive.

> Wes freut er sich?   What is he rejoicing about?

In Modern German the Genitive with these verbs tends to be replaced by a prepositional construction; thus the need for this form wes is diminishing.

Note.—Weshalb? For what reason, wherefore?

(*g*) Note the construction was + Genitive.

> Was ist Gutes daran?   What good is there in it?
>
> (*Cf.* French: Qu'est-ce qu'il y a de bon?)

(*h*) The adverbial compound with **wo(r)=**.

Whenever the interrogative pronoun representing things is governed by a preposition, the adverbial compound consisting of **wo=** + preposition must be used (**wor=** if the preposition begins with a vowel). (*Cf.* **42** (*g*).)

(i) This compound is possible with: **an, auf, aus, bei, durch, für, gegen, hinter, in, mit, nach, neben, über, unter, um, von, vor, zu, zwischen.**

Wir haben lange geplaudert.	We talked for a long time.
Worüber?	About what?
Wozu all das Lesen?	What is the purpose of all the reading?

(ii) This compound may also be used to introduce relative clauses (**52**, Note (i)).

(iii) There is an increasing tendency to use preposition + **was** instead of this adverbial compound:

Frau Braun, ihre Jungs streiten furchtbar. Um was?	Mrs Braun, your boys are having a terrible quarrel. What about?

The use of preposition + **wen** or **wem** when referring to persons probably strengthens this tendency.

(iv) **Was** may be found in the sense of **warum** (why).

Mein Sohn, was birgst du so bang dein Gesicht?	My son, why dost thou so anxiously hide thy face?
Was bist du denn so blaß?	Why are you so pale, then?

51. Interrogative Adjectives.

(*a*) **welcher**, which? is thus declined:

	Singular			Plural
	Masc.	*Fem.*	*Neut.*	
Nom.	welcher	welche	welches	welche
Acc.	welchen	welche	welches	welche
Gen.	welches	welcher	welches	welcher
Dat.	welchem	welcher	welchem	welchen

Welches Wort hat er nicht übersetzt?	Which word has he not translated?
Mit welchem Zug war er gefahren?	Which train had he gone by?

(*b*) **was für (ein)**, what sort of?

(i) In this phrase the für does not govern the following noun or pronoun, which will only be in the Accusative if its function in the sentence requires it to be so.

Was für ein Mann ist er?	What sort of a man is he?
Was für einen Hut wollen Sie?	What sort of a hat do you want?

With plural nouns there is, of course, no indefinite article.

Was für Bäume?   What sort of trees?

(ii) In exclamations.

Was für ein schönes Bild !   What a pretty picture !

NOTE.—The was may be separated from the für.

Was wurden für harte Worte gegen die Jungen gefunden !	What hard words were applied to the young people!

VII. RELATIVE PRONOUNS

52. 1. The **Relative Pronouns** der and welcher are thus declined :

	Masc.	Singular Fem.	Neut.	Plural
Nom.	der	die	das	die
Acc.	den	die	das	die
Gen.	dessen	deren	dessen	deren
Dat.	dem	der	dem	denen

This relative pronoun was derived from, and is almost identical with, the demonstrative pronoun der, die, das. See 117 (*b*).

Nom.	welcher	welche	welches	welche
Acc.	welchen	welche	welches	welche
Gen.	(welches)	(welcher)	(welches)	(welcher)
Dat.	welchem	welcher	welchem	welchen

The genitives in brackets are very rare.

2. Use of der or welcher.

(*a*) Use der when the antecedent is an interrogative, personal, or indefinite pronoun, or a noun used as a vocative.

Niemand, der es gesehen hat.   Nobody who has seen it.

(*b*) Use **welcher** if the relative word is adjectival.

Er murmelte „Dios", welches Wort er von dem Spanier gelernt hatte.	He murmured 'Dios,' which word he had learnt from the Spaniard.

(*c*) Otherwise there is no restriction on the use of either relative pronoun; but there is a tendency to prefer **der, die, das**, etc., because they are shorter. Nevertheless the stylist usually avoids juxtaposition of two identical words.

Das sind die Insekten, die die Blumen zerstören.	Those are the insects which destroy the flowers.

is better rendered: **Das sind die Insekten, welche die Blumen zerstören.**

NOTE.—(i) A compound form composed of **wo=** (or **wor=**) + preposition may be used as a relative when relating to *things*. (*Cf.* **50** (*h, i*).)

There is a tendency to avoid the compound form when referring to a plural antecedent.

Der Tisch, auf dem **auf welchem** } **ich schreibe.** **worauf**	The table on which I write.
Die Häuser, auf die **auf welche** } **es sich bezieht.**	The houses to which it refers.

(ii) After the genitive of the relative pronoun, the definite article is not required in German:

Die Bäume, deren Schönheit er so deutlich beschrieb, . . .	The trees, the beauty of which he described so clearly, . . .

Cf. French: Les arbres dont il décrivit si clairement la beauté.

53. **was** is the Relative Pronoun to be used:

(*a*) After an indefinite neuter antecedent (**das, alles, nichts, wenig, viel**).

Im Bewußtsein, das zu erfüllen, was Volk und Staat verlangen.	In the consciousness of fulfilling that which the people and the State require.
Etwas, was ich unter keinen Umständen dulden werde, ist der Gebrauch von Eselsbrücken.	What I shall not allow on any account is the use of cribs.

(*b*) After a neuter adjective as antecedent.

Er zeigte das Beste, was er tun konnte.	He showed the best he could do.

(*c*) When the antecedent is a whole clause or an idea.

Meine Schwester hat sich endlich einen Hund gekauft, was mir sehr gefällt.	My sister has at last bought a dog, (a fact) which pleases me very much.

(. . . einen Hund gekauft, der mir sehr gefällt would mean 'a dog which I like.')

54. The Relative Pronoun may be omitted in English; in German, as in French, it must never be omitted.

Das Buch, welches er mir geliehen hat.	The book he lent me.
Die Hügel, auf die er hinwies.	The hills he pointed at.

55. (*a*) If the reference is to someone indefinite, the Interrogative Pronoun wer may be used in place of the more clumsy der Mann, der . . . , or derjenige, welcher . . . (he who . . . , the one who . . . , French : *celui qui*).

Wer das getan hat, ist ein unverschämter Kerl.	He who (The one who) has done that is an impudent fellow.
Wem ich diese Symphonie widme, möge auch für ihre Aufführung sorgen.	The one to whom I dedicate this symphony, should also see that it is performed.

Also in proverbs, *e.g.*,

Wer andern eine Grube gräbt, fällt selbst hinein.	Whoso diggeth a pit shall fall therein.

Sometimes the demonstrative element of this use of wer is further emphasized by using as demonstrative der in the main clause :

Wer recht hat, der gibt nicht nach.	He who is right does not yield.
Wem nicht zu raten ist, dem ist nicht zu helfen.	He who cannot be advised cannot be helped (*i.e.*, there is no help for the man who scorns advice).

(*b*) In the same way **was** can be used to represent the idea of 'a thing which,' 'that which,' and may likewise have a demonstrative **das** in the main clause.

Was du heute tun kannst, das verschiebe nicht auf morgen.	Do not put off till to-morrow that which you can do to-day.

NOTE.—**was** can also have an antecedent (**53**).

56. **Wer** and **was** may be followed by **auch** in the sense of 'whoever, whatever.' With this construction the verb may be in the Indicative or the Subjunctive.

Wer sie auch seien.	Whoever they may be.
Was er auch getan hat.	Whatever he has done.

This construction may be strengthened by the addition of **immer.**

Wer sie auch immer sein mögen.	Whoever they may be.

VIII. REFLEXIVE AND RECIPROCAL PRONOUNS

57. The **Reflexive Pronouns** may be shown thus:

Present Tense of **sich waschen** (this shows the Accusative).

ich wasche mich,	I wash myself
du wäschst dich,	thou washest thyself
er wäscht sich,	he washes himself
sie wäscht sich,	she washes herself
es wäscht sich,	it washes itself
man wäscht sich,	one washes oneself
wir waschen uns,	we wash ourselves
ihr wascht euch,	you wash yourselves
sie waschen sich,	they wash themselves

Present Tense of **sich einen König wählen** (this shows the Dative).

ich wähle mir einen König	I choose a king for myself, etc.
du wähl(e)st dir einen König	
er wählt sich einen König	
sie wählt sich einen König	
es wählt sich einen König	

man wählt sich einen König
wir wählen uns einen König
ihr wählt euch einen König
sie wählen sich einen König

Present Tense of spotten used reflexively (this shows the Genitive because spotten takes the Genitive).

ich spotte meiner	I mock or ridicule myself, etc.
du spottest deiner	
er spottet seiner selbst	
sie spottet ihrer selbst	
es spottet seiner selbst	
man spottet seiner selbst	
wir spotten unser(er)	
ihr spottet eur(er)	
sie spotten ihrer selbst	

NOTE.—(i) The selbst in the third person is added to avoid ambiguity; er spottet seiner could mean 'he mocks him' (some other person).

(ii) Be careful to use sich (*not* the personal pronouns) after prepositions, when the pronoun governed by preposition refers to the same person as the subject of the clause.

Er schleppte hinter sich einen leeren Sack.	He was dragging an empty bag behind him.

58. The **Emphatic Adjectives** selbst and selber. They are indeclinable and correspond in function to Latin *ipse*. (Reflexive sich corresponds to Latin *se*.)

Er selbst tötete den Mann.	He himself killed the man.
But: Er tötete sich.	He killed himself.

Note that selbst may be used adverbially ('even') and then usually precedes whatever it qualifies.

Selbst der Hirte freute sich darauf.	Even the shepherd was looking forward to it.

59. Reciprocal Pronouns.

(*a*) The usual pronoun (acc. and dat.) is **einander**. Preposition + **einander** is usually written as one word.

Wir sehen einander nicht oft.	We don't often see one another.
Sie rollten übereinander.	They rolled one over another.

(*b*) The reflexive pronoun may be used when the Reciprocal Pronoun is connected with a verb.

Sie begegneten sich auf dem Marktplatz.	They met one another in the Market.

Where the use of the reflexive pronoun might be ambiguous, the reciprocal idea can be rendered by adding gegenseitig or by using einander as in (*a*) above.
Thus:

Sie lieben sich.	They love themselves.
Sie lieben sich gegenseitig. } Sie lieben einander.	They love one another.

(*c*) The genitive has to be rendered by einer (*fem.* eine) . . . des andern (*fem.* der andern).

Sie spotten einer des andern.	They mock one another.
Sie zerrissen einer des andern Bücher.	They tore one another's books.

But where 'one another' is dependent on a noun, it is usually rendered by einander (dat.). Thus the above sentence is more neatly expressed:

Sie zerrissen einander die Bücher.

IX. GENDER OF NOUNS

60. 1. Natural Gender of Nouns.

Natural Gender, which makes male creatures masculine and female feminine, is observed in German. For example:

der Knabe,	the boy.
die Frau,	the woman.
der Fuchs,	the fox.
die Füchsin,	the vixen.
der Hengst,	the stallion.
die Stute,	the mare.

NOTE, however:

(i)

das Weib,	the woman.
das Fräulein,	the young lady.
das Mädchen,	the girl.

(=lein and =chen are neuter diminutive terminations. See **64** (*a*).)

(ii) Some animal names which do not specify sex, but merely represent the species, are neuter:

> das Schwein, the pig.
> das Pferd, the horse.
> das Schaf, the sheep.
> das Kalb, the calf.
> das Füllen, das Fohlen, the foal, colt.
> das Lamm, the lamb.

To these we might add:

> das Kind, the child.

Unfortunately this cannot be taken as a rule, for there are, among others:

> die Ratte, the rat.
> die Biene, the bee.
> die Wespe, the wasp.
> die Maus, the mouse.

61. 2. Grammatical Gender.

Several conjectures have been put forward to explain why nouns which seem to have no connexion with sex should have taken on masculine or feminine gender. The most plausible is that primitive man was superstitious enough to invest objects around him (*e.g.*, trees, hills, sun, moon) with a spiritual entity, and then with gender.

The student of German should face up to the fact that he must learn the gender of nouns if he wishes to master the language. Such co-ordination and grouping as are possible will be made below, but they will not make it any less true that the gender of each common noun should be known.

62. Masculine (as well as living beings naturally masculine) are:

(*a*) Names of days, months, seasons.

> der Dienstag, Tuesday.
> der Mittwoch, Wednesday.
> (In spite of die Woche, week.)
> der Winter, the winter.
> der Mai, May.

(*b*) Names of winds, points of compass, and most mountains:

> der Süden, the south.

(*c*) Nouns formed from strong verb stems to which nothing has been added:

ber Zug (from ziehen, zog, gezogen), the train.

(*But* bie Zucht, 'breeding,' because a t has been added.)

    Exceptions: bas Schloß, the castle.
                bie Ausfuhr, the export.

(*d*) Nouns ending in =er which denote an agent.

                ber Bäcker, the baker.

(*e*) Nouns ending in =ig, =ich, =icht, =ing, =ling.

                ber Sperling, the sparrow.
                ber Honig, the honey.

    Exceptions: bas Reich, realm.
                bie Pflicht, duty.

63. Feminine (as well as living beings naturally feminine) are:

(*a*) Nouns with the suffixes =heit, =keit, =schaft, =ung, =erei.

                bie Heiterkeit, cheerfulness.
                bie Bäckerei, the baker's shop.

NOTE.—Obviously Aufschwung will be masculine in accordance with **62** (*c*), being derived from schwingen. Nor is the end of the word a suffix.

(*b*) Nouns formed from verb stems to which =e, =t, or =b have been added:

                bie Falle (from fallen), the trap.
                bie Jagb (from jagen), the hunt.

But: ber Fall, the case, in accordance with **62** (*c*).

                bie Flucht (from fliehen), the flight.
                bie Schlacht (from schlagen), the battle.
                bie Hilfe (from helfen), the help.

(*c*) Names of Rivers:

                bie Themse, Thames.
                bie Donau, Danube.

    Exceptions: ber Rhein, ber Main, ber Nedar.

(*d*) Cardinal numerals used as nouns:

                bie beutsche Elf, the German XI.

64. Neuter are:

(a) Nouns with the diminutive suffixes =djen, =lein (sometimes
=el in South Germany and =li in Switzerland):

> das Mädchen, das Mädel, the girl.
> das Lämmchen, the little lamb, lambkin.
> das Röslein, the little rose.

(b) Nouns ending in =tum:

> das Eigentum, the property.

> Exceptions: der Reichtum, wealth.
> der Irrtum, error.

(c) Names of minerals:

> das Blei, lead.
> das Eisen, iron.

> Exceptions: der Stahl, steel (not really a mineral).
> die Bronze, bronze (,, ,,).

(d) Names of countries and towns:

> das heutige Berlin, Berlin of to-day

> Exceptions: die Schweiz, Switzerland.
> die Pfalz, the Palatinate.
> die Türkei, Turkey.
> die Tschechoslowakei, Czechoslovakia.

Names of German districts ending in =gau are usually masculine.

(e) Infinitives used as nouns (the Gerund):

> das Schwimmen, swimming.
> das Essen, the meal.

(f) Letters of the Alphabet:

> großes T, capital T.

(g) Adjectives used as abstract nouns:

> das Gute an ihm, the good, *i.e.*, that which is good, in him.

(h) Nouns ending in =tel which represent fractions:

> das Viertel, the quarter.
> das Fünftel, the fifth.

Note.—The suffix =tel is derived from Teil (part), which is masculine or neuter.

65. Gender of foreign nouns. Generally these retain the gender they had in their own language:

> das Prinzip, Latin (neut.) principium.
> die Theorie, Fr. (fem.) théorie.

(*a*) French masculines in -*age* become feminine in German by analogy with feminines in =e :

> die Etage, Fr. (masc.) étage.

(*b*) Most names of countries are neuter by analogy (**64** (*d*)):

> dieses neue Amerika (despite the Fem. =a ending).

(*c*) Some names of things which in French are masculine become neuter in German:

> das Resultat, le résultat.
> das Porträt, le portrait.

(*d*) The gender of borrowings from English is usually determined by that of the German word nearest in meaning or appearance:

> die Saturday Review, because 'review' reminds one of die Revue.
> der One=Step, because it is der Tanz.
> das Beefsteak, because it is das Fleisch.

X. COMPOUND NOUNS

66. The **Gender** of a Compound Noun is that of the last component, as for example:

> der Uhrmacher, watchmaker.
> die Uhrfeder, watchspring.
> das Uhrwerk, clockwork.

Exceptions:

(i) Der Mittwoch, Wednesday (but die Woche, week).
    Der Abscheu, disgust (but die Scheu, timidity).

(ii) The compounds ending in =mut (der Mut, courage) are masculine, but the following are feminine:

> die Anmut, grace.
> die Demut, humility.
> die Großmut, magnanimity.

> die Langmut, patience.
> die Sanftmut, gentleness.
> die Schwermut, melancholy.

N.B. die Armut, poverty, which has nothing to do with the noun Mut.

(iii) Compounds ending in =voll (adjective) take the gender of the noun immediately before =voll :

> der Mundvoll, mouthful.
> die Handvoll, handful.

(iv) Compound nouns which are really a phrase or a clause are neuter unless the natural gender is strongly felt :

> das Vergißmeinnicht, forget-me-not.
> der Gottseibeiuns, (euphemism for) the devil.

67. Formation of Compound Nouns.

No rules can be given for the formation of compound nouns ; only by observance and care can the student avoid mistakes.

(*a*) In the earlier forms of the language, compounds were formed by juxtaposition, and examples of these and later analogous forms can be found.

> das Hufeisen, horseshoe.
> ein Bäckerwagen, a baker's cart.

(*b*) Some compounds have an e which seems strange at the first sight :

> Tagelohn, day's wages.

This e is not the plural ending but the normal outcome of the O.H.G. (singular) taga which has now disappeared in the normal declension of der Tag. An e is also found after some verb stems :

> das Sterbebett, death-bed.

(*c*) Many compounds have a genitive s :

> das Kriegsgericht, court martial.

In some this s has no etymological justification and is merely by analogy :

> der Liebeshandel, love affair.
> der Hilfslehrer, assistant teacher.

Feminines in =ḥeit, =ḳeit, =ſḍaft, =ung, =tat, =ion, =at, =ut, take this **s** when they form the first part of a compound:

> Woḥltätigḳeitszwecḳe, charitable purposes.
> Deḳorationsmaler, scene painter.

NOTE (i) This **s** may make a difference in meaning:

> die Waſſernot, lack of water.
> die Waſſersnot, distress arising from flooding.
> der Landmann, peasant.
> der Landsmann, compatriot.

(ii) This **s** may not have Genitive force:

> So ſtirbt ein braver Reitersmann.   So a brave trooper dies.
> (*Not* trooper's man.)

·(iii) In a few words the **s** has the force of a plural, although its form is that of a genitive singular:

> die Sḍiffswerft, dockyard (*i.e.*, wharf for ships).

(*d*) The Genitive may not be easily recognized in some compounds:

> Liebfrauenḳirḍe, church of Our Dear Lady.
> der Sonnenſḍein, the sunshine.

(Here the =en is the old weak feminine genitive singular, now obsolete.)

> der Gänſebraten, roast goose.

(Here Gänſe is not plural but an old genitive singular of Gans.)

(*e*) Some show a weak genitive:

> ein Heldentod, a heroic death.

This weak genitive may still stand in compounds although the noun may no longer be weak, *e.g.*,

> das Greiſenalter, senility.

(Nowadays der Greis, *Acc.* den Greis, *Gen.* des Greiſes, old man.)

Some compounds have the weak ending =en merely by analogy:

> der Sinnenrauſḍ, intoxication of the senses.

> (*But* der Sinn, *pl.* die Sinne.)

(*f*) In the compound der Hoḥeprieſter (high priest) the adjective is declined:

> *Nom.*   ein Hoḥerprieſter.
> *Gen.*   des Hoḥenprieſters, etc.

Similarly in bie Lang(e)weile (boredom) the adjective is sometimes declined:

> *Nom.* and *Acc.* bie Lang(e)weile.
> *Gen.* and *Dat.* ber Langenweile.

Aus Langweile or Aus Langerweile, from boredom.

XI. DECLENSION OF NOUNS

68. It should be remembered that

(*a*) The dative plural of all German nouns ends in ₌n:

> ber Mann, bie Männer. *Dat. pl.* ben Männern.
> bie Maus, bie Mäuse. *Dat. pl.* ben Mäusen.

If the noun already ends in ₌n in the nominative plural no additional ₌n is needed in the dative plural.

> bie Frau, bie Frauen. *Dat. pl.* ben Frauen.

A few foreign nouns which make their plural in ₌s take no ₌n in the dative plural:

> bas Auto, bie Autos. *Dat. pl.* ben Autos.

(*b*) Feminine nouns are never inflected in the singular (*i.e.*, they make no change in their ending).

Note.—In M.H.G. many feminine nouns had inflections in the singular, *e.g.*,

> *N.* and *A.* anft, *G.* and *D.* enfte (*cf.* 67 (*d*)).
> *N.* зunge, *A.*, *G.* and *D.* зungen.

In Modern German these inflections in the singular of feminine nouns have only been retained in some compound nouns (67 (*d*)) and in a few fixed expressions:

> Friebe auf Erben.   Peace upon earth.

(*c*) All German nouns begin with a capital letter (except in some scientific works and a few poets, *e.g.* Stefan George).

69. With respect to their declension, nouns can be divided into three main groups—strong, weak, mixed.

1. Strong Nouns.

(*a*) The nominative plural will never be in ₌n.

(*b*) If the noun is masculine or neuter the genitive singular will have the ending ₌s or ₌es.

Add =es to nouns ending in =s, ß, =ſch, =z, and to most monosyllables.

Add =s only to diminutives, nouns in =el, =en, =er, =em, and to
proper names.

NOTE.—The genitive of the prefixed constituents of compound
words is not always formed in accordance with the above rule
because many compound words were formed before the =es ending
was well established.

>Thus we say des Krieges, of the war.
>*But*:   Kriegsrüſtung, munitions.

(*c*) Nominative and accusative singular are the same.

(*d*) If the noun is a masculine or neuter monosyllable the
dative singular may end in =e.

This =e of the dative singular is not used:

  (i) In foreign words: mit dem Lord (not Lorde).
  (ii) When the noun is used immediately after a preposition:
mit Zorn.

(But here a few fixed expressions must have the =e:

>zugrunde gehen, to perish.
>jemanden zu Rate ziehen, to consult someone.
>zu Hauſe, at home.)

(iii) When it would cause a clash of vowels:

>mit dem Pfeil (not Pfeile)und mit dem Bogen.
>auf dem Knie (not Kniee).

(iv) With nouns which are in apposition after an expression of
quantity:

>in einem Glas (not Glaſe) Wein.

2. Weak Nouns.

(*a*) If masculine, these have =(e)n as the inflection for the
Accusative, Genitive, and Dative singular:

>der Graf, den Grafen, des Grafen, dem Grafen.

(*b*) Whatever their gender, they have =(e)n as the inflection
for all the cases of the plural.

(*c*) Never take a modification sign (˝) as the mark of the
plural.

3. Mixed Nouns.

These have their singular strong and their plural weak.

70. Types of Declension.

STRONG

I *Sing.*	II *Sing.*	III *Sing.*	IV *Sing.*
N. -----	N. -----	N. -----	N. -----
A. -------	A. -----	A. -----	A. -----
G. ----- (e)ѕ	G. ----- (e)ѕ	G. ----- ѕ	G. ----- ѕ
D. ----- (e)	D. ----- (e)	D. -----	D. -----
Plur.	*Plur.*	*Plur.*	*Plur.*
N. ----- e	N. --ˉ-- e	N. -----	N. --ˉ--
A. ----- e	A. --ˉ-- e	A. -----	A. --ˉ--
G. ----- e	G. --ˉ-- e	G. -----	G. --ˉ--
D. ----- en	D. --ˉ-- en	D. ----- n	D. --ˉ-- n

In this class are:

In this class are:

In this class are:

In this class are:

I

1. Masc. monosyllables which cannot take ˙˙.
2. Masc. in ₌ig, ₌ich, ₌icht, ₌ing.
3. [1] Fem. in ₌nis[2] and ₌fal.
4. Neut. in ₌nis,[2] ₌fal, and ₌icht.

II

1. Some masc. monosyllables.
2. One neut. monosyllable: das Floß,raft.
3. [1] The following feminine monosyllables:

Art, axe
Bank, bench
Braut, bride
Bruft, breast
Fauft, fist
Frucht, fruit
Gans, goose
Hand, hand
Kraft, power
Kuh, cow
Luft, air
Luft, desire
Macht, might
Magd, maid
Maus, mouse
Nacht, night

III

1. Neut. in ₌el, ₌en, ₌er, except Klofter.
2. Masc. in ₌el, ₌en, ₌er, except those listed in the next column.

IV

1. das Klofter, convent.
2. [1] die Mutter, mother.
die Tochter, daughter.
3. These masc:

Acker, field
Apfel, apple
Bruder, brother
Faden, thread
Garten, garden
Graben, ditch
Hafen, harbour
Hammer, hammer
Handel, quarrel
Laden, shop
Mangel, lack
Mantel, cloak
Nagel, nail
Ofen, stove
Sattel, saddle

[1] Feminines, of course, take no inflection in the singular.
[2] Nouns in ₌nis double the s before an unstressed e, *e.g.*, das Bekenntnis, des Bekenntniffes, die Bekenntniffe.

Nuß, nut
Stadt, town
Wand, wall
Wurst, sausage

Schaden, damage
Schnabel, beak
Schwager, brother-in-law
Vater, father
Vogel, bird

STRONG V	WEAK	MIXED
Sing.	*Sing.*	*Sing.*
N. -----	N. ----- (e)	N. -----
A. -----	A. ----- (e)n	A. -----
G. ----- (e)s	G. ----- (e)n	G. ----- (e)s
D. ----- (e)	D. ----- (e)n	D. ----- (e)
Plur.	*Plur.*	*Plur.*
N. --⸚-- er	N. ----- (e)n	N. ----- (e)n
A. --⸚-- er	A. ----- (e)n	A. ----- (e)n
G. --⸚-- er	G. ----- (e)n	G. ----- (e)n
D. --⸚-- ern	D. ----- (e)n	D. ----- (e)n

In this class are:

1. Most neuter monosyllables.

2. Nouns in =tum.

In this class are:

1. [1] Fem. in =heit, =keit, =schaft, =ung.

2. [1] Fem. in =el, =er, except Mutter and Tochter.

3. Masc. in =e which are names of living beings.

4. Also these masc.:

In this class are:

1. The following masc.:

Bauer,[2] peasant
Dorn, thorn
Forst, forest
Lorbeer, laurel
Mast, mast
Nachbar, neighbour
Schmerz, pain
See, lake
Staat, state (country)
Stachel, sting
Strahl, ray

=================

Weak nouns continued from centre column.

5. Many foreign loan words with stress on the last syllable:

Advokat, lawyer
Assistent, assistant
Diamant, diamond
Elefant, elephant
Husar, hussar
Kamerad, comrade
Kandidat, candidate

Ahn, ancestor
Bär, bear
Bayer, Bavarian (*plur.* Bayern)
Bursch, fellow
Christ, Christian
Fink, finch
Fürst, prince
Geck, fop
Graf, count
Held, hero
Herr, Mr, gentleman (*sing.* oblique cases,

2. These neuters:

Auge, eye
Bett, bed
Ende, end
Hemd, shirt
Insekt, insect
Interesse, interest
Ohr, ear

[1] Feminines, of course, take no inflection in the singular.

[2] Also weak.

Komet, comet
Kommandant, com-
  mander
Monarch, monarch
Musikant, musician
Philosoph, philosopher
Planet, planet
Poet, poet
Präsident, president
Regent, regent
Rekrut, recruit
Sergeant, sergeant
Soldat, soldier
Student, student

Herrn, *pl.* Herren)
Hirt, shepherd
Lump, scamp
Mensch, man, human
  being
Narr, fool
Oberst, colonel
Ochs, ox
Prinz, prince
Spatz, sparrow
Tor, fool
Ungar, Hungarian
  (*plur.* Ungarn)
Vorfahr, ancestor
  (*See preceding column.*)

3. Masculines in =or
which shift the voice
stress in the plural:
'Doktor, doctor
  (*plur.* Dok'toren)
Pro'fessor, professor
'Autor, author

71. Special Declensions.

(*a*) Das Herz (heart) and der Sporn (spur) are thus declined:

	Singular	Plural
Nom.	das Herz	die Herzen
Acc.	das Herz	die Herzen
Gen.	des Herzens	der Herzen
Dat.	dem Herzen	den Herzen
Nom.	der Sporn	die Sporen
Acc.	den Sporn	die Sporen
Gen.	des Sporn(e)s	der Sporen
Dat.	dem Sporn(e)	den Sporen

(*b*) A few masculines are declined in all cases (except the Nom.
Sing.) as if the Nom. Sing. ended in =en, *e.g.*:

	Singular	Plural
Nom.	der Name	die Namen
Acc.	den Namen	die Namen
Gen.	des Namens	der Namen
Dat.	dem Namen	den Namen

These nouns are:

> der Buchstabe,[1] letter (of alphabet).
> der Friede, peace.
> der Funke, spark.
> der Gedanke,[1] thought.
> der Glaube, faith.

[1] These sometimes have a weak Genitive.

> der Haufe, heap.
> der Name,[1] name.
> der Same,[1] seed.
> der Wille, will.
> der Schade (*pl.* Schäden), damage.
> der Fels,[1] rock.

(*c*) Feminines which are formed from masculine nouns by adding =in have plural in =innen, *e.g.*:

> der Graf, the count.
> die Gräfin, the countess, *pl.* die Gräfinnen.

(*d*). There are in conversational German the following plurals in =s:

die Mädels, the girls.	Literary forms die Mädel.
die Jungs or die Jungens, } the boys.	die Jungen.
die Kerls, the fellows.	die Kerle.

(*e*) Nouns with the Italian, Latin, or Greek endings =a, =i, =o, =on, =um, =os, =(ism)us change the ending to =en in the plural.

der Katechismus	die Katechismen	catechism
das Drama	die Dramen	drama
das Konto	die Konten	account
das Studium	die Studien	study
das Kolleg(ium)	die Kollegien	course of lectures
das Konzil(ium)	die Konzilien	council (ecclesiastical)
das Prinzip(ium)	die Prinzipien	principle
die Firma	die Firmen	firm
der Globus (*G.* des Globus)	die Globen	globe
das Epos (*G.* des Epos)	die Epen	epic
der Heros (*G.* des Heros)	die Heroen	hero
das Individuum	die Individuen	individual
der Typ(us)	die Typen	type

So also:

das Material	die Materialien	material
das Mineral	die Mineralien	mineral
das Fossil	die Fossilien	fossil

[1] These sometimes have a weak Genitive.

(*f*) A few grammatical terms keep their Latin plurals:

das Neutrum	die Neutra	neuter
das Pronomen	die Pronomina	pronoun
das Imperfektum	die Imperfekta	Imperfect
(also Imperfekt	Imperfekte)	
das Verbum	die Verba	verb
(also Verb	Verben)	
der Kasus	die Kasus	case

Also:

der Musikus	die Musizi	musician
das Jus	die Jura	law (as a university subject)

(*g*) Nouns with plural in =s are:

  (i) Some foreign nouns.

das Sofa	die Sofas
die Lady	die Ladys (also Ladies)

  (ii) Some parts of speech, not really nouns, but used as such.

        das A   die As (the letter 'a')
    seine furchtbaren Neins, his terrible negatives.

  (iii) Family names (**72** (*d*)).

Meyers sind nicht zu Hause.   The Meyers are not at home.

72. Proper Names.

A general principle is that the name is not inflected if preceded by the article.

(*a*) Names of persons make a Genitive in =s whether masculine or feminine.

Karls Vater. Gretas Hut.

  (i) But if an article is used with the name (**34** (*g*)) the =s is dropped.

    Der Vater des jungen Karl. Der Hut der kleinen Greta.

  (ii) Genitive in =ens and dative in =en are also found.

    Von Andromedens Spielen.
    Phaon legt Melitten die Hand auf die Schulter (Grillparzer, *Sappho*).

This Genitive in =ens is now only popular in Hansens, Maxens, Fritzens.

(iii) Relics of an old weak declension are found in compounds, *e.g.*, Marienkirche. St Mary's Church.

(*b*) If two or more names referring to the same person are used, the last only has the Genitive ₌s.

Neben der gewissenhaften Regie Dr. Hermann Schaffners ist die Arbeit Friedrich Franz Stampes zu erwähnen.	Together with Dr Hermann Schaffner's conscientious production we must mention the work of Friedrich Franz Stampe.
Kurt von Hagenaus Bücher.	Kurt von Hagenau's books.
Die Bücher Kurt von Hagenaus.	The books of Kurt von Hagenau.

NOTE.—Medieval names with von take ₌s with the first name:

> Wolframs von Eschenbach Parzival und Titurel.
> Die Werke Wolframs von Eschenbach

(because Eschenbach is felt to be a place-name and not an integral part of the man's name).

(*c*) Note the declension of

(i)	*Nom.*	Jesus Christus	Jesus Christ
	Acc.	Jesum Christum	
	Gen.	Jesu Christi	
	Dat.	Jesu Christo	

But this is not always followed in Modern German.

„Wir bekennen Christus nicht als einen ethischen Helden sondern als einen Heiland und Herrn."

(ii) Other biblical names:

> Johanniskirche, St John's church.
> Petrikirche, St Peter's church.

(*d*) Family names add ₌s in the plural if the members of the family are referred to.

die Schmidts, the members of the Smith family.

But: die Schiller dieser Welt, the people like Schiller.

73. Titles.

(*a*) The title Herr is always inflected.

> das Haus Herrn Webers.
> das Haus des Herrn Geheimrates Weber.
> Herrn Geheimrat Webers Haus.

NOTE.—In addressing a letter use Herrn (*i.e.*, accusative after an, which is usually omitted).

(*b*) (i) It is usual to have §err or §rau before a title (but not before a royal title).

§err ßrofeffor Müller, Professor Müller.

(ii) A wife used to be allowed to use her husband's title (preceded by §rau); this practice was discouraged by a government regulation issued in March 1934, but it is quite probable that it will persist for some time.

Thus in addressing the wife of Professor Heinrich, one said §rau ßrofeffor, and letters to her were addressed §rau ßrofeffor §einrich.

(iii) §err, §rau (or §räulein) may be placed before a noun indicating relationship.

§hre §rau Mutter, your mother.

Only persons who are not relatives use this form, as it is too circumspect for intercourse between relatives.

(*c*) The title Dr. usually remains uninflected. See **72** (*b*).

(*d*) Title + Proper Name form a unit; one or the other is declined.

(i) If the definite article is used with the title, both article and title will be inflected.

Das Denkmal des Kaifers Jofef II. (des zweiten).

(ii) If the definite article is not used, inflect the name, not the title.

Das Denkmal Kaifer Jofefs II.

74. Titles of Books, etc., are declined unless they are qualified by a preceding explanatory noun.

Aus Schillers Räubern.
Aus den Räubern von Schiller.

But Aus Schillers Drama „Die Räuber."

NOTE.—Der Dichter des Fauft (the author of *Faust*), because Faust is a proper name. See **72** (*a*) (i).

75. Geographical Names.

(*a*) Names of mountains and rivers have an article and regular inflection.

die Mündung des Rheins, the mouth of the Rhine.
die Höhe des Libanons, the height of Lebanon.

But many names of foreign rivers do not take inflection.

Den Oberlauf des Bug ent=   Along the upper course of the
lang.   river Bug.

This use of name without inflection is spreading, and by analogy the names of German rivers and mountains are found without inflection.

(*b*) Names of countries and places are inflected if they stand in the genitive without article.

Die Bewohner Berlins.   The inhabitants of Berlin.

But if the article is used the name is not inflected.

Die Bewohner des heutigen   The inhabitants of present-day
Berlin.   Berlin.

(*c*) Place-names ending in =s or =z do not make a Genitive in =s (they cannot have =es as that ending is not used for proper names).

Avoid the Genitive with such nouns, *e.g.*:

die Quellen von Teplitz.   ⎱
die Quellen der Stadt Teplitz. ⎰ The springs of Teplitz.

76. Names of Months usually drop the =s of the Genitive.

Anfang Juli. In the beginning of July.

If the name is used in front of the noun on which it depends, the =s is used.

Des Februars Stürme.   The storms of February.
Or die Stürme des Februar.

N.B.—März will *never* have an =es (75 (*c*)).

77. Names of Days in the genitive.

(*a*) Used adverbially they take =s.

Er kommt immer des Mon=   He always comes on Monday.
tags (or Montags).

(*b*) Otherwise they follow the general rule (**72**) and take no =s after des.

Im Laufe des Freitag. In the course of Friday.

78. (*a*) Nouns with **no plural** form :

der Abel, nobility.	das Wild, game
die Asche, ashes, embers.	die Butter, butter.
die Beute, booty.	das Eis, ice.
der Bodensatz, dregs.	der Kaffee, coffee.

der Hafer, oats.	das Obst, fruit.
der Hopfen, hops.	der Rauch, smoke.
der Putz, finery.	

Names of sciences ending in =if :

> die Physik, physics.

(b) Some of the above and the following are plural in English but singular in German:

> die Brille, spectacles, glasses (pair of).
> eine Schere, a pair of scissors.
> eine Zange, a pair of tongs.
> die Hose (also plural), trousers.
> die Kaserne, the barracks.
> der Lohn, wages.
> das Protokoll, minutes of a meeting.
> das Hauptquartier, headquarters.
> das Hochland, the Highlands (Scotland).
> das Mittelalter, Middle Ages.
> die Treppe, the stairs.

NOTE.—All these nouns in (b) except das Mittelalter may be used in the plural in German, *e.g.*, zwei Scheren, two pairs of scissors.

79. Nouns with a special plural.

Singular	*Plural*
der Atem, breath	Atemzüge
das Bestreben, endeavour	Bestrebungen
der Betrug, fraud	Betrügereien
der Dank, thanks	Danksagungen (expression of thanks)
das Erbe, inheritance	Erbschaften
der Friede, peace	Friedensverträge (peace treaties)
das Glück, luck	Glücksfälle (cases of good fortune)
das Unglück, misfortune	Unglücksfälle (unfortunate occurrences)
der Regen, rain	Regenfälle
der Schnee, snow	Schneefälle
der Tod, death	Todesfälle
der Rat, advice	Ratschläge (pieces of advice)
die Liebe, love (abstract)	Liebschaften (amours, love affairs)
der Mord, murder	Mordtaten (also Morde, the regular plural)

der Wahn, illusion	Wahnvorstellungen
der Kohl, cabbage	Kohlarten (types of cabbage)
	Kohlköpfe (cabbages)
der Lohn, reward	Belohnungen
das Lob, praise	Lobsprüche
die Vorsicht, caution	Vorsichtsmaßregeln (precautions)
der Bau, building	Bauten

80. Nouns with double plurals.

das Band	Bande, bonds	Bänder, ribbons

(*cf.* also:

der Band	Bände, volumes.
die Bande	Banden, gangs, bands.)

die Bank	Bänke, benches	Banken, banks (financial)
das Gesicht	Gesichter, faces	Gesichte, visions
der Laden	Läden, shops	Laden, shutters
das Land	Länder, countries	Lande, lands (poetic) (also Niederlande, Netherlands)
das Licht	Lichter, lights	Lichte, candles
das Wort	Wörter, single words	Worte, connected words

N.B.

der Mann	Männer, men	Mannen, vassals

(i) There is a special plural form of **Mann,** identical with the singular, used in measuring the strength of a military force.

Eine Armee von 50 000 Mann.

(ii) In many compounds =mann makes the plural in =leute, *e.g.*:

Seemann	Seeleute, seamen
Fuhrmann	Fuhrleute, carriers
Kaufmann	Kaufleute, merchants

But notice

Ehemann	Eheleute, married people
	Ehemänner, married men
Hauptmann	Hauptleute, captains
	Hauptmänner, chief men
Staatsmann	Staatsmänner, statesmen
Ehrenmann	Ehrenmänner, men of honour
Schneemann	Schneemänner, snowmen
Ersatzmann	Ersatzmänner, substitutes

XII. ADJECTIVES

Declension of Adjectives

81. It is convenient to divide adjective declensions into three types:

I. The declension used after the Definite Article der, and limiting words declined like it: dieſer, this; jener, that; jeder, every, each; welcher, which (interr. adjective); mancher, many (a); ſolcher, such.

II. The declension used after the Indefinite Article ein, and the following limiting words declined like ein: fein, no, not a; the Possessive Adjectives mein, my; dein, thy; ſein, his, its; unſer, our; euer, your; ihr, her, their; Ihr, your (polite form).

III. The declension used when the adjective stands before the noun without article or limiting word.

82. These three types are illustrated below. Two simple rules may help:

(a) The endings of the Definite Article must be found either in the adjective or in the preceding word.

(b) If the adjective is

(i) not in the nominative or accusative, and is

(ii) not required to indicate case,

its ending will be =(e)n.

83.

	I *Def. Art., etc., + Adj.*	II *Indef. Art., etc., + Adj.*	III *Simple Adj. + Noun*	*Ending needed to show Case*
Masculine				
N.	der gute Wein	ein guter Wein	guter Wein	=er
A.	den guten Wein	einen guten Wein	guten Wein	=en
G.	des guten Wein(e)s	eines guten Wein(e)s	guten (gutes) Wein(e)s	—
D.	dem guten Wein(e)	einem guten Wein(e)	gutem Wein(e)	=em
Feminine				
N.	die rote Tinte	eine rote Tinte	rote Tinte	=e
A.	die rote Tinte	eine rote Tinte	rote Tinte	=e
G.	der roten Tinte	einer roten Tinte	roter Tinte	=er
D.	der roten Tinte	einer roten Tinte	roter Tinte	=er

NEUTER

N.	das gute Bier	ein gutes Bier	gutes Bier	=(e)s
A.	das gute Bier	ein gutes Bier	gutes Bier	=(e)s
G.	des guten Bier(e)s	eines guten Bier(e)s	guten (gutes) Bier(e)s	—
D.	dem guten Bier(e)	einem guten Bier(e)	gutem Bier(e)	=em

PLURAL (all genders)

ein has no plural;
plural with Posses-
sive Adjective is:

N.	die =en	---	seine alten Bücher	=e	---	=e
A.	die =en	---	seine alten Bücher	=e	---	=e
G.	der =en	---	seiner alten Bücher	=er	---	=er
D.	den =en	--- n	seinen alten Büchern	=en	--- n	—

Everything in Dat. Plur. ends in =n.

84. An adjective used predicatively is not declined.

Innerhalb eines Monats sind die Bäume grün geworden.	Within a month the trees have become green.
Wie kommt's, daß du so traurig bist, Da alles froh erscheint?	How is it you are so sad when all else is gay?

NOTE.—A superlative adjective will, of course, be declined under any circumstances (95 and 96).

85. An adjective which depends on an article or on a limiting adjective is always declined.

ein schönes Mädchen, a beautiful girl.
der neue Apparat, the new set (wireless).
dieser große Mann, this big man.

Kennen Sie ihn? Wen? Den ältesten.	Do you know him? Whom? The eldest.
Alles geben die Götter, die unendlichen, Ihren Lieblingen ganz.	The eternal gods give everything to their favourites in entirety.

NOTE.—After an adjective do not use a pronoun to correspond to the English 'one' or 'ones.'

der Faule, the lazy one.
die Größeren, the bigger ones.

86. An adjective qualifying and standing before a noun is declined.

Der Sommer hat lange Tage.   Summer has long days.
Rote Blumen.   Red flowers.

But:

    Blumen rot wie Feuer.   Flowers red as fire.

NOTE.—In poetry the adjective is often found undeclined before its noun; especially when the noun is masculine and in the nominative, or neuter and in the nominative or accusative.

Saure Wochen, frohe Feste !
Sei dein künftig Zauberwort !

87. Two or more adjectives standing before a noun are declined alike.

mit einem guten alten Mann.
frisches fließendes Wasser.

NOTE.—(i) There is a special declension after **alle** in the plural. Thus :

Nom.	alle guten Leute	all good people
Acc.	alle guten Leute	
Gen.	aller guten Leute	
Dat.	allen guten Leuten.	

Beide (both) and **sämtliche** (all) usually require the same declension as **alle**.

(ii) The declension of an adjective after numeral adjectives and indefinite numeral adjectives is not settled. Thus :

Nom.	einige alte Bücher	some old books
Acc.	einige alte Bücher	
Gen.	einiger alten (or alter) Bücher	
Dat.	einigen alten Büchern	

88. Adjectives and participles used as nouns keep their adjectival declension. Thus :

Singular

Nom.	der Reisende	ein Reisender
Acc.	den Reisenden	einen Reisenden
Gen.	des Reisenden	eines Reisenden
Dat.	dem Reisenden	einem Reisenden

Plural

Nom.	die Reisenden	Reisende
Acc.	die Reisenden	Reisende
Gen.	der Reisenden	Reisender
Dat.	den Reisenden	Reisenden

Thus the adjective deutſch gives:

> der Deutſche, the German. ein Deutſcher, a German.

The past participle gefangen gives:

> der Gefangene, the prisoner. ein Gefangener, a prisoner.
>
> (Exception: der Junge, the lad. ein Junge, a lad.)

NOTE.—Adjectives so used are written with a capital letter. (See 7 (*a*) (ii).)

89. Derſelbe declines both components and is written as one word, unless the contracted form of preposition + definite article is used.

Mit denſelben Gebärden.	With the same gestures.
Am ſelben Abend.	On the same evening.

90. Adjectives in =er, formed from the names of towns, are never declined.

Im Kaſſeler Staatstheater.	In the state theatre at Cassel.
Der Göttinger Muſenalma= nach.	The Göttingen "Almanach of the Muses."

(*Not* Göttingener, which would be clumsy.)

NOTE.—Some towns make an adjective in =iſch; this is written with a small letter, as kölniſch, of Cologne, except in established titles such as:

> Die Kölniſche Zeitung.
> Die Hamburgiſche Dramaturgie.

91. Adjectives of colour used as nouns are not declined if the noun is abstract.

Das Bild hat zuviel vom Schwarz.	There's too much black about the picture.

But: das Schwarze, the bull's eye (target).

92. A few set pairs of adjectives used without an article are not declined:

Alt und jung; reich und arm.	Old and young; rich and poor.
Schwarz auf weiß.	In black and white, *i.e.*, in writing.

93. The names of languages are sometimes declined, sometimes not.

Das Englisch der Universitäten.	The English of the Universities.
Übersetzen Sie ins Deutsche.	Translate into German.
Im Deutschen, auf Deutsch.	In German.
Das Mittelhochdeutsche.	Middle High German.
Im Mittelhochdeutschen.	In Middle High German.
Der Anfang des Neuhochdeutschen.	The beginning of New High German.

94. The adjective 'full of . . . ' is expressed in German by:

(a) **voll von** + Dative.

(b) **voll** + Genitive.

(c) **voller.** This is invariable, but is usually only found before an unqualified noun.

Thus:

Ein Korb voller Kirschen, *or* ein Korb voll von Kirschen. }	A basket full of cherries.
Ein Korb voll der schönsten Kirschen.	A basket full of the finest cherries.

COMPARISON OF ADJECTIVES

95. Ascending Comparison.

1. The Comparative form is made by adding **=er,** and the Superlative by adding **=st** to the Positive.

If the Positive ends in **=e, =r** only is added for the Comparative; the Superlative takes **=est** if the Positive ends in **=s, =sch, =st, =ß,** or if it is monosyllabic and ends in **=d** or **=t.**

Positive	*Comparative*	*Superlative*
klein	kleiner	der kleinste
rund	runder	der rundeste
falsch	falscher	der falscheste
weise	weiser	der weiseste
weiß	weißer	der weißeste

NOTE: See also **98.**

96. The Superlative.

2. There are two aspects of the Superlative, for instance: (a) the highest (Relative Superlative), (b) very high (Absolute Superlative).

(a) Relative Superlative.

The Superlative form of the adjective expresses the highest degree of a quality in a subject (person or thing) *either*:

(i) when compared with some other person or thing

(der, die, das, =ste, or =este).

Thus in:

Dieser Baum ist der schönste im Wald,	This tree is the most beautiful in the wood,

we are comparing this tree with the other trees.

And in:

Werther war das bekannteste Werk Goethes,	*Werther* was the best known of Goethe's works,

we assert that *Werther*, compared with Goethe's other works, was the best known.

Or (ii) where there is no sense of comparison with other persons or things, but where the subject is compared with itself

(am =sten or =esten).

Thus in:

Dieser Baum ist am schönsten im Frühling,	This tree is most beautiful in spring,

we are comparing the various states of beauty of one and the same tree.

(b) Absolute Superlative.

When the adjective expresses the highest degree without any sense of comparison, the adverbs sehr (very), höchst, äußerst (extremely) and the like are used before the Positive form of the adjective.

Dieser Baum ist sehr schön.	This tree is most beautiful.
Ein höchst auffallendes Kleid.	A most striking dress.
Er ist sehr unglücklich.	He is most unfortunate.
Eine äußerst interessante Geschichte.	A most interesting story.

N.B.—aller (Gen. plur. of all) is sometimes prefixed to the Superlative form to strengthen the idea.

Die allerneueste Mode.	The very latest fashion.

(sehr is not used to strengthen a Superlative.)

97. The **Comparative**.

(*a*) 'Than' after a Comparative is **als**.

> **Er ist größer als ich.** He is taller than I.

Denn is also used, particularly before **je**.

> **Luftfahrt ist heute not-** To-day aviation is more neces-
> **wendiger denn je.**   sary than ever.

NOTE.—(i) **denn** must be used to render 'than' in order to avoid the juxtaposition of **als als**.

> **Als Künstler ist er größer denn** He is greater as an artist than
> **als Mensch.**   as a man.

(ii) Do not render 'than' after a Comparative by **wie**; it is condemned by many Germans as journalese.

(*b*) The English double Comparative is usually rendered by **immer** + Comparative.

> **Genf wird immer leerer.** Geneva is getting more and
>   more empty.

But **leerer und leerer** is possible; Goethe often has a peculiar form:

> **Naß und nässer wird's im** It is growing wetter and wetter
> **Saal.**   in the hall.

(*c*) The Comparative is used occasionally in an absolute sense without any idea of comparison with other things or persons; as in

> **die neueren Sprachen**, modern languages; **ein jüngerer
> Lehrer**, a rather young teacher.

(*d*) When two qualities of the same person or thing are being contrasted the ordinary comparative is replaced by **mehr** + Positive.

> **Er ist mehr klug als redlich.** He is more clever than honest.

(*e*) The English Comparative introduced by 'all the more' is rendered by **um so** + Comparative.

> **Leider fand der Großkampf-** Unfortunately on the day of
> **tag nicht den erwarteten** the big contest the attend-
> **Besuch, was um so be-** ance was not up to expecta-
> **dauerlicher ist, als die sport-** tions, which is all the more
> **liche Ausbeute allgemein** regrettable as the sport
> **zufriedenstellte.**   offered gave general satis-
>   faction.

98. Changes in Stem in Comparisons.

(*a*) Some common monosyllabic adjectives modify their stem vowel in comparative and superlative forms. They are:

alt, old	groß, big	kalt, cold	nah, near
arg, bad	hart, hard	klug, clever	scharf, sharp
arm, poor	hoch, high	kurz, short	schwach, weak
grob, coarse	jung, young	lang, long	schwarz, black
			stark, strong

Thus: jung, jünger, der, die, das jüngste, am jüngsten.
    young, younger, youngest.

b) The following are irregular:

groß, größer,   der, die, das größte,   am größten.
gut, besser,   der, die, das beste,   am besten.
        (*Cf.* English good, better, best.)

viel, mehr,   der, die, das meiste,   am meisten.
        (*Cf.* English much, more, most.)

wenig, weniger,	der, die, das wenigste,	am wenigsten.
or minder,	der, die, das mindeste,	am mindesten.
nah, näher,	der, die, das nächste,	am nächsten.
hoch, höher,	der, die, das höchste,	am höchsten.

NOTE.—In the Positive, hoch drops its c whenever it is inflected:
    die hohen Berge, the high mountains.

99. Adjectives ending in =el, =en, =er (unstressed) may drop the e of their ending when their inflection contains e; this will be the case in the Comparative.

tapfer, brave: ein tapfrer (or tapferer) Soldat, a brave soldier.
golden, golden: die goldnen (or goldenen) Ringe, the golden rings.
edel, noble: die edlern (or edleren) Familien, the more noble families.

NOTE.—(i) Such adjectives retain the e in the Superlatives, as in
    die edelsten Familien, the most noble families.

(ii) It is now obligatory, in prose, to drop the e of the ending in the case of adjectives ending in =el.
    Das edle Blut (*not* edele).

100. The **Descending Comparison** of Adjectives is formed by using, before the Positive, weniger or minber (less) for the Comparative, and am wenigſten or am minbeſten (least) for the Superlative form.

Ich bin weniger elenb, als ich früher war.	I am less miserable than I used to be.
Ein weniger ſalziges Brot.	A less salty bread.
Von allen Königen war er am wenigſten kriegeriſch.	Of all the kings he was the least warlike.

NOTE.—Sometimes a superlative with wenigſt or minbeſt may be found:

Die wenigſt bekannten Werke Goethes.	Goethe's least known works.

101. Comparison of Equality expressed in English by 'as . . . as,' 'just as . . . as' is in German:

ſo . . . wie, ebenſo . . . wie.

Er iſt nicht ſo groß wie ſein Bruder.	He is not as big as his brother.
Er hat ebenſoviel wie ich getrunken.	He has drunk just as much as I have.

'The' in 'the more . . . the more,' 'the less . . . the less,' is rendered by:

je . . . beſto, or je . . . umſo, or je . . . je.

Aber je mehr ich über ihn nachbachte, beſto mehr entglitt er mir.	The more I thought about him the more he escaped me.
Je beſſer er ſchreibt, umſo leichter wirb er eine Stelle finben.	The better he writes the more easily will he find a post.
Je weniger er bavon weiß, beſto weniger wirb er leiben.	The less he knows about it the less will be his suffering.

XIII. ADVERBS

102. Adjectives as Adverbs.

Adjectives without inflection are used as Adverbs in German in the Positive and Comparative degree.

Er ſingt ſehr gut.	He sings very well.
Der Wind fuhr ſo traurig durch die Äſte.	The wind passed so sadly through the branches.
Er ſprach klarer als gewöhn= lich.	He spoke more clearly than he usually does.

NOTE.—Remember not to construe as an adjective an unin-flected word of adjectival form which qualifies another adjective adverbially.

Mit göttlich erhabenen Leh= ren.	With doctrines divinely sub-lime.
Der ewig treue König.	The king for ever faithful.

103. Irregular Comparison of Adverbs.

(a) gern(e), *gladly, willingly*; lieber, am liebſten. This adverb is usually rendered by a verb in English.

Ich gehe gern ins Kino.	I like going to the cinema.
Er geht lieber ins Theater.	He prefers to go to the theatre.
Am liebſten gehen wir in die Oper.	We like going to the opera best of all.

(b) bald, *soon*; eher, *sooner, rather*; baldigſt, *as soon as possible*.

(c) The normal Comparative of oft is öfter; the form öfters means *rather often, quite often. Cf.* **97** (*c*).

104. Descending Comparison of Adverbs and Comparisons of Equality.

The descending comparison of adverbs is formed by using before the Positive form weniger or minder (less) for the Com-parative, and am wenigſten or am mindeſten (least) for the Superlative form.

Als ich ihn erblickte, fuhr er weniger ſchnell.	When I caught sight of him he was driving less quickly.
Welcher von den Knaben be= nahm ſich am wenigſten vernünftig?	Which of the boys behaved the least sensibly?

The Comparisons of Equality are expressed in just the same way as those of adjectives (**101**).

Er ſingt ebenſo ſchön wie ich.	He sings just as beautifully as I do.

(Further examples of adverbs in comparisons of equality are given in **101**).

105. Superlative of Adverbs.

There are two forms:

(*a*) The Relative Superlative—which is used whenever there is any sense of comparison with or reference to other persons, things, or occasions.

Bon allen Schülern lernt er am schnellsten.	Of all the boys he learns most quickly.

(*b*) The Absolute Superlative—which is used when no comparison is involved.

Er denkt aufs klarste.	He thinks most clearly.

We can see some reason for this form of the Superlative with auf, if we look upon it as meaning 'towards, in the direction of that which is most clear.'

A few **Irregular Superlatives** of Adverbs:

(i) In =st.

längst, for a long while	höchst, greatly, very much
äußerst, extremely	innigst, most affectionately

möglichst, as much as possible (qualifying other words)

e.g., Er kommt immer möglichst spät.	He always comes as late as possible.

(ii) With im (*not* am), usually after nicht.

nicht im geringsten, not in the least.

(iii) In =(s)tens.

höchstens, at the very most.
erstens, in the first place, first of all.
zweitens (etc.), in the second place.
spätestens, at the very latest.
wenigstens, at (the very) least.

106. Formation of Adverbs.

(*a*) As we have seen in 102, the adjective is used in German without inflection as an adverb.

(*b*) Phrases with the Genitive provide many adverbial forms (19). Thus derart (from der Art) is often used as a synonym for so.

Der Dreißigjährige Krieg hat Deutschland derart zerrüttet, daß es mehr als ein Jahrhundert gebraucht hat, um sich davon zu erholen.	By the Thirty Years' War, Germany was thrown into such disorder that she took more than a century to recover.

Further examples are:

ſeltſamerweiſe, strangely.
verbürgtermaßen, as can be guaranteed.
rechts, to (or on) the right.
links, to (or on) the left.

(*c*) Other adverbial terminations added to adjectives or nouns are =wärts and =lich.

herzlich, heartily.
inniglich, affectionately.
mündlich, by word of mouth.
ſchriftlich, in writing.
nordwärts, northward.
ſüdwärts, southward.

(*d*) Occasionally adverbs are formed from noun phrases.

Die techniſch beileibe nicht ſchlechte Mannſchaft.	The team whose technical performance is by no means bad.

NOTE.—Lange (adv.) has an e and is thus different from lang (adj). This e is sometimes found with gern and fern.

107. Some common adverbs and their idiomatic uses.

auch.

(i) *Also, too.*

Wir werden auch kommen.	We will come too.

(ii) *Even.*

Typen dieſer beiden Gattungen beſtehen zwar auch heute.	Types of these two species exist indeed even to-day.

bald.

(i) *Soon.*

Wir werden bald zurückkommen.	We shall soon come back.

(ii) bald . . . bald, *now . . . now.*

Er guckte bald rechts, bald links.	He looked now to the right, now to the left.

dennoch, *after all.*

Er iſt dennoch gekommen.	He has come after all.

doch.

(i) Concessive adverb, *after all, yet, nevertheless.*

Er ist doch gekommen.	He has come after all.

(Not quite so strong as dennoch.)

(ii) Gives a note of pleading to an Imperative.

Sagen Sie es doch, wenn Sie es nötig haben.	*Do* say so if you need it.

(iii) As an affirmative answer to a negative question or suggestion.

Du hast mein Buch nicht mitgebracht — Doch !	You haven't brought my book with you—Oh, yes I have !

(*Cf.* French *si.*)

einmal or mal.

(i) Usually einmal (not abbreviated to mal) means *once.*

Es war einmal ein König.	Once upon a time there was a king.

(ii) With nicht, *not even.*

Er kann nicht mal den kleinsten Wunsch erfüllen.	He cannot fulfil even the slightest wish.

(iii) May emphasize a word or phrase, especially an Imperative.

Sehen Sie mal her ! Just look here !

erst.

(i) *First.*

Erst muß man bezahlen. You must first pay.

(ii) *Only* or *not until* (with an expression of time).

Erst um drei Uhr ist er zurückgekommen.	He did not come back until three o'clock.

geschweige denn, *much less* (only in the sense indicated below).

Er beherrscht die Sprache nicht genügend, um eine Unterhaltung führen, geschweige denn als Dolmetscher dabei mitwirken zu können.	He hasn't sufficient command of the language for conversation, much less (*or* not to mention) interpreting.

ja, besides being the affirmative adverb (yes), has the meaning of *indeed, truly.*

Das ift ja Unfinn.   That is indeed nonsense.

fchon.

(i) *Already.*

Es ift fchon fechs Uhr.   It is already six o'clock.

(ii) *As early as.*

Schon in feinem zehnten   When he was no more than ten
  Jahre zeichnete er fich   he distinguished himself
  aus.

(iii) *No doubt, surely.*

Er wird fchon kommen.   He will surely come.

wohl.

(i) With expressions indicating state of health, it himself 'well.'

Ich befinde mich fehr wohl   I am very well here.
  hier.

'Well' should otherwise be rendered by gut.

Er fingt fehr gut.   He sings very well.

NOTE.—A comparative wohler is sometimes found.

Wieviel wohler wäre mir's, wenn ich von dem Streit der politifchen Elemente abgefondert, den Wiffenfchaften und Künften, wozu ich geboren bin, meinen Geift zuwenden könnte.

(ii) Is an adverb of supposition, *perhaps, I dare say, I suppose.*

Er ift wohl jetzt hier.   I suppose he's here by now.

NOTE.—Do not confuse lauter (adv.), *merely, nothing but,* with the adj. laut, *loud,* and the adj. lauter, *clear, pure.*

Das ift lauter Unfinn.   That is sheer rubbish.
Mit lauter Stimme.   In a loud voice.
Lauteres Gold   Pure gold.

XIV. NUMERALS

108. Numeral Adjectives, Cardinals and Ordinals, are as follows:

	Cardinal	*Ordinal*
0	null	
1	eins	der, die, das erſte
2	zwei	„ „ „ zweite
3	drei	„ „ „ dritte
4	vier	„ „ „ vierte
5	fünf	„ „ „ fünfte
6	ſechs	„ „ „ ſechſte
7	ſieben	„ „ „ ſiebente
8	acht	„ „ „ achte
9	neun	„ „ „ neunte
10	zehn	„ „ „ zehnte
11	elf	„ „ „ elfte
12	zwölf	„ „ „ zwölfte
13	dreizehn	„ „ „ dreizehnte
14	vierzehn	„ „ „ vierzehnte
15	fünfzehn	„ „ „ fünfzehnte
16	ſechzehn	„ „ „ ſechzehnte
17	ſiebzehn	„ „ „ ſiebzehnte
18	achtzehn	„ „ „ achtzehnte
19	neunzehn	„ „ „ neunzehnte
20	zwanzig	„ „ „ zwanzigſte
21	einundzwanzig	„ „ „ einundzwanzigſte
22	zweiundzwanzig	„ „ „ zweiundzwanzigſte
23	dreiundzwanzig	„ „ „ dreiundzwanzigſte
	etc.	
30	dreißig	„ „ „ dreißigſte
31	einunddreißig	„ „ „ einunddreißigſte
	etc.	
40	vierzig	„ „ „ vierzigſte
50	fünfzig	„ „ „ fünfzigſte
60	ſechzig	„ „ „ ſechzigſte
70	ſiebzig	„ „ „ ſiebzigſte
80	achtzig	„ „ „ achtzigſte
90	neunzig	„ „ „ neunzigſte
100	hundert	„ „ „ hundertſte
101	hundert(und)eins	„ „ „ hundert(und)erſte

102	hundert(und)zwei	der, die, das hundert(und)zweite
	etc.	
120	hundertzwanzig	„ „ „ hundertzwanzigste
	etc.	
130	hundertdreißig	„ „ „ hundertdreißigste
	etc.	
200	zweihundert	„ „ „ zweihundertste
	etc.	
1 000	tausend	„ „ „ tausendste
1 001	tausendeins	„ „ „ tausendunderste
	etc.	
2 000	zweitausend	„ „ „ zweitausendste

109. (*a*) It will be noticed that the Ordinals are formed from the Cardinals by adding the termination ₌t for numbers below 20, ₌ſt for those above 20. The forms ſechzig, ſiebzig, der, die, das erſte, dritte, achte are slightly irregular.

(*b*) The English *one* is:

(i) ein, eine, ein (the indefinite article) if followed by a noun. See 38.

(ii) einer, eine, eines (or eins) if used as a pronoun.

(iii) eins in counting when no noun follows and the idea of gender is not to the fore.

(*c*) Adjectives formed by adding ₌er to multiples of ten which end in ₌ig are invariable, as die neunziger Jahre, the nineties.

(*d*) zwei and drei have genitives—zweier and dreier; and datives—zweien and dreien.

These are used if there is no other word to show the case.

Zu vieren.	In fours, four by four.
Die Freundſchaft zweier Dichter.	The friendship of two poets.

But observe:

Die beiden Dichter.	The two poets.
Wir beide.	Both of us.

(*e*) Cardinal numerals are feminine when used in the sense of 'the figure 2, etc.'

Die Vier iſt zu groß.	The four is too big.

(*f*) hundert and tausend may be used as neuter nouns with the meaning 'a group of a hundred, a thousand.' (*Cf.* French: une centaine, un millier.) When so used they make their plural in =e.

Hunderte von Lämmern lie= fen umher.	Hundreds of lambs were run- ning about.

110. Numeral Nouns.

(*a*) Note ein paar (invariable), *a few*; ein Paar, *a pair*, as:

> mit ein paar Worten, in a few words.
> ein Paar Schuhe, a pair of shoes.
> ein Paar Eier, a couple of eggs.

(*b*) 1 000 000, eine Million.
2 000 000, zwei Millionen.
1 000 000 000, eine Milliarde (plural =n).
1 000 000 000 000, eine Billion (plural =en).

NOTE.—In German printing commas are not used to separate sets of three figures (10, 1 (*a*)).

(*c*) With the exception of die Hälfte (the half) fractions are neuter, and are made by adding =tel:

> $\frac{1}{4}$, ein Viertel.
> $\frac{1}{8}$, ein Achtel.
> $\frac{3}{4}$, drei Viertel.
> $\frac{1}{3}$, ein Drittel.

NOTE.—To translate the English word *half*:
(i) The noun is die Hälfte. (See 47).
(ii) After whole numbers 'and a half' is translated by =undeinhalb, which is not declined.

> Mit zweiundeinhalb Bogen Papier.   With 2½ sheets of paper.

But 1½ is anderthalb and this construction is occasionally found in

> drittehalb 2½.
> viertehalb 3½.

These two compounds are rather rare and should be avoided in favour of the use of =undeinhalb.

(iii) Notice the following:

> ein halber Tag, half a day.
> der halbe Tag, half the day.
> eine halbe Stunde, half an hour.
> in einer halben Stunde, in half an hour.

In den anderthalb Jahrhunderten, die seither vergangen sind.	In the hundred and fifty years which have since passed.

III. Compound Numeral Forms.

(*a*) erſtens, firstly   drittens, etc., thirdly, etc.
     zweitens, secondly   leßtens, lastly

But : zuerſt, at first   zuleßt, at last

(*b*) einmal, once   manchmal, often
     zweimal, twice   das erſte Mal, the first time
     dreimal, etc., three times,   das zweite Mal, the second
       thrice, etc.   time

NOTE.—dreimal vier iſt zwölf, $3 \times 4 = 12$.
        das Einmaleins, the multiplication table.
        ein einziges Mal, once only.
        zum vierten Mal, for the fourth time.
        zum erſten Mal, erſtmalig, erſtmals, for the first time.

(*c*) einfach, simple (*i.e.*, not com-   einfältig, simple (*i.e.*, unin-
     plex)   telligent)
     zweifach, twofold   zweifältig (rare), twofold
        (zwiefach and zwiefältig are also found.)

     mannigfach, manifold   mannigfaltig (rare), manifold
                               (*N.B.* no Umlaut.)

Die mannigfachen Verſuchungen.   The manifold temptations.

(*d*) einerlei, of one kind.
     zweierlei, of two kinds, two kinds of.
     dreierlei, of three kinds, three kinds of.
     allerlei, of all kinds, all kinds of.
     mancherlei, vielerlei, of many kinds, various, divers.

Ein Garten mit allerlei Ro-   A garden with all kinds of roses.
ſen.
Er brachte zweierlei Hefte.   He brought two kinds of ex-
                           ercise books.

NOTE.— (i) This numeral in =erlei is invariable.
       (ii) Es iſt mir einerlei.   It's all the same to me.
                            It doesn't matter.

(*e*) je is used with numerals in the sense of *each*.

Ausverkauf ! Hemden je zwei   Sale ! Shirts two marks each !
   Mark !
Sie bekamen je vier.   **They got four each.**

112. The 24-hour system is used in official timing.

(*a*) Railway time-tables, ship's logs.

18.35 D=zug nach Aachen.

6.35 p.m. Corridor train to Aix-la-Chapelle.

(*b*) Wireless programmes.

22.30 Lokale Nachrichten.

10.30 p.m. Local News.

(*c*) Theatre advertisements.

Donnerstag, 20 Uhr. Der fliegende Holländer.

Thursday, 8 p.m. The Flying Dutchman.

(*d*) Church announcements.

Friedenskirche 10 Uhr P. Rogge; 14½ Uhr, Taufen, P. Rogge; 18 Uhr, P. Martens.

NOTE.—In conversation the 12-hour system is used by older people and by people in the country. Younger people in the towns are extending the use of the 24-hour system to conversation.

113. Time of Day.

(*a*) Note the following:

Wieviel Uhr ist es? or Wie spät ist es?

What time is it?

Um wieviel Uhr soll ich Sie wecken?

At what time am I to wake you?

Es ist zehn Uhr (morgens or vormittags).

It is ten o'clock (in the morning).

Es ist zwölf Uhr or Es ist mittag.

It is twelve o'clock (noon).

Es ist ein Uhr (here ein is invariable).

It is one o'clock.

Kurz vor ein Uhr.

Shortly before one o'clock.

Um viertel[1] nach eins.

At a quarter past one.

Um viertel[1] (auf) zwei—is common in South and Central Germany.

At a quarter past one.

Es ist halb drei.

It is half-past two (*i.e.*, half of the third hour).

Um halb vier.

At half-past three.

[1] In telling time by the clock, this may be written with a small or large letter.

Um halb eins.	At half-past twelve.
Um zehn Minuten vor sechs.	At ten minutes to six.
Es ist (ein) Viertel[1] vor vier.	It is (a) quarter to four.
Es ist drei Viertel[1] (auf) vier —common in South and Central Germany.	It is (a) quarter to four.

Thus a general rule is: Use vor for English *to*, nach for English *past*, except for the half hours.

(*b*) Official timing is spoken as follows:

> 10.55, zehn Uhr fünfundfünfzig.
> 9.30, neun Uhr dreißig.
> 8.05, acht Uhr fünf.
> 18.20, achtzehn Uhr zwanzig.

114. Dates.

(*a*) Days—Sonntag, Montag, Dienstag, Mittwoch, Donnerstag, Freitag, Sonnabend (Samstag in the South).

(*b*) Months—Januar, Februar, März, April, Mai, Juni, Juli, August, September, Oktober, November, Dezember.

Note.—The month is Au'gust, the name 'August.

(*c*) Seasons (Jahreszeiten) — Frühling, Sommer, Herbst, Winter.

Note.—All the above words are masculine and generally have the definite article. See **34** (*b*) (*c*) (*d*).

(*d*) What is the date? Der wievielte ist heute? or Den wievielten haben wir heute?

Es ist der vierte März.	It is the fourth of March.
Am fünfundzwanzigsten Juni.	On the 25th of June.

The date on a letter is:

den 25sten Oktober 1933.	25th October, 1933.
Or den 25. Oktober 1933.	
Or 25.x.33.	

Im Jahre 1815 (read achtzehnhundertfünfzehn).	In 1815.
Am Dienstag.	On Tuesday.
Am Mittwoch.	On Wednesday.

Note.—In this use, the contracted form am is not replaceable by an dem; an dem would only be used if the dem were a demonstrative or if it were qualified.

[1] See note, p. 92.

An dem Mittwoch, als er ſtarb.   On the Wednesday when he died.

The same principle applies to im with names of months.

(e) Several common adverbial phrases of time.

> morgen, to-morrow.
> (der Morgen, morning.)
> morgen früh, to-morrow morning.
> morgen abend, to-morrow evening.
> geſtern abend, last night *or* yesterday evening.
> vorgeſtern, the day before yesterday.
> übermorgen, the day after to-morrow.
> heute, to-day.
> heute morgen, this morning.
> heute abend, this evening, to-night.
> heute vor acht Tagen, a week ago to-day.
> heute über acht Tage, ⎫ a week from to-day.
> heute in acht Tagen, ⎰ to-day week.
> vor zwanzig Jahren, twenty years ago.
> alle zwei Tage, every other day.
> vor einigen Tagen (or neulich), the other day.
> den (or am) andern Tag,   ⎫
> den (or am) nächſten Tag, ⎬ the next day.
> den (or am) folgenden Tag, ⎭

XV. POSSESSIVE ADJECTIVES AND PRONOUNS

115. 1. Possessive Adjectives.

The Personal Pronoun	*Its Possessive Adjective*
ich	mein
du	dein
er	ſein
ſie	ihr
es	ſein
wir	unſer
ihr	euer
ſie	ihr
Sie	Ihr

These adjectives are declined like the Indefinite Article, *e.g.*:

	Masc.	*Singular* *Fem.*	*Neut.*	*Plural*
Nom.	mein	meine	mein	meine
Acc.	meinen	meine	mein	meine
Gen.	meines	meiner	meines	meiner
Dat.	meinem	meiner	meinem	meinen

Sie besuchte ihren Vater.	She was visiting her father.
Das ist sein Haus.	That is his house.

NOTE.—The e before the r in unser and euer may be omitted when the inflection contains e.

Das sind unsre (unsere) Bücher.
Die Gesundheit eurer (rarely euerer) Kinder.

2. Possessive Pronouns.

(*a*) After the verbs sein, werden, bleiben, scheinen, the possessive adjectives mein, dein, sein, unser, euer, **without inflection,** should render the English Possessive Pronoun if it merely indicates ownership.

Der Hund ist mein.	The dog is mine.
Allmählich ist es dein geworden.	Gradually it has become yours.

NOTE.—ihr (her, their), Ihr (your) are not used without inflection.

Das Haus ist Ihres.	
Das Haus ist das Ihre.	The house is yours (as in (*b*) below).
Das Haus ist das Ihrige.	
Das Haus gehört Ihnen.	

(*b*) If comparison between things of the same nature is indicated or hinted at, one of the following three forms must be used. Take mein as an example:

	Masc.	*Fem.*	*Neut.*	*Plur.*
(i) *Nom.*	meiner	meine	mein(e)s	meine
Acc.	meinen	meine	mein(e)s	meine
Gen.	meines	meiner	meines	meiner
Dat.	meinem	meiner	meinem	meinen

This only differs from the declension of the Possessive Adjective in the nominative (masc. and neut.) and the accusative (neut. sing.). It has, in fact, the endings of the Definite Article (**32**).

Sein Pferd und meines.   His horse and mine.

(ii) *Sing.*

> der meine, die meine, das meine,
> den meinen, die meine, das meine, etc.

    Plur.

> die meinen, etc. (as in 83. I).

Seine Bücher und die meinen lagen auf dem Tisch.	His books and mine lay on the table.
Ist das Ihre Feder? Nein, sie ist die seine.	Is that your pen? No, it is his.

(iii) der meinige, die meinige, das meinige, etc. (as in 83. I).

Seine Handschuhe sind nicht zu finden; die meinigen sind zu klein.	His gloves are not to be found; mine are too small.
Welches von diesen beiden ist das deinige?	Which of these two is yours?

Thus:

My father and his were together.	Mein Vater und seiner waren zusammen.
	Or Mein Vater und der seine waren zusammen.
	Or Mein Vater und der seinige waren zusammen.

116. (a) The forms der, die, das meine (or meinige) may be used (with a capital letter) as independent nouns having no reference to any previous nouns:

Das Meinige, das Meine.	My property, my share, my own.
Ich habe das Meinige getan.	I have done my duty, my part.
Die Seinen, die Seinigen. (*Cf.* Latin: *sui*.)	His family, his friends, his people.

(b) Note the rendering of the English idiom which has the Possessive Pronoun in the Genitive:

einige seiner Gedichte. einige von seinen Gedichten. einige Gedichte von ihm.	some poems of his.
ein Buch von mir. eines meiner Bücher. eines von meinen Büchern.	a book of mine.

XVI. DEMONSTRATIVE ADJECTIVES AND PRONOUNS

117. The **Demonstrative Adjectives** and **Pronouns** in German are:

1. der, die, das, this, that; *plur.* these, those.

(*a*) As a Demonstrative Adjective der is declined like the definite article (**32**), but it takes more voice stress in pronunciation. It is common in conversation.

Mit Bengeln der Art kann man nichts anfangen.	One can do nothing with rascals of that type.
An dem und dem Ort.	In such and such a place.

(*b*) As a Demonstrative Pronoun it is thus declined:

		Singular		Plural
	Masc.	*Fem.*	*Neut.*	
Nom.	der	die	das	die
Acc.	den	die	das	die
Gen.	dessen	deren	dessen	deren
		derer		derer
	(des)	(der)	(des)	(der)
Dat.	dem	der	dem	denen

Apart from some of the Genitive forms, this is like the relative pronoun (**52**).

Note.—The Genitives of the Demonstrative Pronoun der:—

(i) The form des, der, des, *plur.* der, is rare save in poetry, biblical language, and compounds such as:

deshalb, deswegen, therefore, on account of that.

(ii) derer (sing. and plur.) is used as antecedent to a following relative clause:

Die Verpflegung derer, die daran leiden.	The care of those who suffer from it.

(iii) When the Demonstrative Pronoun refers to persons and is in the gen. plur. and is qualified by a dependent phrase, the derer form is used.

Er versuchte sich an seine Kameraden zu erinnern; aber die Namen derer des ersten Jahrganges hatte er schon vergessen.	He tried to remember his school-fellows but he had already forgotten the names of those in the first year.

(iv) In other cases the forms beſſen, beren, beſſen, *plur.* beren, should be used.

(v) beſſen, beren, beſſen, *plur.* bere⁊, may also be used in place of the possessive adjectives to avoid ambiguity:

Karl grüßte ſeinen Freund   Karl greeted his friend and the
   und beſſen Frau.   latter's wife.

(ſeine Frau would mean Karl's wife.)

Marie übernahm Gretchens   Mary took over Margaret's
   Stelle, benußte beren In=   position, used her instru-
   ſtrumente und hatte ähn=   ments, and was likewise suc-
   lichen Erfolg.   cessful.

(beren makes it quite clear that the Inſtrumente were
   Gretchen's; had they been Marie's (the subject) the
   possessive adjective ihre would have been used.)

118. 2. bieſer, this, and jener, that. These may be used as Demonstrative Adjectives or Pronouns. They are declined like the definite article. Thus:

	Masc.	Singular Fem.	Neut.	Plural
Nom.	bieſer	bieſe	bieſes	bieſe
Acc.	bieſen	bieſe	bieſes	bieſe
Gen.	bieſes	bieſer	bieſes	bieſer
Dat.	bieſem	bieſer	bieſem	bieſen

Dieſer junge Mann.   This young man.
Ich kenne jene alte Methode, I know that old method, but
   bieſe aber iſt mir ganz neu   this one is quite new to me.

NOTE.—(i) bies is often used for bieſes, especially with the verb ſein (*cf.* **42** (*f*)) and even with a plural verb.

Dies iſt ſein neueſter Roman. This is his most recent novel.
Dies ſind die ſchönſten   These are the finest flowers.
   Blumen.

(ii) bieſer refers to an object nearer at hand in time or space, jener to an object more remote. Thus the pronoun jener can translate the English 'the former,' and bieſer 'the latter.' (*Cf.* French *celui-là, celui-ci.*)

Die beiden Brüder, Karl und Fritz, wohnten einmal hier; sie sind aber schon lange fort. Dieser ist jetzt Pfarrer in Hamburg, jener fiel im Kriege.	The two brothers, Charles and Fred, once lived here, but they have been gone for a long time; the former fell in the war, the latter is a parson in Hamburg.

It will be seen that the order of the pronouns is reversed in English; the German comparison is usually in the order **dieser . . . jener**, the English—'the former . . . the latter.' (**36** (*e*).)

(iii) **jener** means: that one yonder, the former, the notorious, the well-known.

English sometimes has 'that' in *none* of these senses; when that is the case, it should be rendered by **dieser** or **der**.

E.g. Ach ! der hat keine Ehre.	Oh! that fellow hasn't any honour.

119. 3. **derjenige, diejenige, dasjenige**, this (one), that (one). It is always written as one word and declines both constituents. See **83**. I.

> *Acc.* **denjenigen, diejenige, dasjenige.**
> *Gen.* **desjenigen, derjenigen, desjenigen, etc.**
> *Pl.* **diejenigen, etc.**

(*a*) As a Demonstrative Adjective it is very emphatic or precise and is thus common in legal phraseology.

Er war damit beschäftigt, denjenigen Fall zu studieren, in dem ich Advokat war.	He was busy studying that particular case in which I was an advocate.
Dort hatte sie diejenigen Gegenstände zusammengehäuft, die ihr am besten gefielen.	She had there gathered those objects which she liked best.

(*b*) As a pronoun it is always followed by:

(i) A relative clause.

Wer hat die Scheibe zerbrochen?	Who has broken the window?
Derjenige, der (or welcher) eben wegläuft.	The one who is just running away.

It should not be confused with the use of **wer** illustrated in **55** (*a*). **Wer** (he who; the one who) is vague; **derjenige, welcher** (the one who) is more definite and indicates some specific person.

(ii) A dependent genitive.

Alle Katzen lagen tot; auch diejenige der Frau Keller.	All the cats were dead; Mrs Keller's too.

Note.—It is not usual to omit the demonstrative with a genitive as we do in English.

Seine Mütze und diejenige (or die) seines Bruders.	His cap and his brother's.

(iii) A prepositional phrase.

Diejenigen im Garten sind schon lange tot.	Those in the garden have been dead for some time.

120. 4. derselbe, dieselbe, dasselbe, the same; adjective or pronoun.

It is inflected like derjenige and is written as one word unless there is a contraction of preposition + definite article (33).

Es ist derselbe Mann.	It is the same man.
Am selben Abend.	On the same evening.

Note.—It is sometimes used in writing in place of a personal pronoun (but its use is not considered good style) :—

(i) to avoid the juxtaposition of sie sie.

Da liegt die Feder. Reichen Sie mir dieselbe, bitte !	There is the pen. Please hand it to me

(instead of: Reichen Sie sie mir ! which, in fact, is not to be objected to at all).

(ii) after such prepositions as make no adverbial compound (42(g).)

Das Gebet war so lang, daß wir während desselben beinahe einschliefen (better: daß wir dabei fast einschliefen.	The prayer was so long that we almost fell asleep during it.

121. 5. Solcher, solche, solches, such.

(a) As an Adjective solcher is declined like dieser.

solcher Wein, such wine.
solche Leute, such people.
solchen Kindern, to such children.

(b) As a Pronoun it may have demonstrative force.

Dieses Buch ist für solche, die keine Zeit haben, die große Ausgabe zu lesen.	This book is for those who (for such as) have no time to read the large edition.

(*c*) To translate 'such a.'

(i) Solch ein—here folch is invariable.

>Solch ein Lehrer! Such a teacher!
>Solch eine Frau! Such a woman!

(ii) ein folcher—declined like an adjective preceded by the indefinite article.

Er ift ein folcher Narr. He is such a fool.
Eines folchen Mannes. Of such a man.

When 'such' is followed by another adjective, fo is required in German; thus:

Ein fo früher Tod. Such an early death.
Bei fo fchlechtem Wetter. In such bad weather.

XVII. THE VERB

122. There are two main classes of verbs:

(*a*) **Transitive,** *i.e.,* verbs that require a complement in the accusative.

Er öffnete das Fenfter. He opened the window.
Wir haben das Buch gelefen. We have read the book.

(*b*) **Intransitive,** *i.e.*:

(i) Verbs that require no complement.

>Er weinte. He wept.
>Ich eilte davon. I hurried away.

(ii) Verbs that take a complement in the genitive or dative or after a preposition.

Er bedurfte des Geldes. He needed the money.
Er gehorcht feinem Vater. He obeys his father.
Ich zweifle an feiner Treue. I have doubts about his fidelity.

123. Some verbs may be used either transitively or absolutely.

Er fingt ein altes Lied (trans.). He sings an old song.
Er fingt fehr fchön (absol.). He sings very beautifully.
Ich habe einen Brief ge= I have written a letter.
fchrieben (trans.).
Was tut Karl? Er fchreibt an What is Karl doing? He is
feine Mutter (absol.). writing to his mother.

124. (*a*) Transitive verbs may also be used **reflexively** (57).

These have pronoun objects which refer to the subject and may be rendered in English either by a reflexive verb, as

> Er wäſcht ſich.   He is washing himself.

Or by a simple verb, as

> Er freut ſich daran.   He rejoices thereat.

(For a list of common reflexive verbs, see **174** (*b*) and **191**.)

(*b*) Transitive and intransitive verbs may also be used **impersonally.**

Such are found only in the 3rd person singular and usually have **es** as subject. This **es** may sometimes be understood.

> Es mangelt ihm an Geld.   He lacks money.
>
> Mich dünkt, er wird nicht   Methinks he will not live long.
> lange leben.

(For a list of common impersonal verbs, see **171**.)

125. Moods.

(*a*) Indicative (der Indikativ). This is the mood which expresses reality, certainty, or likelihood.

(*b*) Subjunctive (der Konjunktiv). Generally expresses possibility or uncertainty, but for a fuller treatment of its use, see **198** to **213**.

(*c*) Imperative (der Imperativ). Is the mood which expresses commands, requests, and warnings.

(*d*) Infinitive (der Infinitiv).

126. Voice.

(*a*) The Active (das Aktiv), as the name implies, is the form of the verb used when the subject is considered as the agent, the doer of the action.

> Siegfried hat den Drachen   Siegfried has slain the dragon.
> erſchlagen.

hat . . . erſchlagen is in the Active Voice because it represents Siegfried's action.

(*b*) The Passive (das Paſſiv) is the voice used when the subject is considered as being affected by the action, or as undergoing something (Latin *passus*, from the verb 'to suffer').

> Der Drache iſt von Siegfried   The dragon has been slain by
> erſchlagen worden.   Siegfried.

ift . . . erſ$c$lagen worden is in the Passive because it indicates what has happened to the subject.

127. The **Tenses** in German are:

(*a*) Present (das Präſens), the use of which corresponds closely to that of the English Present. It should be remembered, however, that German uses the Present with a future sense more frequently than English; this is especially so in conversation.

Ich leſe es heute abend.	I will read it to-night.

(*b*) Perfect (das Perfektum), used as in English, except that the German Perfect is often found in conversation where English would have a past tense.

Kurz, es hat ſich zerſchlagen.	In a word, the idea came to grief.

(*c*) Imperfect (das Imperfektum). This is used, as in English, in the narration of past events.

Note.—With the following words:

ſeit (preposition)	since, for
ſchon ⎫ (adverbs) bereits ⎭	already
erſt	only
lange	for a long time

German uses (i) the Present when the action began in the past and is continuing (English has Perfect).

Wie lange ſind Sie hier?	How long have you been here?
Ich wohne Bötticherſtraße ſeit 1944.	I have been living in Bötticher-strasse since 1944.
Er ſtudiert Philoſophie ſeit drei Jahren.	He has been studying philosophy for three years.

(ii) the Imperfect when the action began at a more remote time in the past and was continuing.

Sie ſchliefen ſeit zwei Stunden, als er ankam.	They had been sleeping for two hours when he arrived.

This construction is similar to the French with *depuis*.

Ils l'attendaient depuis vingt minutes.	They had been waiting for her for twenty minutes.

This use may be expressed briefly thus:—With the above-mentioned words

> when 'has (have) been doing' = 'has (have) been doing *and still is (are)*' German uses Present;
> when 'had been doing' = 'had been doing *and still was (were)*' German uses Imperfect.

(*d*) Pluperfect (das Plusquamperfektum), used as in English.

(*e*) Future (das Futurum), used as in English, except that German has also a 'Future of Probability,' *e.g.*:

> Er wird wohl krank sein.   He is probably ill.

(*f*) Future Perfect (das Futurum Perfekti), used as in English, except that German has also a 'Future Perfect of Probability.'

> Sie werden wohl da gewesen   They were probably there.
> sein.

(*g*) Conditional (das Konditional).

(*h*) Conditional Perfect (das Konditionalis Perfekti).

128. Other verb forms are:

The Present Participle (das Partizipium Präsentis).
The Past Participle (das Partizipium Präteriti).

These have no special form to indicate person, number, or tense.

129. For purposes of **Conjugation** German verbs may be regarded as falling into two main groups, weak and strong.

1. Weak Verbs.

(*a*) The Past tense is formed by adding to the stem the terminations

=te	Thus, lob=en, to praise	ich lobte, I praised
=test		du lobtest
=te		er, sie, es lobte
=ten		wir lobten
=tet		ihr lobtet
=ten		sie lobten

(*b*) The Past Participle is formed by prefixing ge= to the stem (except in the cases indicated in Note (i) below) and adding the termination =t; thus, for example, the Past Participle of loben is gelobt, praised.

2. Strong Verbs.

(*a*) The 2nd and 3rd person singular Present Indicative have a change of vowel in some strong verbs (see **166** and **168**).

(*b*) The Past tense is formed by changing the stem vowel and using the following endings:

---	Thus, ſing=en, to sing	id) ſang, I sang
-- ſt		bu ſangſt
---		er, ſie, es ſang
-- en		wir ſangen
-- (e)t		ihr ſangt
-- en		ſie ſangen

(*c*) The Past Participle is formed by prefixing ge= to the stem (except in the cases indicated in Note (i) below) and adding the termination =en. Thus the Past Participle of ſingen is geſungen, sung.

NOTE.—(i) ge= is prefixed to the stem with the Past Participle of all verbs, except verbs of foreign origin in =ieren (ſtubieren, past part. ſtubiert), and verbs which have an inseparable prefix (erfahren, begleiten, past part. erfahren, begleitet). See **195. 1**.

(ii) There is a small group of verbs which add =te, etc., to make the Past tense and which also change the vowel of the stem. These will be dealt with under the heading 'Mixed Verbs' (**167**).

130. (*a*) CONJUGATION OF **Werden**

Infinitives : Present, (3u) werden, *to become.*
Perfect, geworden (3u) ſein.

Participles : Present, werbend.
Past, geworden, worden. See **131. 1** (*d*).

INDICATIVE	SUBJUNCTIVE

Present

id) werde	id) werde
bu wirſt	bu werbeſt
er, ſie, es wirb	er, ſie, es werbe
wir werden	wir werden
ihr werbet	ihr werbet
ſie werden	ſie werden

Imperative

  2nd p. sing. **werbe !** become
  1st p. plur. **werben wir !** let us become
  2nd p. plur. **werbet !** become
  Polite form, sing. and plur. **werben Sie !** become

Note.—See also **45** (*c*).

Imperfect

ich wurbe (warb is poetical)	ich würbe
du wurbeſt	du würbeſt
er, ſie, es wurbe	er, ſie, es würbe
wir wurben	wir würben
ihr wurbet	ihr würbet
ſie wurben	ſie würben

Perfect

ich bin geworben	ich ſei geworben
du biſt geworben	du ſeieſt geworben
er, ſie, es iſt geworben	er, ſie, es ſei geworben
wir ſind geworben	wir ſeien geworben
ihr ſeid geworben	ihr ſeiet geworben
ſie ſind geworben	ſie ſeien geworben

Pluperfect

ich war geworben	ich wäre geworben
du warſt geworben	du wäreſt geworben
er, ſie, es war geworben	er, ſie, es wäre geworben
wir waren geworben	wir wären geworben
ihr wart geworben	ihr wäret geworben
ſie waren geworben	ſie wären geworben

Future

ich werbe werben	ich werbe werben
du wirſt werben	du werbeſt werben
er, ſie, es wird werben	er, ſie, es werbe werben
wir werben werben	wir werben werben
ihr werbet werben	ihr werbet werben
ſie werben werben	ſie werben werben

Future Perfect

ich werde geworden sein	ich werde geworden sein
du wirst geworden sein	du werdest geworden sein
er, sie, es wird geworden sein	er, sie, es werde geworden sein
wir werden geworden sein	wir werden geworden sein
ihr werdet geworden sein	ihr werdet geworden sein
sie werden geworden sein	sie werden geworden sein

Conditional

ich würde werden
du würdest werden
er, sie, es würde werden   *No Subjunctive*
wir würden werden
ihr würdet werden
sie würden werden

Conditional Perfect

ich wäre geworden
du wärest geworden
er, sie, es wäre geworden   *No Subjunctive*
wir wären geworden
ihr wäret geworden
sie wären geworden
Or ich würde geworden sein   (This form is less usual)
du würdest geworden sein
er, sie, es würde geworden sein, etc.

(b) Conjugation of Sein

Infinitives: Present, (zu) sein, *to be.*
           Perfect, gewesen (zu) sein

Participles: Present, seiend.
           Past, gewesen.

INDICATIVE	SUBJUNCTIVE

Present

ich bin	ich sei
du bist	du seiest
er, sie, es ist	er, sie, es sei
wir sind	wir seien
ihr seid	ihr seiet
sie sind	sie seien

Imperative

2nd p. sing. ſei ! be
1st p. plur. ſeien wir ! let us be
2nd p. sing. ſeid ! be
Polite form, sing. and plur. ſeien Sie ! be

NOTE.—See also 45 (*c*).

INDICATIVE	SUBJUNCTIVE

Imperfect

ich war	ich wäre
du warſt	du wäreſt
er, ſie, es war	er, ſie, es wäre
wir waren	wir wären
ihr waret	ihr wäret
ſie waren	ſie wären

Perfect

ich bin geweſen	ich ſei geweſen
du biſt geweſen	du ſeieſt geweſen
er, ſie, es iſt geweſen	er, ſie, es ſei geweſen
wir ſind geweſen	wir ſeien geweſen
ihr ſeid geweſen	ihr ſeiet geweſen
ſie ſind geweſen	ſie ſeien geweſen

Pluperfect

ich war geweſen	ich wäre geweſen
du warſt geweſen	du wäreſt geweſen
er, ſie, es war geweſen	er, ſie, es wäre geweſen
wir waren geweſen	wir wären geweſen
ihr waret geweſen	ihr wäret geweſen
ſie waren geweſen	ſie wären geweſen

Future

ich werde ſein	ich werde ſein
du wirſt ſein	du werdeſt ſein
er, ſie, es wird ſein	er, ſie, es werde ſein
wir werden ſein	wir werden ſein
ihr werdet ſein	ihr werdet ſein
ſie werden ſein	ſie werden ſein

Future Perfect

ich werde gewesen sein	ich werde gewesen sein
du wirst gewesen sein	du werdest gewesen sein
er, sie, es wird gewesen sein	er, sie, es werde gewesen sein
wir werden gewesen sein	wir werden gewesen sein
ihr werdet gewesen sein	ihr werdet gewesen sein
sie werden gewesen sein	sie werden gewesen sein

Conditional

ich würde sein
du würdest sein
er, sie, es würde sein   *No Subjunctive*
wir würden sein
ihr würdet sein
sie würden sein

Conditional Perfect

ich wäre gewesen
du wärest gewesen
er, sie, es wäre gewesen   *No Subjunctive*
wir wären gewesen
ihr wäret gewesen
sie wären gewesen
Or ich würde gewesen sein   (This form is less usual)
du würdest gewesen sein
er, sie, es würde gewesen sein, etc.

(c) CONJUGATION OF **Haben**

Infinitives : Present, (zu) haben, *to have.*
Perfect, gehabt (zu) haben.

Participles : Present, habend.
Past, gehabt.

INDICATIVE	SUBJUNCTIVE
Present	
ich habe	ich habe
du hast	du habest
er, sie, es hat	er, sie, es habe
wir haben	wir haben
ihr habt	ihr habet
sie haben	sie haben

Imperative

> 2nd p. sing. ɦabe ! have
> 1st p. plur. ɦaben wir ! let us have
> 2nd p. plur. ɦab(e)t ! have
> Polite form, sing. and plur. ɦaben Sie ! have

Note.—See also **45** (*c*).

Imperfect

ich ɦatte	ich ɦätte
du ɦatteſt	du ɦätteſt
er, ſie, es ɦatte	er, ſie, es ɦätte
wir ɦatten	wir ɦätten
ihr ɦattet	ihr ɦättet
ſie ɦatten	ſie ɦätten

Perfect

ich ɦabe gehabt	ich ɦabe gehabt
du ɦaſt gehabt	du ɦabeſt gehabt
er, ſie, es ɦat gehabt	er, ſie, es ɦabe gehabt
wir ɦaben gehabt	wir ɦaben gehabt
ihr ɦabt gehabt	ihr ɦabet gehabt
ſie ɦaben gehabt	ſie ɦaben gehabt

Pluperfect

ich ɦatte gehabt	ich ɦätte gehabt
du ɦatteſt gehabt	du ɦätteſt gehabt
er, ſie, es ɦatte gehabt	er, ſie, es ɦätte gehabt
wir ɦatten gehabt	wir ɦätten gehabt
ihr ɦattet gehabt	ihr ɦättet gehabt
ſie ɦatten gehabt	ſie ɦätten gehabt

Future

ich werde ɦaben	ich werde ɦaben
du wirſt ɦaben	du werdeſt ɦaben
er, ſie, es wird ɦaben	er, ſie, es werde ɦaben
wir werden ɦaben	wir werden ɦaben
ihr werdet ɦaben	ihr werdet ɦaben
ſie werden ɦaben	ſie werden ɦaben

Future Perfect

ich werde gehabt haben	ich werde gehabt haben
du wirst gehabt haben	du werdest gehabt haben
er, sie, es wird gehabt haben	er, sie, es werde gehabt haben
wir werden gehabt haben	wir werden gehabt haben
ihr werdet gehabt haben	ihr werdet gehabt haben
sie werden gehabt haben	sie werden gehabt haben

Conditional

ich würde haben	
du würdest haben	
er, sie, es würde haben	*No Subjunctive*
wir würden haben	
ihr würdet haben	
sie würden haben	

Conditional Perfect

ich hätte gehabt	
du hättest gehabt	
er, sie, es hätte gehabt	*No Subjunctive*
wir hätten gehabt	
ihr hättet gehabt	
sie hätten gehabt	
Or ich würde gehabt haben	(This form is less usual)
du würdest gehabt haben	
er, sie, es würde gehabt haben, etc.	

(d) Conjugation of a Regular Weak Verb in the Active Voice

Infinitives: Present, (zu) loben, *to praise.*
Perfect, gelobt (zu) haben.

Participles: Present, lobend.
Past, gelobt.

INDICATIVE	SUBJUNCTIVE

Present

ich lobe	ich lobe
du lobst	du lobest
er, sie, es lobt	er, sie, es lobe
wir loben	wir loben
ihr lobt	ihr lobet
sie loben	sie loben

Imperative

    2nd p. sing. lobe ! praise
    1st p. plur. loben wir ! let us praise
    2nd p. plur. lob(e)t ! praise
    Polite form, 2nd p. sing. and plur. loben Sie ! praise

NOTE.—See also 45 (*c*).

Imperfect

ich lobte	The same as the Indicative
du lobteſt	throughout
er, ſie, es lobte	
wir lobten	
ihr lobtet	
ſie lobten	

Perfect

ich habe gelobt	ich habe gelobt
du haſt gelobt	du habeſt gelobt
er, ſie, es hat gelobt	er, ſie, es habe gelobt
wir haben gelobt	wir haben gelobt
ihr habt gelobt	ihr habet gelobt
ſie haben gelobt	ſie haben gelobt

Pluperfect

ich hatte gelobt	ich hätte gelobt
du hatteſt gelobt	du hätteſt gelobt
er, ſie, es hatte gelobt	er, ſie, es hätte gelobt
wir hatten gelobt	wir hätten gelobt
ihr hattet gelobt	ihr hättet gelobt
ſie hatten gelobt	ſie hätten gelobt

Future

ich werde loben	ich werde loben
du wirſt loben	du werdeſt loben
er, ſie, es wird loben	er, ſie, es werde loben
wir werden loben	wir werden loben
ihr werdet loben	ihr werdet loben
ſie werden loben	ſie werden loben

Future Perfect

ich werde gelobt haben	ich werde gelobt haben
du wirst gelobt haben	du werdest gelobt haben
er, sie, es wird gelobt haben	er, sie, es werde gelobt haben
wir werden gelobt haben	wir werden gelobt haben
ihr werdet gelobt haben	ihr werdet gelobt haben
sie werden gelobt haben	sie werden gelobt haben

Conditional

ich würde loben	
du würdest loben	
er, sie, es würde loben	*No Subjunctive*
wir würden loben	
ihr würdet loben	
sie würden loben	

Conditional Perfect

ich hätte gelobt	
du hättest gelobt	
er, sie, es hätte gelobt	*No Subjunctive*
wir hätten gelobt	
ihr hättet gelobt	
sie hätten gelobt	
Or ich würde gelobt haben	(This form is less usual)
du würdest gelobt haben	
er, sie, es würde gelobt haben, etc.	

(e) Conjugation of a Strong Verb in the Active Voice

Infinitives: Present, (zu) singen, *to sing*.
               Perfect, gesungen (zu) haben.

Participles: Present, singend.
             Past, gesungen.

INDICATIVE	SUBJUNCTIVE

Present

ich singe	ich singe
du singst	du singest
er, sie, es singt	er, sie, es singe
wir singen	wir singen
ihr singt	ihr singet
sie singen	sie singen

Imperative

> 2nd p. sing. ſinge ! sing
> 1st p. plur. ſingen wir ! let us sing
> 2nd p. plur. ſing(e)t ! sing
> Polite form, 2nd p. sing. and plur. ſingen Sie ! sing

NOTE.—See also 45 (*c*).

Imperfect

ich ſang	ich ſänge
du ſangſt	du ſängeſt
er, ſie, es ſang	er, ſie, es ſänge
wir ſangen	wir ſängen
ihr ſang(e)t	ihr ſänget
ſie ſangen	ſie ſängen

Perfect

ich habe geſungen	ich habe geſungen
du haſt geſungen	du habeſt geſungen
er, ſie, es hat geſungen	er, ſie, es habe geſungen
wir haben geſungen	wir haben geſungen
ihr habt geſungen	ihr habet geſungen
ſie haben geſungen	ſie haben geſungen

Pluperfect

ich hatte geſungen	ich hätte geſungen
du hatteſt geſungen	du hätteſt geſungen
er, ſie, es hatte geſungen	es, ſie, es hätte geſungen
wir hatten geſungen	wir hätten geſungen
ihr hattet geſungen	ihr hättet geſungen
ſie hatten geſungen	ſie hätten geſungen

Future

ich werde ſingen	ich werde ſingen
du wirſt ſingen	du werdeſt ſingen
er, ſie, es wird ſingen	er, ſie, es werde ſingen
wir werden ſingen	wir werden ſingen
ihr werdet ſingen	ihr werdet ſingen
ſie werden ſingen	ſie werden ſingen

Future Perfect

ich werde gesungen haben	ich werde gesungen haben
du wirst gesungen haben	du werdest gesungen haben
er, sie, es wird gesungen haben	er, sie, es werde gesungen haben
wir werden gesungen haben	wir werden gesungen haben
ihr werdet gesungen haben	ihr werdet gesungen haben
sie werden gesungen haben	sie werden gesungen haben

Conditional

ich würde singen
du würdest singen
er, sie, es würde singen   *No Subjunctive*
wir würden singen
ihr würdet singen
sie würden singen

Conditional Perfect

ich hätte gesungen
du hättest gesungen
er, sie, es hätte gesungen   *No Subjunctive*
wir hätten gesungen
ihr hättet gesungen
sie hätten gesungen
Or ich würde gesungen haben   (This form is less usual)
du würdest gesungen haben
er, sie, es würde gesungen haben, etc.

131.   NOTES ON **Werden, Sein,** AND **Haben**

I. **werden**

(*a*) As an independent verb, werden means 'to become.'

Er ist alt geworden.	He has grown old.
Im April werden die Bäume grün.	In April the trees become green.

(NOTE.—bekommen means 'to get,' 'obtain.')

(*b*) It is the auxiliary used to form the future and conditional tenses of all verbs.

Um halb vier werden wir da sein.	We shall be there at half-past three.
Ich würde gehen, wenn ich Zeit hätte.	I should go if I had time.

(*c*) It is the auxiliary used to form all the tenses of the actional passive voice.

Vor Sonnenaufgang wurde er erschossen.	He was shot before sunrise.
Er wird von vielen gehaßt.	He is hated by many.

(*d*) When werden is used as an independent verb, its past participle is geworden; when it is used as the auxiliary to form the passive, the past participle worden is used.

Er ist reich geworden.	He has become rich.
Er ist gehaßt worden.	He has been hated.
Sie wird begleitet worden sein.	She will have been accompanied.

2. sein

(*a*) As an independent verb, sein means 'to be.'

Er ist zwanzig Jahre alt.	He is twenty.

(*b*) sein is the auxiliary verb used to form the perfect infinitive and the perfect and pluperfect tenses of:

(i) sein, to be   bleiben, to remain
    werden, to become   verschwinden, to disappear
    geschehen, to happen   erscheinen, to appear
    gelingen, to succeed   anbrechen, to dawn

Sie war sofort verschwunden.	She had disappeared immediately.
Wir sind nicht lange geblieben.	We did not stay long.
Es scheint um drei Uhr geschehen zu sein.	It seems to have happened at three o'clock.

(ii) intransitive verbs which indicate change of state, *e.g.*:

    sterben, to die   erwachen, to wake up
    einschlafen, to fall asleep   entstehen, to arise
    ertrinken, to drown   genesen, to recover, get better

Er wird wohl eingeschlafen sein.	He will probably have fallen asleep.
Ein Kind ist geboren.	A child has been born.
Er ist gestern abend gestorben.	He died last night.

(iii) intransitive verbs of motion, *e.g.* :

fommen, to come	wandern, to wander
gehen, to go	folgen, to follow

Ihnen waren die Sozialde= mokraten gefolgt.	The Social Democrats had followed them.
Er soll durch den Wald ge= kommen sein.	He is said to have come through the wood.
Sie waren über die Berge gewandert.	They had wandered over the mountains.

Note.—begegnen, *to meet*, takes sein.

fortfahren, *to drive away* (intrans.), takes sein.

But: fortfahren, *to continue* (intrans.), takes haben.

tanzen, *to dance*, normally takes haben; but if there is a sense of dancing from one place into another, sein is used.

durchreisen (durch being separable and taking voice stress), *to pass through*, takes sein.

durchreisen (durch being inseparable and the stem reis= taking voice stress), *to travel all over*, takes haben.

Wir waren damals nur schnell durchgereist.	We only passed quickly through then.
In den Ferien haben wir ganz Schottland durchreist.	We travelled all over Scotland in the holidays.

durchgehen, *to go through* durchwandern, *to wander through* durchziehen, *to travel through* anlaufen, *to call at* (a port) anfahren, *to rebuke*	These may be found conjugated with sein even when they are used transitively. The idea of motion in the simple verb seems to predominate.

In conversation the past participle of a simple verb of motion (such as gehen or kommen) may sometimes be understood after the auxiliary sein. This omission is rare in the North.

Heute vormittag nun, wie er fortging, nach Brennholz zu suchen, bin ich zu seiner Frau auf das Schiff.	This morning when he went off to look for firewood I went to his wife on the ship.

3. haben

(*a*) As an independent verb haben means 'to have.'

Die Kirche hat keinen Turm.	The church has not got a tower

(b) It is the auxiliary verb used to form the perfect infinitive and the perfect and pluperfect tenses of all transitive verbs and of all verbs which do not take ſein as an auxiliary.

Wir haben den Film ſchon geſehen.	We have already seen the film.
Ich hatte ihn nicht lange gekannt.	I had not known him long.

4. The omission of the auxiliaries haben and ſein.

The auxiliary of the perfect or pluperfect tense may be omitted in a subordinate clause:

Ich war geräuſchlos eingetreten und hielt mich ſtill, bis er geendet.	I had come in quietly and stood silent until he had finished.

This omission is common where it avoids the juxtaposition of two uses of the same verb:

Da er ein ziemlich unnützes Männlein geweſen, war er nicht imſtande, es zu tun.	As he had been rather a useless little fellow he was unable to do it.

NOTE.—This omission should not be made in the case of a perfect or pluperfect tense which has a past participle the same in form as the infinitive. (176 (*e*) (ii); 236, 4.)

132.   PECULIARITIES OF SOME WEAK VERBS

(a) Weak verbs whose stem ends in consonant ₌b, ₌t, ₌m, or ₌n insert an e before an inflectional ₌t or ₌ſt, in order to avoid clumsy groups of consonants. Thus:

>antworten: (imperfect) ich antwortete, du antworteteſt, er antwortete.
>
>bilden: (present tense) ich bilde, du bildeſt, er bildet.
>   (past participle) gebildet.
>
>öffnen: (present tense) ich öffne, du öffneſt, er öffnet, etc.
>   (imperfect) ich öffnete, du öffneteſt, er öffnete, etc.
>   (past participle) geöffnet.

NOTE.—Weak verbs whose stem ends in ₌nn, ₌mm will not need this extra e as these double consonants represent only one sound.

>Therefore: er brummte, wir trennten.

Weak verbs whose stem ends in ₌tt will require the extra e because most of the inflections contain t.

>Therefore: er rettete, du wetteſt, er bittet.

(*b*) Weak verbs whose stem ends in one of the sibilants, =s, =ſ(ch), or =z, insert an e before the ſt inflection of the 2nd person singular, present indicative.

> wälzen: ich wälze, du wälzeſt, er wälzt.
> faſſen: ich faſſe, du faſſeſt (du faßt is also frequently found).
> reiſen: ich reiſe, du reiſeſt (du reiſt is also found).

(*c*) Weak verbs whose infinitive ends in =eln drop the e before the l in the first person singular, present indicative.

> ſchütteln: ich ſchüttle, du ſchüttelſt, er ſchüttelt, etc.
> feſſeln: ich feßle, du feſſelſt, er feſſelt, etc.
> wandeln: ich wandle, du wandelſt, er wandelt, etc.

(*d*) Weak verbs whose infinitive ends in =ern may drop the e before the r when followed by an e, but they frequently retain it.

> wandern: ich wandre (or ich wandere), du wanderſt, er
> wandert, etc.
> zittern: ich zittre (or ich zittere), du zitterſt, er zittert, etc.
> erſchüttern: ich erſchüttre (or ich erſchüttere), du erſchütterſt,
> er erſchüttert, etc.

NOTE.—wandern, *to move from one place to another* (therefore aus=
> wandern, *to emigrate*).
> wandeln, *to stroll along leisurely* (usually poetical or high
> style).
> erſchüttern, *to shake violently* (physically or emotionally).
> ſchütteln, *to shake normally* (e.g., a person's hand or a tree
> to make fruit fall).

(*e*) Those weak verbs whose infinitives end in =eln or =ern drop the e of the =en inflection, 1st and 3rd person plural, present indicative; *e.g.*,

> ſchütteln: wir ſchütteln, ihr ſchüttelt, ſie ſchütteln.
> zittern: wir zittern, ihr zittert, ſie zittern.
> flüſtern: wir flüſtern, ihr flüſtert, ſie flüſtern.

133. CONJUGATION OF A VERB IN THE ACTIONAL
PASSIVE VOICE

(Remember: In the actional Passive Voice *be* is werden, except in the Imperative, and *been* is worden. Every tense of the
Passive Voice has a past participle in it.)

Infinitives: Present, gelobt (zu) werden, *to be praised.*
> Perfect, gelobt worden (zu) ſein, *to have been praised.*

INDICATIVE	SUBJUNCTIVE

Present

I am praised

ich werde gelobt	ich werde gelobt
du wirst gelobt	du werdest gelobt
er, sie, es wird gelobt	er, sie, es werde gelobt
wir werden gelobt	wir werden gelobt
ihr werdet gelobt	ihr werdet gelobt
sie werden gelobt	sie werden gelobt

Imperative

2nd p. sing. sei gelobt ! be praised!
1st p. plur. seien wir gelobt ! let us be praised!
2nd p. plur. seid gelobt ! be praised!
Polite form, sing. and plur. seien Sie gelobt ! be praised!

Imperfect

I was praised

ich wurde gelobt	ich würde gelobt
du wurdest gelobt	du würdest gelobt
er, sie, es wurde gelobt	er, sie, es würde gelobt
wir wurden gelobt	wir würden gelobt
ihr wurdet gelobt	ihr würdet gelobt
sie wurden gelobt	sie würden gelobt

Perfect

I have been praised

ich bin gelobt worden	ich sei gelobt worden
du bist gelobt worden	du seiest gelobt worden
er, sie, es ist gelobt worden	er, sie, es sei gelobt worden
wir sind gelobt worden	wir seien gelobt worden
ihr seid gelobt worden	ihr seiet gelobt worden
sie sind gelobt worden	sie seien gelobt worden

Pluperfect

I had been praised

ich war gelobt worden	ich wäre gelobt worden
du warst gelobt worden	du wärest gelobt worden
er, sie, es war gelobt worden	er, sie, es wäre gelobt worden
wir waren gelobt worden	wir wären gelobt worden
ihr wart gelobt worden	ihr wäret gelobt worden
sie waren gelobt worden	sie wären gelobt worden

Future

I shall be praised

idy werbe gelobt werben	idy werbe gelobt werben
bu wirst gelobt werben	bu werbest gelobt werben
er, sie, es wirb gelobt werben	er, sie, es werbe gelobt werben
wir werben gelobt werben	wir werben gelobt werben
ihr werbet gelobt werben	ihr werbet gelobt werben
sie werben gelobt werben	sie werben gelobt werben

Future Perfect

I shall have been praised

idy werbe gelobt worben sein	idy werbe gelobt worben sein
bu wirst gelobt worben sein	bu werbest gelobt worben sein
er, sie, es wirb gelobt worben sein	er, sie, es werbe gelobt worben sein
wir werben gelobt worben sein	wir werben gelobt worben sein
ihr werbet gelobt worben sein	ihr werbet gelobt worben sein
sie werben gelobt worben sein	sie werben gelobt worben sein

Conditional

I should be praised

idy würbe gelobt werben	
bu würbest gelobt werben	
er, sie, es würbe gelobt werben	*No Subjunctive*
wir würben gelobt werben	
ihr würbet gelobt werben	
sie würben gelobt werben	

Conditional Perfect

I should have been praised

idy wäre gelobt worben	
bu wärest gelobt worben	
er, sie, es wäre gelobt worben	*No Subjunctive*
wir wären gelobt worben	
ihr wäret gelobt worben	
sie wären gelobt worben	

Or id) würde gelobt worden   (This form is less usual)
        fein
     du würdeft gelobt worden
        fein
er, fie, es würde gelobt worden
        fein, etc.

134. The Passive with fein.

The auxiliary of the Passive Voice is (with the exception of
the Imperative) werden. There is also a Passive formed with the
auxiliary fein. English uses *to be* in both cases, and it is hard
for the English student to appreciate the need in German for
two forms of the Passive Voice. The Passive with werden (133)
may be called the actional Passive, because it describes *action*;
the Passive with fein may be called the statal Passive, because
it describes a *state*. Consider the following sentences:

Als id) herankam, {wurde das Fenfter zerbrochen (1).
                  {war das Fenfter zerbrochen (2).

Both these are translated in English, rather ambiguously—
'When I came the window was broken.'

There is no ambiguity in the German: (1) means—At the
moment of my arrival someone broke the window; (2) means
—When I arrived the window was already in a broken condition.

So also:

Um neun Uhr {wird der Weihnachtsbaum gefchmückt (3).
             {ift der Weihnachtsbaum gefchmückt (4).

(3) At nine o'clock the decoration of the Christmas tree begins;
(4) By nine o'clock the tree already stands decorated.

135. (*a*) Only verbs which govern an accusative can be turned
directly into the Passive.

Active

Er fchlug den Hund mit einem   He beat the dog with a stick.
   Stock.

Passive

Der Hund wurde von ihm   The dog was beaten by him
   mit einem Stock gefchlagen.   with a stick.

Thus what was the accusative in the active form becomes the
nominative in the Passive.

(b) Verbs governing a genitive or dative (172-4) cannot be turned directly into the Passive. They must be rendered impersonally with or without es

Es muß ihm bei diesem heißen Wunsche geholfen werden.	In this ardent desire he must be helped.
Ihrer wurde gespottet. } Es wurde ihrer gespottet. }	She was mocked.

(For other ways of rendering an English Passive idea, see 188.)

136.   CONJUGATION OF A REFLEXIVE VERB

Infinitives: Present, sich (zu) erinnern.
Perfect, sich erinnert (zu) haben.

Participles: Present, sich erinnernd.
Past—not used alone.

INDICATIVE	SUBJUNCTIVE

Present

ich erinnere mich (daran), etc.   ich erinnere mich (daran), etc.

Imperative

2nd p. sing. erinnere dich !
1st p. plur. erinnern wir uns !
2nd p. plur. erinnert euch !
Polite form 2nd p. sing. and plur. erinnern Sie sich

Imperfect

ich erinnerte mich (daran), etc.   ich erinnerte mich (daran), etc.

Perfect

ich habe mich (daran) erinnert, etc.   ich habe mich (daran) erinnert, etc.

Pluperfect

ich hatte mich (daran) erinnert, etc.   ich hätte mich (daran) erinnert, etc.

Future

ich werde mich (daran) erinnern, etc.   ich werde mich (daran) errinern, etc.

Future Perfect

ich werde mich (daran) erinnert haben, etc.   ich werde mich (daran) erinnert haben, etc.

Conditional

idⱼ würbe midⱼ (baran) erinnern,   *No Subjunctive*

Conditional Perfect

idⱼ ḥätte midⱼ (baran), erinnert,   *No Subjunctive*
etć.

Or idⱼ würbe midⱼ (baran) erinnert   (This form is less usual)
ḥaben, etc.

NOTE.—A reflexive verb may also have its reflexive pronoun in
the genitive or the dative; see 57 for the forms which must then
be used.

(57 gives the present tense of a reflexive verb in full.)

LISTS OF STRONG VERBS ARRANGED ACCORDING
TO ABLAUT

Ablaut is the change of vowel in the various parts of strong
verbs. Thus the Ablaut of ſingen, ſang, geſungen is i, a, u, and
that of meiben, mieb, gemieben is ei, ie, ie.

In the Ablaut series given below verbs are shown in the
Infinitive, the Imperfect 3rd p. sing., and the Past Participle,
with meaning. The vowel in brackets is that of the stem in the
2nd and 3rd person singular, present indicative; it is given only
if it is different from that of the other persons of the present
indicative.

Thus in 138 the Ablaut is ei, ie, ie, and the singular of the
present indicative of bleiben will be:

idⱼ bleibe, bu bleibſt, er bleibt.

In 150 the Ablaut is e, (i), a, o, and the singular of the present
indicative of ſterben will be:

idⱼ ſterbe, bu ſtirbſt, er ſtirbt.

Where necessary, the quantity is indicated in brackets after
the Ablaut.

137. ei, i, i (short i).

beißen	biß	gebiſſen	to bite
ſidⱼ befleißen	ſidⱼ befliß	ſidⱼ befliſſen	to apply oneself to
bleidⱼen*	blidⱼ	geblidⱼen	to fade*

* NOTE: Usually found in compounds, *e.g.*, erbleidⱼen, to grow
pale; verbleidⱼen, to fade; bleidⱼen (meaning to bleach) is weak.

gleichen	glich	geglichen	to resemble
gleiten	glitt	geglitten	to slip, to slide
			(but begleiten, to accompany, is weak)
greifen	griff	gegriffen	to seize
kneifen	kniff	gekniffen	to nip
leiden	litt	gelitten	to suffer
pfeifen	pfiff	gepfiffen	to whistle
reißen	riß	gerissen	to tear
reiten	ritt	geritten	to ride (horse)
schleichen	schlich	geschlichen	to slink
schleifen	schliff	geschliffen	to whet (a knife), to grind
schmeißen	schmiß	geschmissen	to hurl, smite, fling
schneiden	schnitt	geschnitten	to cut
schreiten	schritt	geschritten	to stride
streichen	strich	gestrichen	to stroke, cross out, paint
streiten	stritt	gestritten	to strive, contend, quarrel
weichen	wich	gewichen	to yield

138. ei, ie, ie.

bleiben	blieb	geblieben	to remain
gedeihen	gedieh	gediehen	to thrive
leihen	lieh	geliehen	to lend
meiden	mied	gemieden	to avoid
preisen	pries	gepriesen	to praise
reiben	rieb	gerieben	to rub
scheiden	schied	geschieden	to separate, divorce
scheinen	schien	geschienen	to shine, seem
schreiben	schrieb	geschrieben	to write
schreien	schrie	geschrie(e)n	to scream, yell
schweigen	schwieg	geschwiegen	to be silent
speien	spie	gespie(e)n	to spew, vomit, spit
steigen	stieg	gestiegen	to mount, climb
treiben	trieb	getrieben	to drive on, impel
weisen	wies	gewiesen	to point
zeihen	zieh	geziehen	to accuse

139. ie, o, o (short o).

fließen	floß	geflossen	to flow
genießen	genoß	genossen	to enjoy
gießen	goß	gegossen	to pour
kriechen	kroch	gekrochen	to creep
riechen	roch	gerochen	to smell
schießen	schoß	geschossen	to shoot
sieden	sott	gesotten	to boil (*trans.*)

N.B.—triefen, troff (or triefte), getrieft, to drip.

140. e, (i), o, o (all vowels short).

dreſchen	droſch	gedroſchen	to thresh
fechten	focht	gefochten	to fight
flechten	flocht	geflochten	to plait
melfen	molf	gemolfen	to milk
		(also weak)	
quellen	quoll	gequollen	to gush
ſchmelzen	ſchmolz	geſchmolzen	to melt (*intrans.*)
ſchwellen	ſchwoll	geſchwollen	to swell (*intrans.*)

141. i, o, o (all vowels short).

glimmen	glomm	geglommen	to glimmer, burn faintly
flimmen	flomm	geflommen	to climb

142. (*a*) au (äu), o, o (short o).

ſaufen	ſoff	geſoffen	to drink (of animals)
			to guzzle (of humans)

(*b*) a, o, o (short o).

ſchallen	ſcholl	geſchollen	to sound forth (usually weak)

N.B.—rächen (to revenge) is weak except for a past participle gerochen.

143. ie, o, o (long o).

biegen	bog	gebogen	to bend
bieten	bot	geboten	to offer
erfieſen	erfor	erforen	to choose (poet.)
fliegen	flog	geflogen	to fly
fliehen	floh	geflohen	to flee
frieren	fror	gefroren	to freeze
ſtieben	ſtob	geſtoben	to fly up (as dust, Staub)
verlieren	verlor	verloren	to lose
wägen	wog	gewogen	to weigh (also weak)
wiₑgen	wog	gewogen	to weigh
			to rock (usually weak in this sense)

144. e, o, o (all vowels long).

heben	hob	gehoben	to lift
ſcheren	ſchor (also	geſchoren	to shear; to concern
(*Pres.* 2 & 3 *p.*	ſcherte)		(*reflexively*) to be off
sing. ſchierſt,			
ſchiert or ſcherſt,			
ſchert)			
weben	wob	gewoben	to weave (occasionally weak)
bewegen	bewog	bewogen	to induce
			(bewegen, to stir (emotions), to shift (things), is weak)

145. au, o, o (long o).

ſaugen	ſog	geſogen	to suck
ſchnauben	ſchnob	geſchnoben	to snort

(ſchrauben, to screw, is usually weak, but there is a past participle verſchroben = distorted, eccentric.)

146. ü, o, o (all vowels long).

lügen	log	gelogen	to tell a lie
trügen	trog	getrogen	to deceive

147. ä, o, o (all vowels long).

gären	gor	gegoren	to ferment
ſchwären	ſchwor	geſchworen	to fester (also weak)

NOTE: ſchwören, ſchwor (or ſchwur), geſchworen, to swear an oath; (fluchen, to curse).

148. i, a, u (all vowels short).

binden	band	gebunden	to bind
dingen	dang	gedungen	to hire (also weak)
	(usually dingte)		
dringen	drang	gedrungen	to press, penetrate
finden	fand	gefunden	to find
gelingen	gelang	gelungen	to succeed (*impersonal*)
klingen	klang	geklungen	to sound
ringen	rang	gerungen	to wrestle
ſchlingen	ſchlang	geſchlungen	to wind, twine, swallow
ſchwinden	ſchwand	geſchwunden	to disappear
ſchwingen	ſchwang	geſchwungen	to swing
ſingen	ſang	geſungen	to sing
ſinken	ſank	geſunken	to sink
ſpringen	ſprang	geſprungen	to spring, jump
ſtinken	ſtank	geſtunken	to stink
trinken	trank	getrunken	to drink
winden	wand	gewunden	to wind
zwingen	zwang	gezwungen	to compel

N.B.—ſchinden, ſchund (or ſchand), geſchunden, to flay.

149. i, a, o (all vowels short).

beginnen	begann	begonnen	to begin
gewinnen	gewann	gewonnen	to win, gain
rinnen	rann	geronnen	to run (of liquids)
ſchwimmen	ſchwamm	geſchwommen	to swim, float
ſinnen	ſann	geſonnen	to ponder
		(also geſinnt, in sense of ' disposed towards')	
ſpinnen	ſpann	geſponnen	to spin

150. e (i), a, o (e, a, o short).

bergen	barg	geborgen	to shelter
bersten	barst	geborsten	to burst
(2 & 3 p. sing.			
pres. berstest			
(birst), berstet			
(birst)			
gelten	galt	gegolten	to be worth, to be valid
			(gelten als (or für) = to pass for, to be con-
			sidered as)
schelten	schalt	gescholten	to scold
sterben	starb	gestorben	to die
verderben	verbarb	verborben	to spoil

werben used to belong to this class, and the old past tense warb is still found in poetry and archaic style.

151. ä, a, o (all vowels long).

gebären	gebar	geboren	to bear (children)

152. e (i), a, o (a long, other vowels short).

brechen	brach	gebrochen	to break
erschrecken	erschrak	erschrocken	to be frightened
sprechen	sprach	gesprochen	to speak
stechen	stach	gestochen	to stab, sting
stecken	stak	gesteckt	to be sticking in
	(also steckte)		(shows irregularity in the past participle)
treffen	traf	getroffen	to hit, to meet

153. e (ie), a, o (all vowels long).

befehlen	befahl	befohlen	to command
empfehlen	empfahl	empfohlen	to recommend
stehlen	stahl	gestohlen	to steal

154. e (i), a, e (a long, other vowels short).

essen	aß	gegessen	to eat
fressen	fraß	gefressen	to eat (of animals or like animals)
messen	maß	gemessen	to measure
vergessen	vergaß	vergessen	to forget

155. e (ie), a, e (all vowels long).

geben	gab	gegeben	to give
(2 & 3 *pers.*			
sing. pres.			
gib[t, gibt)			
genefen	genas	genefen	to recover (from illness)
(2 & 3 *p. sing.*			
pres. gene(fe)ft,			
geneft)			
gefdjehen	gefdjah	gefdjehen	to happen
lefen	las	gelefen	to read

156. i, a, e (long a and e).

bitten	bat	gebeten	to ask, request
fitzen	faß	gefeffen	to be sitting

157. ie, a, e (long a and e).

liegen	lag	gelegen	to be lying

158. a (ä), u, a (long u, short a)

baden	buf (also	gebaden	to bake
	badte)		
fdjaffen	fdjuf	gefdjaffen	to create, produce
(2 & 3 *pers.*			
sing. pres.			
fdjaffft, fdjafft)			

(fdjaffen, to procure, bring about, is weak)

wadjfen	wudjs	gewadjfen	to grow (to wax)
wafdjen	wufdj	gewafdjen	to wash

159. a (ä), u, a (all vowels long).

fahren	fuhr	gefahren	to go, to drive (*intrans.*)
graben	grub	gegraben	to dig
laden	lub	geladen	to load, invite
fdjlagen	fdjlug	gefdjlagen	to strike

160. a (ä), ie, a (short a).

fallen	fiel	gefallen	to fall
halten	hielt	gehalten	to hold, keep
laffen	ließ	gelaffen	to let, to leave, to cause,
			to have (a thing done)

161. a (ä), ie, a (long a).

blaſen	blies	geblaſen	to blow
raten	riet	geraten	to advise

(*Pres.* 3 *pers sing.* rät).

162. au, ie, au.

hauen	hieb	gehauen	to hew, hack

(*Pres.* 2 & 3
pers. sing.
hauſt, haut)

laufen	lief	gelaufen	to run

(*Pres.* 2 & 3
pers. sing.
läufſt, läuft)

163. ei, ie, ei.

heißen	hieß	geheißen	to be called, to mean, to bid

164. o (ö), ie, o (long o).

ſtoßen	ſtieß	geſtoßen	to push, to thrust

165. a (ä), i, a (all vowels short).

fangen	fing	gefangen	to catch
hängen (also	hing	gehangen	to be hanging
hangen)			

(hängen (weak), to hang up (*trans.*))

166. A general rule for the formation of the present tense of
strong verbs:

Strong verbs with a in the stem take ä in 2nd and 3rd person
singular present.

Strong verbs with short e in the stem take i in 2nd and 3rd
person singular present.

Strong verbs with long e in the stem take ie in 2nd and 3rd
person singular present.

167. MIXED VERBS

Infinitive	Imperfect 1st and 3rd Sing.	Past Part.	Meaning	Impf. Subj. 1st and 3rd Sing.
brennen	brannte	gebrannt	to burn	brennte
nennen	nannte	genannt	to name	nennte
kennen	kannte	gekannt	to know (See Note (*a*) below)	kennte

rennen	rannte	gerannt	to race	rennte
senden	sandte (or sendete)	gesandt (or gesendet)	to send	sendete
wenden	wandte (or wendete)	gewandt (or gewendet)	to turn	wendete
bringen	brachte	gebracht	to bring	brächte
denken	dachte	gedacht	to think	dächte

NOTE.—(*a*) kennen corresponds to French *connaître* (Scots *ken*) and means 'to know a person, place or thing.'

Kennen Sie Herrn Schmidt?	Do you know Mr Schmidt?
Kennst du das Land, wo die Zitronen blühn . . .?	Know'st thou the land where citrons bloom . . .?

wissen corresponds to French *savoir* and means 'to know a fact.' Its Pres. Ind. is: ich weiß, du weißt, er weiß, wir wissen, ihr wißt, sie wissen; its Pres. Subj.: ich wisse, du wissest, er wisse, etc.; its Past Ind.: ich wußte; its Past Subj.: ich wüßte, etc.; its Past Part.: gewußt.

Ich kenne den Mann vom Ansehen, aber ich weiß nicht, wie er heißt.	I know the man by sight but I don't know his name.
Ich weiß, wo Herr Schmidt wohnt.	I know where Mr Schmidt lives.
Wir wissen, daß er hier war.	We know that he was here.
Das weiß ich schon lange.	I have known that for some time.

(*b*) The two forms of senden and wenden may be used indiscriminately, but for a few fixed expressions:

> verwandt, related.
> ein Verwandter, a relative.
> der Gesandte, the ambassador.
> ein Gesandter, an ambassador.
> gewandt, skilful.

Apart from these the tendency seems to be in favour of an increasing use of the forms wendete, gewendet; sendete, gesendet.

(*c*) There is another word 'to send,' schicken (weak). This reminds one of Bismarck's retort to the ambassador who complained that German had frequently two words to represent the same thing, and who instanced schicken and senden, adding that he saw no difference between them. Bismarck is said to have replied:

> Sie sind wohl ein Gesandter, aber kein geschickter.

(*d*) The impersonal verb bünken offers some interesting forms:
bünken, bünkte, gebünkt (less common: beuchte (bäuchte) gebeucht).

(From M.H.G. mich bünkt, mich buhte).

(i) The Umlaut of bünkt was extended to the Past and gave bäuchte, which became beuchte.

(ii) From this Past a new Present was formed, mich beucht, which is still found in archaic style.

(iii) The original Present bünkt gave rise to an analogical form of the Imperfect, bünkte, which now is considered the correct modern form.

168.   ALPHABETICAL LIST OF STRONG, MIXED, AND IRREGULAR VERBS

NOTE.—(i) Verbs marked * have fein as the auxiliary to make the perfect infinitive, the perfect, and pluperfect tenses; verbs not so marked have haben.

(ii) The 2nd and 3rd person singular of the present indicative will have the same stem vowel as the infinitive unless otherwise indicated.

(iii) Of the imperative only the 2nd person singular is given as the other forms are made quite regularly from the present tense. Those verbs which change a of the stem to ä in the 2nd and 3rd person singular, present indicative, have unmodified a in the imperative 2nd person singular.

Those verbs which change e of the stem to i (except stechen and werden) and those which change e of the stem to ie in the 2nd and 3rd person singular, present indicative, retain the change in the imperative 2nd person singular and drop the ending e of the indicative mood.

(iv) With verbs other than those referred to in (iii) above, there are sometimes two forms of the imperative 2nd person singular, one with e and one without e. Originally e was found with strong verbs. To-day this distinction is not always observed; the form with e is often used in poetry and where the sentence rhythm requires it. The general tendency, however, is to use the form without e.

(v) If two forms are given, it should be understood that the one in brackets is optional. If one form in brackets occurs, it should be understood that it is rare. If in the Imperative column no form is given, it should be understood that the verb has no 2nd p. sing. Imperative.

Infin.	Impf. Ind.	Past Part.	Meaning	2 & 3 p. Sing. Pres.	Imper.	Impf. Subj.
backen	backte (also buk)	gebacken	to bake	bäckſt bäckt	backe	backte (büke)
bedürfen	bedurfte	bedurft	to need	bedarfſt bedarf	bedürfe	bedürfte
befehlen	befahl	befohlen	to command	befiehlſt befiehlt	befiehl	beföhle
befleißigen (ſich)	befliß[1]	befliſſen	to apply oneself	befleißige	befleißige	befleißigte
beginnen	begann	begonnen	to begin		beginne	begänne
beißen	biß	gebiſſen	to bite	beißt beißt	beiße	biſſe
bergen	barg	geborgen	to hide	birgſt birgt	birg	bürge
berſten*	barſt	geborſten	to burst	berſteſt (birſt) berſtet (birſt)	berſte (birſt)	berſte
betrügen	betrog	betrogen	to deceive		betrüge	betröge
bewegen[2]	bewog	bewogen	to induce	bewegſt bewegt	bewege	bewöge
biegen	bog	gebogen	to bend		biege	böge
bieten	bot	geboten	to offer		biete	böte
binden	band	gebunden	to bind		binde	bände
bitten	bat	gebeten	to request		bitte (bitt')	bäte
blaſen	blies (blus)	geblaſen	to blow	bläſt bläſt	blaſe	blieſe (blüſe)

[1] From an old infinitive befleißen, now rarely used.

[2] (bewegen = to stir (emotions), to shift (things), is weak.)

Infin.	Impf. Ind.	Past Part.	Meaning	2 & 3 p. Sing. Pres.	Imper.	Impf. Subj.
bleiben*	blieb	geblieben	to remain		bleibe	bliebe
bleichen*¹	blich	geblichen	to fade		bleiche	bliche
braten	briet	gebraten	to roast	brätst brät	brate	briete
brechen	brach	gebrochen	to break	brichst bricht	brich	bräche
brennen	brannte	gebrannt	to burn		brenne	brennte
bringen	brachte	gebracht	to bring		bringe	brächte
denken	dachte	gedacht	to think		denke	dächte
dingen	dingte (dang)	gedungen	to hire		dinge	dingte
dreschen	drosch	gedroschen	to thresh	drischst drischt	drisch	drösche
dringen	drang	gedrungen	to press to urge		dringe	dränge
dürfen	durfte	gedurft (dürfen)	to be allowed	darfst darf	(dürfe)	dürfte
empfehlen	empfahl	empfohlen	to recommend	empfiehlst empfiehlt	empfiehle	empföhle
erkiesen	erkor	erkoren	to choose (poet.)		erkiese	erköre
erlöschen*	erlosch	erloschen	to be extinguished	erlischst erlischt	erlisch	erlösche
erschrecken*	erschrak	erschrocken	to be frightened	erschrickst erschrickt	erschrick	erschröcke (erschräke)
erwägen	erwog	erwogen	to consider		erwäge	erwöge

¹ NOTE: See NOTE on p. 124.

134

essen	aß	gegessen	to eat	ißt / ißt	iß	äße
fahren*¹	fuhr	gefahren	to go, drive (vehicle)	fährst / fährt	fahre	führe
fallen*	fiel	gefallen	to fall	fällst / fällt	falle	fiele
fangen	fing	gefangen	to catch	fängst / fängt	fange	finge
fechten	focht	gefochten	to fight / to fence	fichtst / ficht	ficht (fechte)	föchte
finden	fand	gefunden	to find		finde	fände
flechten	flocht	geflochten	to plait	flichtst / flicht	flicht (flechte)	flöchte
fliegen*	flog	geflogen	to fly	fliegt / fliegt	fliege	flöge
fliehen*	floh	geflohen	to flee		fliehe	flöhe
fließen*	floß	geflossen	to flow	fließt / fließt	fließe	flösse
fressen	fraß	gefressen	to eat (of animals)	frißt / frißt	friß	fräße
frieren	fror	gefroren	to freeze		friere	fröre
gären	gor	gegoren	to ferment		gäre	göre
gebären	gebar	geboren	to bear (children)	gebierst / gebiert	gebäre (gebier)	gebäre
geben	gab	gegeben	to give	gibst / gibt	gib	gäbe
gedeihen*	gedieh	gediehen	to thrive	gedeiht	gedeihe	gediehe
gehen*	ging	gegangen	to go	geht	geh	ginge

¹ NOTE: but fahren = to drive a car etc. has haben as auxiliary.

135

Infin.*	Impf. Ind.	Past Part.	Meaning	2 & 3 p. Sing. Pres.	Imper.	Impf. Subj.
gelingen*	gelang	gelungen	to succeed (impers.)			gelänge
gelten	galt	gegolten	to be worth / to be valid / to pass for	giltst / gilt	gilt (gelte)	gölte
genesen*	genas	genesen	to recover (from illness)	gene(se)st / genest	genese	genäse
genießen	genoß	genossen	to enjoy	genießt / genießt	genieße	genösse
geschehen*	geschah	geschehen	to happen (impers.)	geschieht		geschähe
gewinnen	gewann	gewonnen	to win / to gain		gewinne	gewönne
gießen	goß	gegossen	to pour	gießt / gießt	gieße	gösse
gleichen / gleiten	glich / glitt	geglichen / geglitten	to resemble / to glide / to slip		gleiche / gleite	gliche / glitte
glimmen	glomm	geglommen	to burn faintly		glimm	glimmte (glömme)
graben	grub	gegraben	to dig	gräbst / gräbt	grabe	grübe
greifen / haben	griff / hatte	gegriffen / gehabt	to seize / to have	hast / hat	greife / habe	griffe / hätte
halten	hielt	gehalten	to hold, keep	hältst / hält	halt (hatte)	hielte

Infinitive	Preterite	Meaning	Past Participle	Present	Imperative	Subjunctive
hängen (hangen)	hing	to be hanging	gehangen	hängst / hängt	hänge	hinge
hauen	hieb (haute)	to hew	gehauen		haue	hiebe (haute)
heben	hob	to lift	gehoben		hebe (heb')	höbe
heißen	hieß	to be called / to bid, to mean	geheißen	heißt / heißt	heiße	hieße
helfen	half	to help	geholfen	hilfst / hilft	hilf	hülfe (hälfe)
kennen	kannte	to know	gekannt		kenne	kennte
klimmen*	klomm	to climb	geklommen		klimme	klimmte (klömme)
klingen	klang	to sound	geklungen		klinge	klänge
kneifen	kniff	to pinch / to nip	gekniffen		kneife	kniffe
kommen*	kam	to come	gekommen		komm	käme
können	konnte	to be able	gekonnt	kannst / kann		könnte
kriechen*	kroch	to creep	gekrochen		krieche	kröche
laden	lud	to load / to invite	geladen	lädst (ladest) / lädt (ladet)	lade	lüde
lassen	ließ	to let, leave / to cause	gelassen	läßt / läßt	laß	ließe
laufen*	lief	to run	gelaufen	läufst / läuft	laufe	liefe
leiden	litt	to suffer	gelitten		leide	litte
leihen	lieh	to lend	geliehen		leihe	liehe

137

Infin.	Impf. Ind.	Past Part.	Meaning	2 & 3 p. Sing. Pres.	Imper.	Impf. Subj.
lesen	las	gelesen	to read	liest / liest	lies	läse
liegen	lag	gelegen	to lie		liege (lieg')	läge
lügen	log	gelogen	to tell a lie		lüge	löge
meiden	mied	gemieden	to avoid		meide	miede
melken	molk (melkte)	gemolken (gemelkt)	to milk		melke	mölke (melkte)
messen	maß	gemessen	to measure	mißt / mißt	miß	mäße
mögen	mochte	gemocht (mögen)	to like	mag / mag	(möge)	möchte
müssen	mußte	gemußt (müssen)	to have to	mußt / muß		müßte
nehmen	nahm	genommen	to take	nimmst / nimmt	nimm	nähme
nennen	nannte	genannt	to name		nenne	nennte
pfeifen	pfiff	gepfiffen	to whistle	pfeift / pfeift	pfeife	pfiffe
preisen	pries	gepriesen	to praise	preist / preist	preise	priese
quellen	quoll	gequollen	to spring forth	quillst / quillt	quelle (quill)	quölle
raten	riet	geraten	to advise	rätst / rät	rate	riete
reiben	rieb	gerieben	to rub	reibst / reibt	reibe	riebe
reißen	riß	gerissen	to tear	reißt / reißt	reiße	rißse

Infinitive	Present (3rd sing.)	Meaning	Past Participle	Preterite	Imperative	Imperf. Subjunctive
reiten[1]*		to ride (horse)	geritten	ritt	reite	ritte
rennen[1]*		to race	gerannt	rannte	renne	rennte
riechen		to smell	gerochen	roch	rieche	röche
ringen		to wrestle	gerungen	rang	ringe	ränge (ringte)
rinnen*		to flow	geronnen	rann	rinne	rönne
rufen		to call	gerufen	rief	rufe	riefe
saufen	säufst / säuft	to drink (animals)	gesoffen	soff	saufe	söffe
saugen		to suck	gesogen	sog	sauge	söge
schaffen		to create	geschaffen	schuf	schaffe	schüfe
schallen[2]		to sound	geschollen (also geschallt)	scholl	schalle	schölle
scheiden		to separate / to depart (takes sein in this meaning)	geschieden	schied	scheide	schiede
scheinen		to seem / to shine	geschienen	schien	scheine	schiene
schelten	schiltst / schilt	to scold	gescholten	schalt	schilt	schölte
scheren	schierst (or scherst) / schiert (or schert)	to shear	geschoren	schor (also scherte)	schere (or schier)	(schöre) / scherte

[1] NOTE: takes haben as auxiliary when transitive.

[2] (schallen (weak), to sound is more usual; schellen (weak), to ring.)

Infin.	Impf. Ind.	Past Part.	Meaning	2 & 3 p. Sing. Pres.	Imper.	Impf. Subj.
ſchieben	ſchob	geſchoben	to shove	ſchiebt	ſchiebe	ſchöbe
ſchießen	ſchoß	geſchoſſen	to shoot	ſchießt	ſchieße	ſchöſſe
ſchinden	ſchund	geſchunden	to flay		ſchinde	ſchünde
ſchlafen	ſchlief	geſchlafen	to sleep	ſchläfſt, ſchläft	ſchlafe	ſchliefe
ſchlagen	ſchlug	geſchlagen	to strike	ſchlägſt, ſchlägt	ſchlage	ſchlüge
ſchleichen*	ſchlich	geſchlichen	to sneak into, to slink		ſchleiche	ſchliche
ſchleifen	ſchliff	geſchliffen	to whet, grind, to slip		ſchleife	ſchliffe
ſchleißen	ſchliß	geſchliſſen	to slit	ſchleißt	ſchleiße	ſchliſſe
ſchließen	ſchloß	geſchloſſen	to close	ſchließt	ſchließe	ſchlöſſe
ſchlingen	ſchlang	geſchlungen	to wind, to swallow		ſchlinge	ſchlänge
ſchmeißen	ſchmiß	geſchmiſſen	to smite, to fling	ſchmeißt	ſchmeiße	ſchmiſſe
ſchmelzen¹*	ſchmolz	geſchmolzen	to melt	ſchmilzeſt, ſchmilzt	ſchmilz	ſchmölze
ſchnauben	ſchnob	geſchnoben	to snort		ſchnaube	ſchnöbe (ſchnaubte)
ſchneiden	ſchnitt	geſchnitten	to cut		ſchneide	ſchnitte
ſchreiben	ſchrieb	geſchrieben	to write		ſchreibe	ſchriebe

¹ NOTE: takes haben as auxiliary when transitive.

ſchreien	ſchrie	geſchrie(e)n	to cry out, to shriek		ſchreie	ſchree
ſchreiten*	ſchritt	geſchritten	to stride, to step		ſchreite	ſchritte
ſchwären	ſchwor	geſchworen	to fester		ſchwäre	ſchwäre
ſchweigen	ſchwieg	geſchwiegen	to be silent		ſchweige	ſchwiege
ſchwellen[1]*	ſchwoll	geſchwollen	to swell	ſchwillſt, ſchwillt	ſchwill	ſchwölle
ſchwimmen*	ſchwamm	geſchwommen	to swim, float		ſchwimme	ſchwömme
ſchwinden*	ſchwand	geſchwunden	to disappear		ſchwinde	ſchwände
ſchwingen	ſchwang	geſchwungen	to swing		ſchwinge	ſchwänge
ſchwören	ſchwor (or ſchwur)	geſchworen	to swear		ſchwöre	ſchwüre (ſchwörte)
ſehen	ſah	geſehen	to see	ſiehſt, ſieht	ſieh(e)	ſähe
ſenden	ſandte (ſendete)	geſandt (geſendet)	to send		ſende	ſendete
ſieden	ſott	geſotten	to boil (trans.)		ſiede	(ſötte) ſiedete
ſingen	ſang	geſungen	to sing		ſinge	ſänge
ſinken*	ſank	geſunken	to sink		ſinke	ſänke
ſinnen	ſann	geſonnen	to think, to muse		ſinne	ſänne (ſönne)
ſitzen	ſaß	geſeſſen	to sit (be sitting)		ſitze (ſitz')	ſäße
ſollen	ſollte	geſollt (ſollen)	(various) (v. 177)	ſollſt, ſoll	(ſolle)	ſollte

[1] NOTE: takes haben as auxiliary when transitive.

Infin.	Impf. Ind.	Past Part.	Meaning	2 & 3 p. Sing. Pres.	Imper.	Impf. Subj.
ſpeien	ſpie	ge|ſpie(e)n	to spit, vomit		ſpeie	ſpiee (ſpeite)
ſpinnen	ſpann	ge|ſponnen	to spin		ſpinne	ſpönne
ſprechen	ſprach	ge|ſprochen	to speak	ſprichſt / ſpricht	ſprich	ſpräche
ſprießen¹	ſproß	ge|ſproſſen	to sprout	ſprießt / ſprießt	ſprieße	ſpröſſe
ſpringen*	ſprang	ge|ſprungen	to jump		ſpringe	ſpränge
ſtechen	ſtach	ge|ſtochen	to sting	ſtichſt / ſticht	ſtich	ſtäche
			to stab			
ſtecken	ſtak (ſteckte)	ge|ſteckt	to be sticking in	ſteckſt / ſteckt	ſtecke	ſtäke
(ſtecken)	ſteckte		to place			
ſtehen	ſtand	ge|ſtanden	to be standing	ſtehſt / ſteht	ſtehe (ſteh)	ſtände (ſtünde)
ſtehlen	ſtahl	ge|ſtohlen	to steal	ſtiehlſt / ſtiehlt	ſtiehl (ſtehl)	ſtähle (ſtöhle)
ſteigen*	ſtieg	ge|ſtiegen	to mount	ſteigſt / ſteigt	ſteige (ſteig)	ſtiege
ſterben*	ſtarb	ge|ſtorben	to die	ſtirbſt / ſtirbt	ſtirb	ſtürbe
ſtieben²	ſtob	ge|ſtoben	to fly up (as dust), scatter		ſtiebe	ſtöbe
ſtinken	ſtank	ge|ſtunken	to stink		ſtinke (ſtink)	ſtänke

¹ Note: used with ſein or haben.
² Note: takes haben as auxilary when transitive.

Infinitive	Preterite	Past participle	Meaning	Present		Subjunctive
stoßen[1]	stieß	gestoßen	to push / to thrust	stößt / stößt	stoße (stoß)	stieße
streichen	strich	gestrichen	to stroke / to cross out		streiche (streich)	striche
streiten	stritt	gestritten	to strive / to contend		streite (streite)	stritte
tragen	trug	getragen	to carry / to wear	trägt / trägt	trage (trag)	trüge
treffen	traf	getroffen	to hit / to meet	trifft / trifft	triff	träfe
treiben[1]	trieb	getrieben	to drive on, drift		treibe (treib)	triebe
treten*	trat	getreten	to tread / to step	trittst / tritt	tritt	träte
triefen	troff (triefte)	getrieft	to drip		triefe (trief)	(tröffe) triefte
trinken	trank	getrunken	to drink		trink (trinke)	tränke
trügen	trog	getrogen	to deceive		trüg (trüge)	tröge
tun	tat	getan	to do	tust / tut	tu (tue)	täte
verderben	verdarb	verdorben	to spoil	verdirbst / verdirbt	verdirb	verdürbe
verdrießen	verdroß	verdrossen	to vex	verdrießt / verdrießt	verdrieß (verdrieße)	verdrösse
vergessen	vergaß	vergessen	to forget	vergißt / vergißt	vergiß	vergäße

[1] NOTE: takes haben as auxiliary when transitive.

Infin.	Impf. Ind.	Past Part.	Meaning	2 & 3 P. Sing. Pres.	Imper.	Impf. Subj.
verlieren	verlor	verloren	to lose		verliere (verlier)	verlöre
wachſen*	wuchs	gewachſen	to grow	wächſt wächſt	wachſe	wüchſe
wägen	wog	gewogen	to weigh (trans.)	wägt	wäge	wöge
wiegen¹	wog	gewogen	to weigh (usually intrans.)	wägt	wiege	wöge
waſchen	wuſch	gewaſchen	to wash	wäſchſt wäſcht	(waſch) waſche	wüſche
weben (occasionally weak)	wob (occasionally weak)	gewoben	to weave		webe (web)	wöbe (webte)
weichen*	wich	gewichen	to yield	weiſt	weiche	wiche
weiſen	wies	gewieſen	to point to show	weiſt	weiſe (weis)	wieſe
wenden	wandte (wendete)	gewandt (gewendet)	to turn		wende	wendete
werben	warb	geworben	to strive after	wirbſt wirbt	wirb	würbe
werden*	wurde (ward)	geworden	to become, etc.	wirſt wird	werde	würde
werfen	warf	geworfen	to throw	wirfſt wirft	wirf	würfe
winden	wand	gewunden	to wind	weißt weiß	winde	wände
wiſſen	wußte	gewußt	to know	weißt weiß	wiſſe	wüßte

¹ wiegen (weak), to rock (cradle).

zeihen	zieh	geziehen	to accuse	zeihe (zeih)	ziehe	
ziehen[1]	zog	gezogen	to pull, go to draw	ziehe	zöge	
zwingen	zwang	gezwungen	to force to compel	zwing (zwinge)	zwänge	

[1] NOTE: takes haben as auxiliary when transitive, otherwise takes sein.

145

169. Verbs which are formed by the addition of a prefix to a strong verb have the same Ablaut as that verb.

Thus:

> greifen, griff, gegriffen, to seize, grasp.
> begreifen, to understand, comprehend.

Das begriff er sofort.	He understood that at once.
Nur mit Mühe hat sie es begriffen.	Only with difficulty did she comprehend this.

> angreifen, to attack.

Der Hund griff mich an.	The dog attacked me.
Er wurde von einem Stier angegriffen.	He was attacked by a bull.

NOTE.—This does not apply to verbs which have been formed from a noun.

der Ratschlag, counsel, gives: ratschlagen, ratschlagte, geratschlagt (to deliberate).

der Antrag, proposal, gives: beantragen, beantragte, beantragt (to propose, put forward a motion).

der Auftrag, commission, task, gives: beauftragen, beauftragte, beauftragt (to commission).

der Anlaß, cause, gives: veranlassen, veranlaßte, veranlaßt (to cause).

die Handhabe, handle, gives: handhaben, handhabte, gehandhabt (to handle, manage).

There is also a verb radebrechen (to 'murder' a language or to speak it imperfectly) which is weak despite brechen, brach, gebrochen, and which gives: radebrechte, geradebrecht.

FACTITIVE VERBS

170. These verbs express the idea of the subject's causing something to happen. They are derived from strong verbs, but are themselves always weak:

Factitive Verbs	*Derived from*
beugen, to bend (*i.e.*, to cause to bend).	biegen, to bend.
erschrecken, to frighten. (erschreckte, erschreckt.)	erschrecken, to be frightened. (erschrak, erschrocken.)
fällen, to fell.	fallen, to fall.
legen, to place, lay.	liegen, to lie.
schwemmen, to flood, wash away.	schwimmen, to swim.

ſenken, to lower.	ſinken, to sink.
ſeßen, to place.	ſißen, to sit.
ſprengen, to blow up; to ride furiously.	ſpringen, to leap.
tränken, to give to drink.	trinken, to drink.
verſchwenden, to squander.	verſchwinden, to vanish.

IMPERSONAL VERBS

171. Impersonal verbs are those that are found only in the 3rd person singular. Some require es a subject:

Es regnet heute. It is raining to-day.

Some require no es if there is another pronoun before the verb:

Mich dürſtet. I am thirsty.

(*But:* es dürſtet mich, although this is less common.)

(*a*) Impersonals describing weather:

es iſt kalt, warm, heiß, it is cold, warm, hot.
es friert, it is freezing.
es ſchneit, it is snowing.
es regnet, it is raining.
es taut, it is thawing.
es hagelt, it is hailing.
es donnert, it is thundering.
es blißt, it is lightning.
es tagt, the day is dawning.
es dunkelt, it is growing dusk.
es dämmert, twilight is falling.

(*b*) Reflexive Impersonals (or used as such); *e.g.*,

Es verſteht ſich.	Of course (*lit.* it is self-evident, self-understood).
Es hört ſich gut in dieſem Theater.	The acoustics in this theatre are good (*lit.* hearing is good).
Es lohnt ſich nicht der Mühe.	It is not worth while.

(*c*) An Impersonal construction often represents English there is' + gerund:

Es klopft.	Someone is knocking at the door (*lit.* there is a knocking).
Es brennt.	Fire! (*lit.* there is a burning) *or* it smarts.
Es zieht furchtbar.	There is an awful draught.

This is also the case with the passive:

Heute wird in Mariaspring getanzt.	There is dancing to-day at Mariaspring.
Es wird jetzt gebetet.	Prayer is being offered up now.

Note that in these Passive Impersonals the es is omitted if some other word begins the clause; thus:

In der Kirche wird jetzt gebetet.

(*d*) Impersonals + Accusative.

es dürstet mich,
mich dürstet,   }I am thirsty; usually: ich habe Durst.
(ich bin durstig),

es hungert mich,
mich hungert,   }I am hungry; usually: ich habe Hunger
(ich bin hungrig),

es friert mich,
mich friert,   }I am cold.
(also personal: ich friere),

es juckt mich, I itch.

es schmerzt mich, it pains me.

es schläfert mich,
(more usual: ich bin schläfrig),}I am sleepy.

es würgt mich, I have a choking feeling.

mich schaudert's,
es schaudert mich,}I am afraid.

mich dünkt (167, Note (*d*)), it seems to me.

Es widert mich (an), das zu tun,
(more usual: es ist mir widerlich,}I loathe doing that.
das zu tun),

(*e*) Impersonals + Dative.

mir ist nicht wohl, I do not feel well.

mir wird kalt, I am beginning to feel cold.

es geht ihm gut, he is well; things are well with him.

mir graut's,
es graut mir,   }I shudder at.
mir graust's,
es graust mir,

es träumt mir (poet.), I dream (more usually ich träume).

es bangt mir, I am afraid.

(*But:* ich bange mich um ihn.)

Es war ihm gelungen, das zu tun.	He had succeeded in doing that.
Ihm war, als ob . . .	He felt as if . . .

(*f*) The passive of verbs which take the genitive or dative must be rendered impersonally (**135** (*b*)).

(*g*) **Es ist** and **es gibt,** *there is, there are.*

es gibt, etc., followed by the Accusative, is used:

(i) to express a general statement without any reference to *restricted* locality.

In Holland gibt es viele Tulpen.	There are many tulips in Holland.

(In Holland implies far too large an area to be considered as 'restricted locality.')

Es gibt einen Typ von Menschen, der keinerlei Verständnis für Musik hat.	There is a type of person devoid of any feeling for music.

Or (ii) to express *natural* result.

In Indien ereignete sich ein Erdbeben; infolgedessen gab es viel Unglück.	There was an earthquake in India; as a result there was much distress.

Or (iii) to make broad, sweeping statements.

Es gibt so vieles, worüber man einig werden kann, und da sollte man nicht zögern, einig zu sein. 　　　　(Bismarck.)	There is so much about which one can come to an agreement, and so one should not hesitate to agree.

es ist, etc., refers to *local* experience.

In meinem Garten waren Tulpen.	There were tulips in my garden.

(In meinem Garten restricts the idea to a comparatively small area.)

Note.—The es of es ist, etc. (meaning *there is*), is omitted in inversion and in subordinate clauses. The es of es gibt is never omitted (**42** (*d*) Note).

(*h*) Note the expression:

　　　　Es kommt darauf an.　It depends.　(**225.**)

172.   VERBS WHICH GOVERN THE DATIVE CASE

(*a*) The following are the commonest verbs which require the dative case when translating the noun or pronoun which is the direct object in English:

ähneln, to resemble.	**Meine Schwester ähnelt ihrer Großmutter.** My sister resembles her grandmother.
ahnen (usually impers.), to have a foreboding.	**Mir ahnt was Böses.** I feel that something evil is going to happen.
behagen, to suit, please (**mißbehagen,** to displease).	**Das Frühlingswetter behagt mir sehr.** Spring weather suits me.
bekommen, to agree with.	**Zuviel Ruhe bekommt mir nicht.** Too much rest does not agree with me.
belieben (usually impers.), to please.	**Wie es Ihnen beliebt.** As you please.
	Wie beliebt? I beg your pardon (*i.e.*, What did you say?).
	(Old fashioned for **Wie bitte?**)
danken, to thank.	**Wir danken Ihnen für Ihre Gastfreundlichkeit.** We thank you for your hospitality.
dienen, to serve.	**Sein Leben lang diente der König seinem Volke.** The king served his people for the whole of his life.
drohen, to threaten.	**Dem Schiff drohte ein Sturm.** A storm threatened the ship.

(**drohen** + dat., to be approaching with the prospect of future danger or discomfort; in other senses use **bedrohen** + acc.)

erliegen, to succumb.	**Er ist einem schweren Anfall erlegen.** He has succumbed to a serious attack.
fehlen, to be lacking.	**Es fehlte ihm an Mut.** He lacked courage.
fluchen, to curse.	**Wir sollten keinem Menschen fluchen.** We ought to curse no man.
folgen, to follow.	**Der Hund ist seinem Herrn gefolgt.** The dog has followed its master.

frommen, fruchten, to avail.	Das frommt uns gar nichts (archaic; use nützen in Modern German). That is of no help to us at all.
gebrechen (usually impers.), to lack.	Es gebricht dem Lande an Nahrungs= mitteln. The country lacks food-stuffs.
gefallen, to please.	Das Konzert hat mir sehr gefallen. I liked the concert very much.
gehorchen, to obey.	Der Soldat muß seinem Offizier ge= horchen. The soldier must obey his officer.
gehören, to belong.	Das Gut gehört dem alten Grafen. The estate belongs to the old count.
gelingen, to succeed (mißlingen, to fail) (both usually impers.)	Dem großen Mediziner Robert Koch ist es gelungen, den Tuberkelbazillus zu entdecken. The great professor of medicine, Robert Koch, suc-ceeded in discovering the bacillus of tuberculosis.
gelten, to be meant for, to concern.	Eine Kugel kam geflogen. Gilt's mir oder gilt es dir? There came a bullet. Is it meant for me or for you?
	Was gilt es mir? What does it matter to me?
glauben, to believe.	Ihm können Sie glauben. You can believe him.

(*But:* glauben an, to believe in, *v. 223.*)

gleichen, to resemble.	Er gleicht seinem Bruder sehr. He resembles his brother very much.
mangeln (usually impers.), to lack.	Es mangelt uns nicht an Gelegen= heiten zum Sprechen. We don't lack opportunities for conversa-tion.
nutzen, nützen, to be of use to.	Der Hund nützt dem Hirten. The dog is useful to the shepherd.
nahen, sich nähern, to approach.	Die Hilfe naht der belagerten Stadt. Help approaches the besieged town.

paſſen, to suit, to fit (of clothes).	**Das paßt mir gar nicht.** That does not suit me at all.
raten, to advise.	**Chriſtus riet dem jungen Manne, ſein Hab und Gut den Armen zu geben.** Christ advised the young man to give his possessions to the poor.
ſchaden, to damage, to be harmful to.	**Nicht alle Inſekten ſchaden dieſer Pflanze.** Not all insects are harmful to this plant.
ſchmeicheln, to flatter.	**Schmeicheln Sie mir nicht!** Don't flatter me.
ſchwanen (impers.), to have a foreboding.	**Mir ſchwant was Unheimliches.** I have a feeling that something weird is about to happen.
ſtehen, to suit.	**Der Hut ſteht Ihnen gut.** The hat suits you.
trauen, to trust.	**Dem konnte ich nie trauen.** I could never trust him.
(mißtrauen, to mistrust.)	

(b) Some verbs require the *personal* object to be in the dative, whereas they may require the accusative for the non-personal direct object. The commonest are:

Verbs of saying, writing:

ſagen, to say, tell.	**Was ſagen Sie mir Neues?** What new thing are you telling?
erzählen, to relate.	**Er erzählte uns Geſchichten.** He used to tell us stories.
antworten, to answer. (**erwidern,** to answer.)	**Sie wollte mir nichts antworten.** She would make no answer at all.

(*But*: To answer a question, a letter, etc., **eine Frage beantworten**, or **auf eine Frage antworten**.)

Verbs of command, permission:

befehlen, to command.	**Das hat er uns befohlen.** He has ordered us to do that.
gebieten, to command, to enjoin.	**Er hat ihr Ruhe geboten.** He has ordered her (to take) rest.
erlauben, to allow. (**geſtatten,** to grant.)	**Das werden Sie mir wohl erlauben.** I suppose you will allow me that.

anvertrauen, to entrust.	Er hat mir seinen Sohn anvertraut. He entrusted his son to me.

Verbs of forgiving:

vergeben, to forgive. (verzeihen, to pardon.)	Vergib mir meine Sünden ! Forgive me my sins.

(*c*) The dative is required with these verbal expressions:

weh tun, to hurt.	Tut's Ihnen weh? Does it hurt you?
leid tun, to cause to be sorry.	Es tut mir furchtbar leid. . . . I am awfully sorry (conversational).
	Die heimatlosen Kinder tun uns wirklich leid. We are really sorry for the homeless children.
zuteil werden, to fall to a person's share.	Das alte Haus ist mir zuteil geworden. The old house has fallen to my share.
zugute kommen, to fall to a person's benefit.	Es wird ihm zugute kommen. It will turn out to his advantage.

(*d*) Verbs which are compounded with the following prefixes (**194, 195**) govern the dative, if the original verb was intransitive:

Inseparable:

ent=　　Der Gefangene war ihnen entkommen. The prisoner had escaped them.

wider=　　Er widerstrebt allen Versuchen. He resists all attempts.

　　　　(Exceptions: enthaupten, to behead + Acc.; entstehen aus, to arise from.)

Separable:

bei=　　Ich pflichte dieser Maßregel bei. I approve of this measure.

　　　　(*But:* Ich füge einen Zettel bei, because fügen is transitive.)

ein=　　Es fiel mir eben ein, daß Sie . . . It just occurred to me that you . . .

　　　　(*But:* Er hat die Bittschrift eingereicht, because reichen is transitive.)

entgegen=　　Sie kam mir entgegen. She came to meet me.

nach=　　Er eifert seinem Vater nach. He is emulating his father.

(*But:* Er stellt die Uhr nach, (He is putting the clock back), because stellen is transitive.

On the other hand, nachstellen, to stalk, takes the dative. Der Wilddieb stellte dem Reh nach. The poacher was stalking the deer.

vor=   Er wollte dem Ausschuß vorstehen. He wanted to control the committee.

(*But:* Wir wollen das Gedicht vortragen, (We intend to recite the poem), because tragen is transitive.)

zu=   Sie ist der Mutter zugeflogen. She has flown to her mother.

(*But:* Machen Sie die Tür zu! (Close the door), because machen is transitive; zuhören, however, takes the Dative: Hören Sie dem Professor zu! Listen to the professor.)

173. With verbs which govern the dative, it is convenient to consider **adjectives which govern the dative.**

Usually the dependent dative precedes the adjectives.

The commonest of these adjectives are:

ähnlich, similar to, like.	Ein Haus ist dem anderen ähnlich. One house is like the other.
angemessen, suitable to.	Eine klare Stimme ist einem Redner angemessen. A clear voice is suitable to an orator.
dankbar, grateful to.	Ich bin Dir dankbar. I am grateful to you.
eigen, peculiar to.	Warmes Klima ist dem Süden eigen. A warm climate is peculiar to the South.
gehorsam, obedient to.	Seid gehorsam eurem Herrn! Be obedient to your master.
gewogen, inclined to, fond of.	Das Glück war ihm hold und gewogen. Fortune was favourable to him.
gleich, equal to, like.	An Würde ist sie ihm sowieso gleich. In the matter of dignity she is his equal in any case.

hold, favourable to.	(See above under gewogen.)
läſtig, troublesome to.	Inſekten ſind den Pferden läſtig. Insects are troublesome to horses.
nahe, near.	Die Schule iſt nahe dem Bahnhof. The school is near the station.
nützlich, useful.	Die engliſche Sprache iſt dem Reiſenden nützlich. English is useful to the traveller.
überlegen, superior to.	Die Mannſchaft war ihrem Gegner überlegen. The team was superior to its opponents.
ſchädlich, injurious to.	Alkohol iſt der Geſundheit ſchädlich. Alcohol is injurious to health.

174.   VERBS WHICH GOVERN THE GENITIVE CASE

(*a*) In poetry and some fixed expressions these verbs govern the genitive.

	Modern Prose Construction
achten, to heed	achten auf + accusative
bedürfen, to need, require	+ genitive
brauchen, to need	+ acc.
begehren, to desire	+ acc.
entbehren, to dispense with	+ acc.
entkleiden (eines Amtes, einer Ehre), to deprive (of an office, an honour)	+ gen.
entraten, to dispense with, to do without	+ acc.
erwähnen, to mention	+ acc. or + gen.
gedenken, to remember, to think of	ſich erinnern an + acc. denken an + acc.
geneſen to give birth to	+ gen. (von + dat. = to recover from).
genießen, to enjoy	+ acc.
harren, to wait for	harren auf + acc.
hoffen, to hope for	hoffen auf + acc.
lachen, to laugh at	lachen über + acc.
pflegen, to take care of, to give oneself up to	+ acc. + gen.
ſchonen, to spare	+ acc.
ſpotten, to mock at	ſpotten über + acc.
vergeſſen, to forget	+ acc.

walten, to discharge the duties of, hold sway over   walten über + acc.

warten, to wait for   warten auf + acc.

zürnen, to be angry about   zürnen über + acc.

(b) Reflexive verbs which take also a genitive object.

sich annehmen (einer Sache), to interest oneself in (a thing).

sich bedenken, to bethink oneself of.

sich bedienen, to make use of (*cf.* French: *se servir de*).

sich befleißen (more usually: sich befleißigen + gen.), to apply oneself to.

sich begeben (des Rechtes, Vorteils), to renounce.

sich bemächtigen, \
sich bemeistern, } to take possession of.

sich bescheiden, to refrain from.

sich besinnen (eines Besseren), to think of something (better).

sich enthalten, to withhold oneself from.

sich entledigen (einer Pflicht, eines Auftrages), to free oneself of, to accomplish (a task).

sich entleeren, to empty itself of.

sich entsinnen, to recollect.

sich (er)freuen, to rejoice in. (See also 225.)

sich erinnern, to remember (usually sich erinnern an + acc.).

sich erwehren, to refrain from.

sich lohnen, to be worth—in the expression: Es lohnt sich der Mühe nicht. It is not worth the trouble.

sich rühmen, to boast of.

sich schämen, to be ashamed of.

sich versehen (in literary language), to expect something of.

sich versichern, to make sure of.

175. With verbs which govern the genitive it is convenient to consider **adjectives which govern the genitive.**

Usually the dependent genitive precedes the adjective. The commonest of these adjectives are:

bedürftig, in need of.

bewußt, conscious of.

eingedenk, mindful of.

fähig, capable of.

gewahr,[1] aware of.

gewärtig, expectant of.

gewohnt,[1] accustomed to (usually gewohnt an + acc.).

gewiß, certain of.
tunbig, acquainted with.
los,[1] rid of.
mächtig, master of.
müde,[1] tired of.
fatt,[1] satiated with, "fed up" with.
fchulbig, guilty of.
ficher, sure of.
teilhaftig, participating in.
überbrüffig, weary of.
verbächtig, suspected of.
verluftig, deprived of.
voll, full of (also + von; 94).
wert,[1] worth.
würbig, worthy of.

[1] (These may also govern the accusative because the old genitive sing. es, *of it*, was later taken to be an accusative.)

MODAL VERBS

176. The **Modal Verbs** are:

bürfen	können	mögen
müffen	follen	wollen

(For meanings see 177.)

(a) The **Present Indicative** is thus conjugated:

ich barf	ich tann	ich mag
bu barfft	bu tannft	bu magft
er barf	er tann	er mag
wir bürfen	wir tönnen	wir mögen
ihr bürft	ihr tönnt	ihr mögt
fie bürfen	fie tönnen	fie mögen
ich muß	ich foll	ich will
bu mußt	bu follft	bu willft
er muß	er foll	er will
wir müffen	wir follen	wir wollen
ihr müßt	ihr follt	ihr wollt
fie müffen	fie follen	fie wollen

NOTE.—In the Present Indicative of the Modals:
  (i) There is no Umlaut in the singular.
  (ii) The plural is regular.
  (iii) The 1st and 3rd person singular forms are always alike.

(*b*) The **Present Subjunctive** is quite regular; it has the infinitive stem throughout and the usual endings, *e.g.*,

> ich könne, du könnest, er könne, wir können, ihr könnet, sie können.

(*c*) The **Past Indicative.** In this tense no Modal verb has an Umlaut. The inflections are those of a weak verb.

> ich durfte, ich konnte, ich mochte, ich mußte, ich sollte, ich wollte.

(*d*) The **Past Subjunctive** restores the Umlaut of the infinitive stem.

> ich dürfte, ich könnte, ich möchte, ich müßte, ich sollte, ich wollte.

(*e*) The **Perfect** and **Pluperfect** tenses.

(i) If there is no other verb dependent on the modal, the regular past participles gedurft, gekonnt, gemocht, gemußt, gesollt, gewollt (note that there is no Umlaut) are used to form these tenses.

Ich habe es gewollt.	I wished it.
Er hat es gekonnt.	He has been able to.

(ii) If there is another verb dependent on the modal, a past participle, identical in form with the infinitive, is used.

Ich habe es oft tun wollen.	I have often wished to do it.
Er hat endlich gehen können.	He has at last been able to go.

(*f*) The other parts of these verbs are regular.
The Imperatives, apart from wolle, are almost unknown.

(*g*) After Modals no zu is required before a dependent infinitive:

> Er wollte gehen.   He wanted to go.

177. Meanings and **uses** of the Modals.

dürfen

(*a*) *may, can* (permission).

Darf ich jetzt spielen?	May I play now? (*i.e.*, Have I permission to play?)

(*b*) *need only to.*

Der Herr Doktor dürfen nur bitten, und ich werde es holen.	You only need to ask, doctor, and I will fetch it.

(*c*) (rarely) *dare.*

Wie dürfen Sie das tun?	How dare you do that?

(*d*) dürfte, the Past Subjunctive, implies a quiet statement of a probability.

Der Direktor dürfte wohl zustimmen.	The headmaster might (and probably will) agree.
Es dürfte von Interesse sein . . . (fixed journalistic expression).	It might be of some interest . . .

können

(*a*) Expresses ability.

Der Blinde kann mittels seiner Finger lesen.	The blind man can read with the help of his fingers.

(*b*) Expresses possibility (especially with the Past Subjunctive).

Das Paket kann doch morgen ankommen. Vielleicht könnte er es Ihnen sagen.	The parcel may arrive to-morrow after all. Perhaps he might tell you.

(*c*) Differentiate between:

Er kann die Zeitung gelesen haben.	He may have read the newspaper.
Er hat die Zeitung lesen können.	He has been able to read the newspaper.
Er könnte die Zeitung gelesen haben.	He might have read the newspaper (*i.e.*, It is quite within the bounds of possibility that he has read it).
Er hätte die Zeitung lesen können.	He could have read the newspaper (*i.e.*, He would have been able to read it).

(*d*) *To know thoroughly (a language).*

Können Sie Deutsch?	Do you know German well?
N.B.—Ich kann nicht umhin, es zu tun.	I can't help doing it.
Dafür kann ich nichts.	I can't help that.

mögen

(a) *To like* (transitive).

Apfelmus mag ich nicht.	I don't like apple sauce.
Wir mögen sie heute nicht lesen.	We don't care to read them to-day.

Especially with Past Subjunctive, sometimes strengthened with gern.

Ich möchte gern wissen, wie er es macht.	I should very much like to know how he does it.

(b) Expresses possibility which has a fair degree of probability.

Sie mögen recht haben.	You may be right (and quite probably so).

(c) Replaces a subjunctive in a 'whoever' clause which has concessive force.

Wer er auch immer sein mag, instead of: Wer er auch sei.	Whoever he may be.

(d) Expresses a third person Imperative idea.

Sie mögen schreiben soviel sie wollen.	Let them write as much as they like.
Er möge (or mag) zusehen, daß es nicht wieder vor= kommt.	Let him see to it that it does not happen again.

müssen

Expresses *compulsion* or *obligation*.

Wir mußten es wiederholen.	We had to repeat it.

Remember to translate

the Present by	'must'
	'has to'
	'have to'
the Past by	'had to'
the Perfect by	'has had to'
	'have had to'
the Pluperfect by	'had had to'

Wir müssen jetzt gehen.	We must (have to) go now.
Wir mußten gehen.	We had to go.

Wir haben immer um 8 Uhr gehen müssen.	We have always had to go at 8 o'clock.
Vor seiner Ankunft hatten wir immer gehen müssen.	Before he came, we had always had to go.

N.B. Ich müßte das eigentlich tun (always with eigentlich). · I really ought to do that.

sollen

(a) Present, *shall* (when it expresses, not futurity or determination, but moral law).

Du sollst deinen Vater und deine Mutter ehren.	Thou shalt honour thy father and mother.

(b) Present, *am to, is to, are to.*
Past,   *was to, were to.*

Er soll die Aufgabe noch einmal schreiben.	He is to write the exercise once more.
Sie sollten in der Pause kommen.	They were to come during 'break.'

(c) Present, *am said to, is said to, are said to.*
Past,   *was said to, were said to.*

Bei den Unruhen sollen insgesamt zwanzig Personen getötet worden sein.	Twenty persons altogether are said to have been killed in the disturbances.
Die Polizei suchte nach dem Dieb, der sich noch in der Gegend umhertreiben sollte.	The police were looking for the thief who was said to be still wandering round in the neighbourhood.

(d) Past Subjunctive, *ought* (to do).
Pluperfect Subjunctive, *ought to have* (done).

Erst am Ende der Mahlzeit sollte man trinken.	One ought not to drink until the end of the meal.
Ich hätte früher schreiben sollen.	I ought to have written earlier.

wollen

(a) *To want, wish.*

Er wollte nicht mitgehen.	He did not want to go with them.
Was Ihr wollt.	What you will (*Twelfth Night*).

(b) *To be on the point of.*

Sie wollten eben gehen, als er kam.	They were just about to go, when he came.

(c) *To intend.*

Wir wollen die Sommer= ferien in der Schweiz zu= bringen.	We intend to spend our sum- mer holiday in Switzerland.

(d) *To claim* (to have done something).

Der Wachtmeister will den Mann im Garten gesehen haben.	The police sergeant claims to have seen the man in the garden.

178. A dependent infinitive after a modal may be omitted, particularly when the dependent verb expresses motion or when it expresses a simple common action.

Haben Sie die Bergner in diesem Stück gesehen? Nein! Na, da müssen Sie unbedingt hin.	Have you seen Bergner in that play? No! Well, you must certainly go.

Notes on the Infinitive

179. A German infinitive is usually introduced by zu, which stands immediately before it. Zu is *not* used before the infinitive in the following circumstances:

(a) In commands which are addressed to the general public.

Nicht hinauslehnen!	Don't lean out!
Einsteigen!	Take your seats!

(b) When it is used as a verbal noun (gerund) (**187** (a)).

Das Weinen der Frauen.	The weeping of the women.

(c) After the modals (**176, 177**).

Er kann heute gehen.	He is able to go to-day.

But: wünschen (to wish) and vermögen (to be able) both take zu.

Er vermag heute zu gehen.	He is able to go to-day.

(d) After lassen (i) when lassen means *to let, allow*.

Er wird sie wohl singen lassen.	I suppose he will allow her to sing.

(ii) When laſſen has a causative force. (See **181** (*a*).)

Er ließ ſich einen Radio= apparat machen.	He had a wireless set made for him.

(*e*) After verbs of perception (seeing, hearing, feeling).

Ich hörte die Vögel ſingen.	I heard the birds singing.
Wir ſahen ihn kommen.	We saw him come (or coming).

(*f*) Usually after helfen (to help), heißen (to bid), lehren (to teach), lernen (to learn), bleiben (to remain), and verbs of motion:

Der Arzt hieß ihn nur Waſſer trinken.	The doctor ordered him to drink water only.
Er lernt ſchwimmen.	He is learning to swim.
Dürfen wir ſchwimmen gehen?	May we go swimming?

Note.—Das heiß ich ſchreiben ! That's what I call writing!

(*g*) After nichts (tun) als:

Sie tut nichts als ſchlafen.	She does nothing but sleep.
Nichts als trinken, eſſen und ſchlafen. Das iſt ſein Leben !	Nothing but drinking, eating, and sleeping. That is his life.

(*h*) In some idioms with haben:

Sie haben gut reden.	It's all very well for them to talk.
Sie hatte einen Mantel von der Schulter hängen.	She had a cloak hanging from her shoulder.

(*i*) As the subject of a verb in proverbs or epigrams:

Früh ins Bett gehen lohnt ſich leicht.	Those who go to bed early obtain an easy reward.

180. The **elliptical infinitive.** The English infinitive after *how*, *where*, or *what* must be rendered in German by a subordinate clause:

Ich weiß nicht, wie ich es aus= drücken ſoll.	I don't know how to express it.
Sagen Sie mir, bitte, was ich tun ſoll !	Please tell me what to do!
Er zeigte ihm, wohin er gehen ſollte.	He showed him where to go.

181. Active Infinitive with passive meaning.

(*a*) After heißen, hören, laſſen, ſehen, the infinitive may have a passive meaning:

Er ließ ihn die Tür öffnen.	He let him open the door (active).
Er ließ die Tür öffnen.	He had the door opened. (He caused the door to be opened) (passive).

(*Cf.* French: *Il a fait ouvrir la porte*).

Er hieß es tun.	He ordered it to be done (passive).
Wir haben ſie (die Nachtigall) ſingen hören.	We have heard it sing (active).
Wir haben ſie (die Lieder) ſingen hören.	We have heard them sung (passive).

NOTE.—Sometimes this causes ambiguity:

Ich höre ihn rufen.	I hear him calling,
	or I hear him called (*i.e.*, someone calling him. This meaning is rare).

To avoid the ambiguity a subordinate clause with wie may be used:

Ich höre, wie man ihn ruft.	I hear someone calling him.

(*b*) After ſein an active infinitive preceded by zu may have passive force:

Das iſt zu vermeiden.	That is to be avoided.
Das Haus iſt zu verkaufen.	The house is to be sold.

182. The Accusative and Infinitive construction.

(The Accusative and Infinitive after verbs of perception, etc., has already been dealt with in **179** (*e*)).

This construction, which is so common in English, cannot always be rendered by an Accusative and Infinitive in German.

Compare:

Ich bat ihn zu kommen.	I asked him to come.
Ich wünſchte, daß er kommen ſollte.	I wanted him to come.
Er riet mir zu gehen.	He advised me to go.

Er verlangte, daß ich gehen sollte.	He required me to go.
Wir bewogen ihn zu kommen.	We induced him to come.
Wir wissen, daß sie Diebe sind.	We know them to be thieves.

183. 'Too' + Adjective + Infinitive.

This may be rendered by a subordinate clause introduced by als daß and having its verb in the subjunctive.

| Sie ist zu klug, als daß sie das nicht einsehen könne. | She is too clever not to be able to see that. |
| Er war zu groß geworden, als daß er seine alten Freunde hätte besuchen können. | He had grown too great to visit his old friends. |

In modern German there is an increasing tendency to use an infinitive construction here as we do in English; particularly when the infinitive idea is simple.

| Er ist zu alt, um das zu tun. | He is too old to do that. |

NOTE.—Beware of 'for there' + infinitive; it is rendered by a subordinate clause in German.

| Es ist dumm, daß zwei solche Läden da sind. | It is stupid for there to be two such shops there. |
| Es nützte nichts, daß man eine Probe abhielt. | It was useless for there to be a rehearsal. |

NOTES ON THE PARTICIPLES
THE PRESENT PARTICIPLE

184. Remember that the German Present Participle is not so common as the Present Participle in English.

(*a*) It may be used as a noun and then takes the usual adjectival inflections.

> der Reisende, the traveller.
> ein Reisender, a traveller.
> die Umstehenden, the bystanders.

(*b*) It may be used as an adjective.

Eine reizende Dame.	A charming lady.
Das Stück war wirklich glänzend.	The play was really splendid.
Der träumende Mund.	"Dreaming Lips."

(*c*) In a few cases, where it has lost much of its participial meaning and taken on adjectival force, it may be used adverbially.

Er spricht fließend Deutsch.	He speaks German fluently.
Es ist aber dringend nötig.	But it is urgently needed.

(*d*) It may be used as an adverb of manner if the action it indicates is really contemporaneous with the verb with which it is connected.

Das Kind ging weinend hin und her.	The child walked up and down crying.

If the action is not contemporaneous, the idea must not be rendered by a present participle, but by a finite verb. (See **187** (*h*) (*h*).)

Er zog seine Feder heraus und unterschrieb den Scheck.	Drawing out his pen he signed the cheque.
Als er durch den Wald ging, bemerkte er eine Fußstapfe.	Going through the forest he noticed a footprint.
Da er seine Mutter nicht sah, ging er nach Hause.	Not seeing his mother he went home.

(*e*) A form preceded by zu, and looking like a Present Participle, is used before nouns in the sense of the Latin gerundive.

Ein zu vermietendes Zimmer.	A room (which is) to be let.
Das wäre ein zu wünschendes Resultat.	That would be a result to be desired.

This form is not a Present Participle, but is developed from the active infinitive with passive meaning (**181** (*b*)).

Dieses Zimmer ist zu vermieten.	This room is to be let.
Dieses Resultat ist zu wünschen.	This result is to be desired.

185. The Participial construction before nouns.

German has no objection to inserting a prepositional phrase before a participle, present or past, which qualifies and precedes a noun.

Das ist die Sprache jener germanischen Könige, für die ein vor den Göttern beschworener Vertrag heilig war.	That is the language of those Teutonic kings to whom a treaty attested in the name of the gods was sacred.

Ein dichter, in der Luft schwe=
   bender Nebel bedeckte den
   Turm.

A thick mist hanging in the air
   covered the tower.

NOTE.—This construction, which has value when used neatly, may
become very clumsy.

Baron von X., der nach einer
   schweren Operation an Herz=
   schwäche verstorbene deutsche
   Ozeanflieger.

Baron von X., the German avia-
   tor who died of heart weakness
   after a serious operation.

186.   THE PAST PARTICIPLE

(*a*) The **Past Participle** may be used to express a short command (often of a military nature).

Stillgestanden !   Attention !
Aufgepaßt !   Look out !

(*b*) When used with a dependent infinitive the Past Participle of

   (i) the modals;
   (ii) lassen, heißen, hören, sehen;
   (iii) (sometimes) lehren, lernen, fühlen, helfen, brauchen,

is replaced by one identical in form with the infinitive, thus:

Ich habe sie gehört.   I have heard her.
But Ich habe sie singen hören.   I have heard her sing.
   Wir hatten ihn allein ge=
   lassen.   We had left him alone.
But Wir hatten uns ein Haus
   bauen lassen.   We had had a house built for
   ourselves.

(*c*) Some Past Participles may be used as nouns. They retain
the usual adjectival inflections.

Niemand konnte dem Ange=
   klagten sein Mitleid ver=
   sagen.   No one could refrain from sym-
   pathizing with the accused.

Er war längere Zeit Ge=
   sandter in Rom.   He was an ambassador in Rome
   for some considerable time.

(*d*) German uses the Past Participle after the verb kommen
(to come), where English has the Present Participle.

Sie kommen stramm anmar=
   schiert.   They come marching smartly
   up.

Das Kind kam ins Haus
   gelaufen.   The child came running into
   the house.

(e) NOTE:

gefeßt baß . . . , supposing that . . .
zugegeben baß . . . , granted that . . .
Trinfgelb eingerechnet, tip included.
abgerechnet, not counting.
abgesehen bavon, baß . . . , apart from the fact that . . .
ausgenommen (baß, wenn), except (that, when).
abgemacht ! agreed !

ENGLISH VERBAL FORM IN -ING

GERUND OR PRESENT PARTICIPLE

187. English makes very frequent use of the verbal form in '-ing'; on the other hand the German Present Participle in ˭enb is restricted in its use (184). Accordingly, particular care should be given to the various ways of rendering this English verbal form in '-ing'; it may be the Gerund (Verbal Noun), or it may be the Present Participle.

(a) The English Gerund used as the **subject or direct object of a verb** is rendered by the German **infinitive** used as a neuter noun.

Sehen ift glauben.	Seeing is believing.
Betteln und Haufieren ift strengftens verboten.	Begging and h a w k i n g a r e strictly forbidden.
Diefes Herumftehen fehe ich nicht gern.	I don't like this standing about.

This German infinitive-noun may be governed by a preposition if the resultant phrase is not too clumsy; for this reason it is rare to find a preposition governing the German infinitive-noun if the noun has a dependent Genitive.

Die Politifer find beherrfcht von einem Nichtverftehen˭wollen oder Nichtverftehen˭fönnen.	The politicians are dominated by inability or unwillingness to understand.
Er fam mit dem Lefen zu Ende.	He finished reading.
Nach dem Infrafttreten des Verfailler Vertrages.	After the coming into force of the Treaty of Versailles.
Beim Wafchen diefer Waren.	In the washing of these goods (*or* On washing these goods).

(*b*) If the English Gerund is **introduced by a personal idea** (*i.e.*, a possessive adjective or a noun in the Genitive), it will be rendered in German by a **subordinate clause**, introduced by baß, wenn, or the like.

Daß Arthur mit ihr zu sprechen wünschte, war ganz begreiflich.	Arthur's wishing to speak to her was quite understandable.
Wenn ich dies trinke, wird es seine Aufgabe erleichtern, nicht wahr?	My drinking this will make his task easier, won't it?
Daß Sie krank waren, hatte damit nichts zu tun.	Your being ill had nothing to do with it.

(*c*) When the English Gerund is **dependent on a noun**, it is usually rendered in German by an **infinitive phrase** with zu (but occasionally by a compound noun).

Er hatte das Vergnügen, sie zu begleiten.	He had the pleasure of accompanying her.
Seine Art, das zu sagen . . .	His way of saying that . . .
Die Kunst zu dichten (*or* die Dichtkunst).	The art of writing poetry.
Wir haben keine Zeit, um hier zu plaudern.	We have no time for talking here.

(*d*) The verbal form in '-ing' as **the object of verbs**.

(i) This will usually be rendered by an **infinitive** with zu.

Er fuhr fort zu reden.	He went on speaking.
Er hat aufgehört, Deutsch zu lernen.	He has stopped learning German.
Vor zehn Jahren fing ich an, in dieser Bank zu arbeiten.	Ten years ago I began working in this bank.

(ii) After verbs of perception and motion, and after lassen (meaning to leave), bleiben, lehren, and lernen, this form will be rendered by an **infinitive** without zu.

Ich ließ die Hand auf ihrer Wange liegen, und in diesem Augenblick fühlte ich eine Träne darauf fallen.	I left my hand resting on her cheek and at that moment I felt a tear fall(-ing) on it.

Dann ſieht man ein rieſiges Stahlgerippe auftauchen.	Then one sees a huge skeleton of steelwork rising up.
Du würdeſt wohl die ganze Nacht tanzen bleiben?	I suppose you would stay dancing the whole night?

Note.—If both the infinitive on which the verbal form in '-ing' depends and the verbal form itself have direct objects, the use of the German infinitive may be too clumsy and can be avoided by using a subordinate clause introduced by wie.

Ich ſah, wie er das Holz hereinbrachte.	I saw him bringing in the wood.
Sie hörten, wie er die Tür leiſe zumachte.	They heard him gently closing the door.

(e) The English Gerund **governed by a preposition.**

It has been shown in (a) above that the German Infinitive-noun form cannot be so freely used after a preposition as can the English Gerund. It is most important to understand the various ways in which German renders the English preposition + Gerund.

(i) Certain German adjectives and verbs require a definite preposition to give them their full meaning (**218** to **234**); for example, beſtehen auf (to insist on) must have the auf to complete the idea.

When the English equivalents of these German adjectives and verbs are followed by Gerunds or Present Participles, they must be rendered in German by an **adverbial form** composed of da(r) and the appropriate preposition + infinitive with zu when the subjects of the two clauses are the same person (thing), or by a daß clause when the subjects differ.

Er iſt ſtolz darauf, Student zu ſein.	He is proud of being a student.
Seine Mutter iſt ſtolz darauf, daß er Student iſt.	His mother is proud of his being a student.
Wir beſtehen darauf, hinzugehen.	We insist on going there.
Wir beſtehen darauf, daß Sie gehen.	We insist on your going.
Eines Abends, als die Kellner gerade damit beſchäftigt waren, ihr Abendeſſen einzunehmen, lief eine Ratte durch den Raum.	One evening when the waiters were busy having their supper, a rat ran across the room.

Das Eisengitter hatte uns davor bewahrt, daß wir durch die Scheiben des Hotels gebrauſt wären.	The iron trellis had prevented us from crashing through the windows of the hotel.

(ii) 'Without' and 'instead of' + Gerund are rendered by ohne . . . zu and anſtatt . . . zu when the subject of the two clauses is the same person (thing), and by ohne daß and anſtatt daß when the subjects differ.

Er ging aus, ohne ein Wort zu ſogen.	He went out without saying a word.
Er folgte mir, ohne daß ich ein einziges Wort geſagt hatte.	He followed me without my having said a single word.
Anſtatt nach Hauſe zu gehen, blieb das Kind im Walde.	Instead of going home the child stayed in the forest.
Anſtatt daß Sie mich be= ſuchen, werde ich zu Ihnen kommen.	Instead of your visiting me I will come to you.

(iii) 'By' + Gerund, indicating manner, or means by which, is rendered by a **subordinate clause** introduced by dadurch . . . daß.

Jakobs Leiſtungen wurden auch dadurch anerkannt, daß man eine amtliche meteorologiſche Station auf ſeinem Grundſtück er= richtete.	Jakob's achievements were also recognized by setting up an official meteorological station on his piece of ground.
Er ſcheuchte die Vögel da= durch, daß er eine Katze im Garten ließ.	He scared the birds by leaving a cat in the garden.

(iv) Note also the rendering of the verbal form in '-ing' in the following :

Er ſagte mir, daß meine Frau Sie beſucht hatte.	He told me about my wife's visiting you.
Er wollte wiſſen, wie man einen Paß bekommt.	He wanted to know about get- ting a passport.
Außer daß ich ihn in der Zeu= genbank ſah, bin ich ihm noch nicht begegnet.	Except for seeing him in the witness-box, I have not yet met him.
Ich bin des Schreibens müde.	I am tired of writing.

(*f*) The English Present Participle which forms **part of an attributive phrase** is usually rendered by a **relative clause.**

Ein Mann, der an der Ecke stand . . .	A man standing at the corner . . .
Das Wirtshaus hat ein Schild, das dieses Sprichwort trägt.	The inn has a sign bearing this proverb.

Note.—In accordance with 185 the participial construction may be used in these cases, but care should be taken to avoid clumsiness.

Ein an der Ecke stehender Mann.	A man standing at the corner.

(*g*) English quite frequently uses a Present Participle to introduce **a phrase which leads up to a main clause.** In German this is usually rendered by a **finite verb.**

The finite verb may make another main clause, linked to the first by und, if the two actions follow one upon the other, as in:

Er öffnete das Fenster und lehnte sich hinaus.	Opening the window he leaned out.
Er rückte seinen Stuhl vor den Ofen und setzte sich.	Drawing his chair up to the stove, he sat down.

(*h*) Finally, an English Participial phrase (with or without preposition) expressing time, cause, and the like should be rendered in German by a subordinate clause introduced by a suitable **conjunction** (als, wenn, da, etc.).

Da er nicht wußte, wo er war, fragte er einen Schutzmann.	Not knowing where he was, he asked a policeman.
Da er nicht glaubte, was ich sagte, wollte er mir nicht helfen.	Not believing what I said, he would not help me.
Während ich durch den Garten ging, hörte ich einen Ruf.	(Whilst) going through the garden, I heard a cry.
Als wir nach Hause bummelten, trafen wir meine Mutter.	Sauntering homewards, we met my mother.
Wenn Sie das tun, werden Sie bestraft werden.	You will be punished for doing that.
Nachdem (ehe *or* bevor) ich das Zimmer verließ, klingelte ich zweimal.	After (before) leaving the room, I rang twice.

The use of the conjunction indem is particularly interesting in this connexion. Indem has no counterpart in English, but conveys the idea of 'in the time that.'

In (*g*) above we have seen that where the two actions follow one after the other, a main clause followed by und renders the participial idea. Where the actions are contemporaneous, a subordinate clause usually renders the participial idea.

In the use of such a subordinate clause it is sometimes difficult to distinguish between als and indem. The difference is one of degree. Indem expresses the parallelism in time (Gleichzeitigkeit) of the two actions more precisely than does als.

Da ! sagte meine Tante, indem sie den Schrank aufmachte.	There! said my aunt, opening the cupboard.
Indem er aus dem Bett stieg, fiel der Alte plötzlich hin.	Getting out of bed, the old man suddenly fell down.

NOTE.—It should be noted that these remarks do not deal with all the possible uses of the English verbal form in '-ing.' It is, however, claimed that most of the difficulties have been treated.

NOTES ON THE PASSIVE VOICE

188. It is not true to say that German avoids the Passive whenever possible; nevertheless, there are **substitutes** for it which can often be used in certain circumstances.

(*a*) The **indefinite pronoun** man with the active may render an English passive if there is no agent idea:

Man sagt.	It is said.
(*Cf.* French: *on dit*.)	
Man kann nur vermuten.	It can only be supposed.

(*b*) Some German verbs are used **reflexively** where English has a passive:

Eine ungemein rohe Tat spielte sich in dieser Wirtschaft ab.	An exceptionally violent deed was done in this inn.
Der Schein wird sich finden.	The banknote will turn up (will be found).
Es fragt sich nur, ob. . . .	It is only to be questioned (It is only questionable) whether. . . . It is only a question whether. . . .

(c) laſſen used reflexively + infinitive may render 'can be
one)':

Das läßt ſich leicht machen.	That can easily be done.
Es läßt ſich daraus erſehen.	It can be seen from that.
Er läßt ſich leicht ermuntern.	He can easily be encouraged.

NOTE.—These alternatives should not be used indiscriminately.

Der Hund wurde von ſeinem Herrn gefunden.	The dog was found by his master.

(Ordinary passive because a definite agent is stated.)

Man fand den Hund in der Schlucht.	The dog was found in the gully.

(No agent is definitely indicated.)

Es wird ſich finden.	It will be found.

(The reflexive construction implies that no definite search will be
made, but that the lost object will turn up in the natural course of
affairs, or in such a way as to suggest its own agency. Thus in the
first sentence in (b) above, eine Tat is considered as being self-acting.)

Es läßt ſich finden.	It can be found.

(This implies the possibility of something being done.)

(d) Remember that after certain verbs English passive infinitives are rendered by a German **active infinitive** (181):

Er hat ſich das Haar ſchneiden laſſen.	He has had his hair cut (*lit.* He has caused his hair to be cut).

(e) (i) Verbs of 'knowing, seeing, hearing, and thinking' used
in the passive, followed by an English present participle or an
infinitive, must be rendered by man + the active.

Man wußte, daß er ein Dieb war.	He was known to be a thief.
Man fand ihn links fahrend.	He was found driving on the left.
Man hörte ſie einbrechen.	They were heard breaking in.
Man dachte, daß ſie hier wären.	They were thought to be here.

(ii) If the above verbs have as subject 'it' pointing forward
to a subordinate clause which is the real sense subject, they
must be rendered by man + the active.

Man ſah, daß er unrecht hatte.	It was seen that he was wrong.
Man meint, daß er ſterben wird.	It is thought that he will die.

(*f*) Remember that verbs which govern the genitive or the dative cannot be turned personally into the passive. An impersonal construction will be required (**135**).

Es wurde mir erlaubt, das zu tun.	I was allowed to do that.

189. German active verbs which are rendered by an English passive.

Sie soll von edler Herkunft sein.	She is said to be of noble birth.
Wir dürfen nicht kommen.	We are not allowed to come.
Wie heißt er?	What is he called? (What is his name?)
Er erschrak vor dieser Erscheinung.	He was frightened of this phenomenon.
Das Schaf ersoff.	The sheep was drowned.
Er ertrank in der See	He was drowned in the sea.
Wie alt mag er wohl sein?	How old is he supposed to be?

SPECIAL CONSTRUCTIONS

190. Construction after verbs of 'believing, confessing, maintaining.' If the subject of such a verb is the same person as the subject of a following dependent clause, the dependent clause may be rendered by the **infinitive** in German.

Wir behaupten, recht zu haben.	We maintain that we are right.
Die Menschen glaubten, durch technische Erfindungen zu einem glücklicheren Leben zu gelangen.	Mankind believed that a happier life could be achieved by technical inventions.

191. Common **Reflexive Verbs** whose English equivalents are not reflexive:

(*a*) With the reflexive pronoun in the dative:

sich einbilden, sich vorstellen, to imagine.
sich anmaßen, to presume.

(*b*) With the reflexive pronoun in the accusative:

sich annehmen einer Sache, to take an interest in a thing.
sich bedienen einer Sache, to use a thing.
sich befinden, to be (health).
sich befleißigen einer Sache, to apply oneself to a thing.
   (Also **sich befleißen,** but the longer form is more usual.)

sich beklagen über eine Sache, to complain of a thing.

sich belaufen auf (ℛℳ 20), to amount to (20 marks).

sich bemächtigen einer Sache, to seize a thing.

sich bemühen um eine Sache, für eine Person, to strive for a thing, for a person.

sich benehmen, to behave (usually well).

sich betragen, to behave (usually badly).

sich besinnen auf eine Sache, to call a thing to mind.

sich bewerben um eine Sache, to apply for a thing.

sich bücken, to stoop.

sich einlassen in eine Sache (sometimes auf eine Sache), to enter into a matter, to engage in a matter.

sich enthalten einer Sache, to abstain or refrain from a thing.

sich entschließen, to resolve.

sich erbarmen einer Person (*or* über eine Person), to have mercy on someone.

sich ereignen, to happen.

sich freuen einer Sache, to enjoy a thing.
   (sich freuen einer Sache is poet.).

sich freuen über eine Sache, to be pleased at a thing.
   (mit einer Sache in S. Germany.)

sich freuen auf eine Sache, to look forward to a thing.

sich ergeben, to surrender, to result *or* follow from.

sich erholen, to recover (from illness).

sich erinnern an eine Sache, to remember a thing.

sich erinnern einer Person, to remember a person.
   (Gen. must be used if object is a personal pronoun.)

sich erkälten, to catch cold.

sich erkundigen nach einer Sache, nach einer Person, to inquire about a thing, a person.

sich fürchten vor einer Sache, vor einer Person, to be afraid of a thing, a person.

sich gewöhnen an eine Sache, an eine Person, to get accustomed to a thing, a person.

sich grämen über eine Sache, um eine Person, to grieve about a thing, for a person.

sich irren, to be mistaken.

sich legen, sich hinlegen, to lie down.

sich nähern einer Sache, einer Person, to approach a thing, a person.

sich nähren von einer Sache, to feed on a thing.

ſich rächen an einer Perſon, to take revenge on a person.

ſich ſchämen über eine Sache, über eine Perſon, to be ashamed
of a thing, a person.

(Sometimes ſich ſchämen einer Perſon.)

ſich ſehnen nach einer Perſon, nach einer Sache, to long for a
person, for a thing.

ſich ſetzen, to sit down.

ſich ſtellen (als ob), to pretend (that).

ſich unterhalten über eine Sache, über eine Perſon, to converse
about a thing, about a person.

ſich unterſtehen, to presume, dare.

ſich verirren, to go astray, lose one's way.

ſich verlaſſen auf eine Perſon, auf eine Sache, to rely on a
person, on a thing.

ſich vorbereiten auf eine Sache, to prepare for a thing.

ſich weigern, to refuse.

ſich widerſetzen einer Sache, einer Perſon, to oppose a thing,
a person.

ſich wundern über eine Sache, to wonder at a thing.

192. These verbs govern the accusative of the person and the
genitive of the thing:

> anklagen, to accuse.
> berauben, to rob.
> beſchuldigen, to accuse.
> entlaſten, to relieve.
> freiſprechen, to acquit.
> verweiſen (des Landes), to banish (from the country).
> würdigen (formal style), to favour with.
> zeihen, to accuse.

Der Richter ſprach ihn des Diebſtahls frei.	The judge acquitted him of the charge of theft.
But: Jemanden von einer Anklage freiſprechen.	To acquit someone of a charge.
Der König verwies den Herzog des Landes.	The king banished the duke.
Sie klagte ihn des Mordes an.	She accused him of the murder.
Er beraubte mich zweier Lämmer (*or* Er raubte mir zwei Lämmer).	He robbed me of two lambs.

193. Common verbs which take two accusatives, one of the person, the other of the thing:

> foften, to cost.
> lehren, to teach.
> nennen, to name.
> fchelten,
> fchimpfen, }to call (someone a fool, etc.).
> taufen, to baptize.
> titulieren, to style, give the title of.

(Sometimes

fragen,	to ask.
Ich wollte Sie eben dies fragen.	I just wanted to ask you this.
But: Jemandem eine Frage ftellen.	To ask someone a question.)
Ich fchelte ihn einen Narren.	I call him a fool.
Sie lehrte mich Deutfch.	She taught me German.
Diefe Reife hat fie viel Geld gefoftet.	This journey has cost her a lot of money.
Man fann ihn faum einen großen Präfidenten nennen.	He can scarcely be called a great president.

SEPARABLE AND INSEPARABLE PREFIXES

194. Prefixes are attached to verbs to give variation in

(i) Meaning:

> *e.g.*, greifen, to grip, seize.
> angreifen, to attack.
> begreifen, to comprehend.

Or (ii) Function:

> antworten, to answer, is intransitive.
> beantworten, to answer, is transitive.

195. Prefixes may be:

1. Inseparable (untrennbar). Arranged in rhyme-form for easy learning these are:

> be=, ge=, ent=, er=,
> emp=, miß=, ver=, zer=.

NOTE.—(*a*) Inseparable prefixes never take voice stress when they are compounded with a verb.

> zer'brechen, to smash in pieces.

(*b*) A verb which has an inseparable prefix requires no extra ge= prefix in the past participle. Thus the past participle of ſtehen is geſtanden; that of entſtehen is entſtanden.

(*c*) As to the meaning of inseparable prefixes, it is difficult to assign a single precise meaning to each prefix, but it may be useful to remember that

be= often makes an intransitive verb transitive.

> ſiegen, to be victorious; beſiegen, to overcome, conquer.

ent= often implies separation.

> binden, to bind; entbinden, to free from.

er= (i) often implies 'obtaining by' (the action of the verb):

> erſtreben, to attain by striving.

Der Bau des Panama=kanals iſt mit ſchweren Opfern an Menſchen=leben erkauft worden.	The building of the Panama Canal **was** achieved at the **cost** of many human lives.

(ii) or has inchoative forces

Heine erblickte das Licht dieſer Welt in der Stadt Düſſeldorf.	Heine *first* beheld **the** light of this world in the town of Düsseldorf.

zer= usually implies 'breaking.'

> legen, to place, zerlegen, to analyse.
> fallen, to fall, zerfallen, to fall to pieces, to decay.

2. **Separable** (trennbar).

Most of the prepositions which govern the accusative and/or the dative may be used as separable prefixes.

Other separable prefixes are: ein, inne, los (in is not used as a separable prefix; ein renders the idea of 'motion into,' *e.g.*, eintreten, to enter).

Note.—(*a*) Separable prefixes always have voice stress.

Wann wird er 'ankommen?   When will he arrive?

(*b*) These prefixes may be separated from the infinitive by zu; but the prefix, the zu, and the verb are all written as one word.

Der Rieſe begann ſofort eine größere Geſtalt anzuneh=men.	The giant at once began to take on a larger shape.

(*But:* Er wollte eine größere Gestalt annehmen, because wollen takes no zu with a dependent infinitive.)

(*c*) They may be separated from the past participle by ge=.

Das hatten wir schon aus= gemacht.	We had already settled that.

(*d*) In a main clause the separable prefix goes to the end of the clause.

Stehen Sie sofort auf !	Stand up at once !
Er schaltete das Licht an.	He switched the light on.

(*e*) In a subordinate clause the separable prefix comes immediately before and is written as part of the verb.

Als er das Licht einschaltete, konnten wir das Kind deut= lich sehen.	When he switched on the light we could see the child clearly.

(*f*) Distinguish between herum and umher.

Herum has the idea of encompassing, encircling, going round.

Er fuhr um die Stadt herum.	He drove round the town, *i.e.*, he kept outside it.

umher has the idea of motion in different directions within a place.

Er fuhr in der Stadt umher.	He drove round (about within) the town.

(*g*) hin and her may be used as separable prefixes:

Er lief hinter ihm her.	He ran behind him.
Setzen Sie sich hin !	Sit down !

They may also be compounded with other prefixes (as in herab, hinauf):

her denotes motion towards a place or person (English 'hither').
hin denotes motion away from a place or person (English 'hence').

Kommen Sie herein ! (very often Herein ! alone).	Come in (*i.e.*, to the place where the speaker is).
Er ging hinein.	He went in (*i.e.*, away from the person or place).
Er ging hinaus.	He went out (*i.e.*, away from the place).
Er kam heraus	He came out (*i.e.*, to someone already outside).

(*h*) There is an increasing tendency in modern German to treat short adjectives, nouns, adverbs, or adverbial phrases as if they were separable prefixes, *either* (i) by compounding them with the verb:

Im Hafen von Constanza ist die Schiffahrt völlig lahmgelegt.	In Constanza harbour the shipping is completely crippled.
Ob diese Verhandlungen zustandekommen, hängt wesentlich von Frankreich ab.	Whether these negotiations come to pass, depends essentially on France.

Or (ii) by putting them to the end of main clauses:

Der Minister legte die Notwendigkeit einer innenpolitischen Entscheidung wie der Reichstagswahl klar.	The minister made clear the need for a decision on the home political front such as that offered by the elections for the Reichstag.
Nur langsam faßte hier die neue Idee Fuß.	Only slowly did the new idea gain a foothold here.
Seit Monaten nimmt er an den Beratungen des Kabinetts teil.	For some months past he has been taking part in Cabinet discussions.

196. 3. Prefixes which are **both separable and inseparable.**

These are: durch, hinter, über, um, unter, voll, wieder, wider. In accordance with the rules given in **195,** 1 and 2, these prefixes will have voice stress when they are separable and will have no voice stress when they are inseparable.

Durch)

Separable	*Inseparable*
'durchblicken, to show (intr.)	durch'blicken, to look through
'durchdringen, to penetrate, get through (intr.)	durch'dringen, to penetrate (trans.)
'durchjagen, to chase through	durch'jagen, to gallop over
'durchreisen, to pass through	durch'reisen, to travel all over
'durchschauen, to look through	durch'schauen, to see through (someone's tricks or thoughts)
'durchschiffen, to sail through	durch'schiffen, to navigate
'durchstreichen, to cross out	durch'streichen, to wander through
	(also: durch'streifen)
'durchziehen, to pull through	durch'ziehen, to travel through

Hinter is rare as a separable prefix. It is sometimes found in popular speech:

Ich wurde hintergeſchickt. I was sent to the back.

better: Ich wurde nach hinten geſchickt.

hinter is usually inseparable:

hinter'laſſen, to leave behind (after death)
hinter'gehen, to deceive.

Über

Separable	Inseparable
'überfahren, to pass over (intr.)	über'fahren, to drive over, to run over (person)
'überführen, to carry over, to transport, to lead across	über'führen, to convict, (eine Leiche), to convey a body
'übergehen, to pass over, to proceed to	über'gehen, to overlook
'überlaufen, to run over, to flow over (intr.)	über'laufen, to run over (trans.) (past part. means 'crowded')
'überlegen, to lay over, to place over	über'legen, to reflect, to consider
'überſetzen, to cross, to ferry over	über'ſetzen, to translate
'überſtehen, to jut out	über'ſtehen, to endure
'übertreten, to step over, to pass	über'treten, to transgress
'überwerfen, to throw over	ſich mit jemandem über'werfen, to fall out with someone

Um

'umgehen, to go round, to deal with	um'gehen, to evade, to turn the flank of an enemy
'umſpannen, to change horses	um'ſpannen, to encompass
'umziehen, to change clothes or residence	um'ziehen, to surround

Unter

Separable	Inseparable
'unterbreiten, to lay under	unter'breiten, to submit something (to inspection) (also: unter'werfen)
'unterſtehen, to stand below	unter'ſtehen, to presume, to dare, to be under command of.
'unterſtellen, to place under	unter'ſtellen, to impute, to submit (oneself) to (authority)

Voll
'vollfüllen, to fill full   voll'strecken or voll'ziehen, to fulfil

Wider. *These compounds are always Inseparable:—*

wider'fahren, to befall
wider'legen, to refute
wider'raten, to dissuade
wider'reden, to contradict
wider'rufen, to retract
wider'setzen, to oppose
wider'sprechen, to contradict
wider'stehen, to resist
wider'streben, to resist
wider'streiten, to conflict with

Other verbs compounded with **wider** may either be separable or inseparable; nor does this affect the meaning.

Wieder
'wiederholen, to fetch back; wieder'holen, to repeat

All other compounds with **wieder** are separable.

Study of the above verbs will show that the **separable verb** usually has a **natural or practical meaning**:

'übersetzen, to ferry over, put across;

whereas the **inseparable verb** usually has a **figurative meaning**:

über'setzen, to translate.

197. Nouns formed from compound verbs usually retain the voice stress of the verb from which they are derived:

über'setzen, to translate; die Über'setzung, the translation.
'ankommen, to arrive; die 'Ankunft, the arrival.

But:

wider'sprechen, to contradict; der 'Widerspruch, the contradiction.
unter'halten, to support; der 'Unterhalt, the support.
unter'richten, to teach; der 'Unterricht, the teaching.

XVIII. USES OF THE SUBJUNCTIVE

198. The clear-cut rules which indicate the use of the subjunctive in Latin and French cannot be paralleled in German. Popular speech tends to use the indicative in some places where the grammarian might demand the subjunctive. The beginning of this replacement of subjunctive by indicative may perhaps be seen in the similarity of certain forms.

ich gehe is both present indicative and present subjunctive.
sie lobten is both past indicative and past subjunctive.

Another tendency is to use a modal auxiliary where once a subjunctive would have been required.

Wer es auch sei.
Wer es auch immer sein mag.}Whoever it may be.

Nevertheless the student cannot afford to indulge in indicatives when his fancy pleases. He should observe the cases when the subjunctive is required and only use the indicative for a definite reason.

199. Reported discourse, questions, writing, thought (*oratio obliqua*) are usually put in the subjunctive.

(*a*) Speech:

Er sagte, er werde morgen kommen.
He said he would come tomorrow.

The verb of saying may be understood from a previous sentence. (This is common in journalistic style.)

Er hat eine Unterredung gewährt, welche die Karten seiner Politik aufgedeckt hat. Das Ziel seiner Träume sei eine wirtschaftliche Union von Prag bis Athen. Eine Revision der ungarischen Grenze komme nicht in Frage. Jeder Versuch in dieser Richtung bedeute Krieg.
He has granted an interview which has revealed the nature of his policy. (He said that) The object of his dreams was an economic union from Prague to Athens, (that) a revision of the Hungarian frontier would not come under consideration, and (that) any attempt in this direction would mean war.

(*b*) Reported Questions:

Er fragte, ob sie wirklich da seien.
He asked whether they were really there.

(*c*) After Verbs of Writing:

Rußland, so schrieb er, grenze wie Frankreich an Deutschland; wie Frankreich müsse es sich getroffen fühlen durch die ungeheure Vergrößerung der preußischen Macht seit 1866.	He wrote that Russia bordered on Germany as did France; and (that), like France, she was bound to feel affected by the immense increase in Prussian power from 1886 onwards.

(*d*) Reported Thought:

Man meinte, eine Bündnisgruppe, die Österreich und England mit Preußen verbinde, könne dem französischen Bündnis Widerstand leisten.	They were of the opinion that a group of alliances which should unite Austria and England with Prussia might offer resistance to the French alliance.

NOTE.—(i) The indicative in indirect statement implies certainty or strong support of an idea:

Er sagt, daß er arm ist.	He says he is poor (and it is true).
Die Krankenpflegerin glaubt, daß er genesen wird.	The nurse believes that he will get better (and the speaker agrees).

(Daß er genesen werde implies that the speaker is not convinced that the nurse's belief is right.)

(ii) German is like English in that it does not necessarily have daß (that) to introduce indirect discourse (**243**). If no daß is used normal word order is observed. But daß is required if the main clause verb is negative.

Ich glaube nicht, daß er recht hat.	I don't believe that he is right.

Daß should also be used if its omission would give cause for confusion:

Dieser Versuch bewies, daß die neue Theorie der Wellenbewegung ganz falsch war.	This experiment proved that the new theory of wave motion was quite false.

To omit daß here would bring die neue Theorie der Wellenbewegung next to bewies, and in quick reading it might be momentarily taken as the object of bewies.

After verbs of feeling daß should not be omitted.

Es tut mir leid, daß Sie dieser Meinung sind.	I am sorry you are of this opinion.

200. The **Tense** of the Subjunctive in indirect discourse; the general rules are:

(*a*) Use the tense which the verb would have had in direct discourse. (This applies to every tense but the Past and the Pluperfect.)

Direct Discourse	*Indirect Discourse*
Jch leſe den Fauſt. Jch las den Fauſt	Er ſagt (or ſagte), er leſe den Fauſt.
Jch habe den Fauſt geleſen. Jch hatte den Fauſt geleſen.	Er ſagt (or ſagte), er habe den Fauſt geleſen.
Jch werde den Fauſt leſen.	Er ſagt (or ſagte), er werde den Fauſt leſen.
Jch würde den Fauſt leſen. etc.	Er ſagt (or ſagte), er würde den Fauſt leſen.

(*b*) Where the following of the above rule in (*a*) would result in a form of the present subjunctive identical with the corresponding person of the present indicative, the past subjunctive may be used:

Er fragte, ob ſie ihn geſehen hätten.	He asked whether they had seen him.

(hätten replaces haben, which is identical with the indicative.)

NOTE.—A further subtle difference is sometimes found between present and imperfect subjunctives:

Man ſagt, daß er arm iſt.	People say that he is poor (and it is known to be true).
Man ſagt, daß er arm ſei.	People say that he is poor (it may be true).
Man ſagt, daß er arm wäre.	People say that he is poor (but we think that he is not).

201. The Subjunctive is used to express the **Imperative** of the 3rd person singular and plural. (And therefore the Imperative of the polite form of address.)

Unter den Mitwirkenden ſeien Hedi Meyer und Trude Tander herausgegriffen.	Among the players let Hedi Meyer and Trude Tander be selected for mention.
Es lebe die Königin !	Long live the queen !
Um Auskunft wende man ſich an die Zentralſtelle.	For information apply to the central office.

202. The **Optative** Subjunctive, so called because it usually expresses a sincere desire:

Wäre ich doch nicht so weit gewandert!	Would that I had not wandered so far!

203. The **Concessive** Subjunctive is very like the Subjunctive of the 3rd person Imperative in function:

Er sei so groß wie ein Baum (or sei er), ich werde ihn doch töten.	He may be as big as a tree, but I'll kill him.
Es koste was es wolle.	Whatever it may cost.
Was er auch sagen möge, er wird es nicht ändern können.	Whatever he may say, he won't be able to alter it.
Wer etwa dies zum erstenmal unter die Augen bekäme.	Whoever might set eyes on this for the first time.

In this function the auxiliary mögen often replaces the subjunctive.

Das mag wohl sein, aber ich bleibe dabei.	That may be so, but I am sticking to my point.

204. The **Imperfect** Subjunctive often replaces the Conditional, and the **Pluperfect** Subjunctive usually replaces the Conditional Perfect.

Ich hätte ihn öfter gesehen, wenn ich Zeit gehabt hätte.	I should have seen him more often if I had had time.

205. The Subjunctive is usually required in a **final clause** (clause of purpose) introduced by damit or auf daß (in order that).

Es läutet, damit man wisse, daß jemand begraben werden soll.	The church bell rings so that people may know that someone is to be buried.

NOTE.—auf daß is usually archaic or poetic.

Luthers Katechismus, 4. Gebot:

Du sollst deinen Vater und deine Mutter ehren, auf daß es dir wohl gehe und du lange lebest auf Erden.	"Honour thy father and mother that thy days may be long in the land which the Lord thy God giveth thee."

Alter Trinkspruch:

Auf daß es uns wohl gehe auf unsre alten Tage!	That it may be well with us in our old age!

206. Conditional Clauses.

(*a*) Probable conditions : in these the indicative is used (they are necessarily mostly in the present).

Morgen gehen wir aufs Land, wenn es schönes Wetter ist.	To-morrow we shall go into the country if it is fine.

(*b*) If the conditional clause really expresses what happened the indicative must be used.

Wenn er gar nicht sprach, war es nicht aus Verzweiflung.	If he did not speak (and we know that he did not) it was not from despair.

(*c*) The present subjunctive in conditional clauses is rare. If a degree of uncertainty or improbability is indicated, use is made of the auxiliary sollen :

Ich werde es Ihnen sagen, wenn er kommt.	I will tell you, if he comes (and he is expected to).
Ich werde es Ihnen sagen, wenn er kommen sollte.	I will tell you, if he should happen to come.

(*d*) If the conditional clause is contrary to what are known to be the facts, or if it merely represents a mental conception, the subjunctive is used.

Wenn ich ein Böglein wär', Flög' ich zu dir.	If I were a little bird I should fly to thee.
Und wenn ihm auch die öffentliche Geltung einer Kunst kein Maßstab für ihre ästhetische Rangordnung schiene, so fände er doch an diesem Tanz etwas Wertvolles.	And even if the public approval of an art should seem to him no standard for its æsthetic valuation (*i.e.*, let us suppose this—a mental conception) he would surely find something of value in this dance.

207. In **Comparative Clauses** (clauses with als wenn or als ob) the subjunctive is required.

Er sieht aus, als ob er tot sei.	He looks as if he is dead.

NOTE.—Any 'if' or 'as if' clause may omit its wenn if it places the verb first in the clause.

| Hätte Napoleon auf die Errichtung der französischen Weltherrschaft verzichtet, wäre er auf die Guillotine geschleift worden. | If Napoleon had renounced the idea of building up a French world-empire he would have been dragged to the guillotine. |
| Sie jubelten, als wäre der Prinz schon da. | They were cheering, as if the prince were already there. |

208. The Subjunctive is required in the **als daß** clause after

(*a*) a comparative:

| Ich wäre eher gestorben, als daß ich das getan hätte. | I would have died rather than have done that. |

(*b*) **zu** + adjective:

| Er ist zu edel, als daß er das getan hätte. | He is too noble to have done that. |

209. The Subjunctive is occasionally required in clauses introduced by **nicht daß**.

| Hat er das Examen bestanden? | Has he passed the examination? |
| Nicht daß ich es wüßte. | Not that I know of. |

210. The Subjunctive is required in clauses introduced by **es sei denn daß, es wäre denn daß,** *unless.*

| Es sei denn, daß es mir bewiesen werde, so kann ich es nicht glauben. | Unless it is proved to me I cannot believe it. |

NOTE.—The past subjunctive of **müssen** sometimes represents this 'unless' idea.

| Ich glaube ihm nicht, so müßte ich es hören (rare). | I can't believe him unless I hear it. |

211. The past subjunctive is sometimes used in questions and exclamations to give a note of query.

| Damit wären wir fertig? | I suppose that's the end of that? |

212. The Subjunctive is found in relative clauses which do not express a known fact, and in which the relative pronoun has the meaning 'such as, or of a type that.'

Er ſucht eine Magd, die Spaniſch könne.	He is looking for a maid who can speak Spanish.
Irgend etwas, was es veränbern könnte, würde man annehmen.	Anything which could alter it would be accepted.

This subjunctive is found in Latin and French. Compare *Elle cherche une bonne qui sache faire la cuisine.*

213. From the uses given above it will be seen that generally the Subjunctive is the mood of uncertainty and wishing, and the Indicative that of fact, certainty, or probability.

XIX. CONJUNCTIONS

214. The following **Co-ordinating Conjunctions** do not affect the position of words in a sentence:

> und, and
> oder, or
> entweder . . . oder, either . . . or
> ſowohl . . . als (wie), both . . . and
> denn, for
> aber ⎫
> allein (poet. or noble style) ⎬ but
> ſondern ⎭

NOTE.—(i) For the use of ſondern two conditions are necessary, the preceding idea must be negative, and the idea coming after 'but' must offer a contrast to that which precedes.

Wir werden das nicht heute, ſondern morgen beſprechen	We will discuss that, not to-day but to-morrow.
Der Junge iſt nicht bös, ſondern ſchalkhaft.	The lad is not bad, but roguish.
Ich will es nicht geſchrieben, ſondern getippt haben.	I want it, not written but typed.

But:

Er wollte nicht warten; aber es gelang uns, ihn zu überreden.	He did not want to wait but we succeeded in persuading him.

(aber, because there is not a contrast.)

(ii) aber may be placed after the subject or after the verb. If it is left in that place in the English translation, it must be rendered by 'however.'

Der Vater aber zürnte nicht.   But the father (*or,* The father,
                                however,) was not angry.

(iii) aber sometimes means *again.*

abermals, once more.
die Abermillionen, the millions and millions.
            (A rather stylized expression.)

215. Subordinating Conjunctions introduce subordinate clauses,
in which the verb comes last (**236** 4).

(*a*) Common Subordinating Conjunctions :

als, when (referring to past obgleich,⎫
   time)   obschon, ⎬ although
bevor,⎫   obwohl, ⎭
ehe, ⎬ before
bis, until   seit,   ⎫ since (time not
da, as, since (stating reason)   (seitdem),⎭ cause)
damit, in order that   so oft, as often as
daß, that   sobald, as soon as
falls, in case   solange, as long as
indem, as, while. (**187** (*h*)) während, whilst
je (+ comparative), the   weil, because
   (more . . .). (**101**)   ⎧ if
nachdem, after   wenn, ⎨ when (present or future
ob, whether   ⎪   time)
                                     ⎩ whenever
                              wie, as (manner not cause)
                              wofern, in as much as

(*b*) To translate the English 'when.'

(i) In questions, direct or indirect, wann.

Wann kommt er?   When is he coming?
Er wußte nicht, wann er   He did not know when he
   kommen würde.   would come.
Er fragte mich, wann ich   He asked me when I wanted
   kommen wollte.   to come.

(ii) With reference to present or future time, wenn.

Wenn er kommt, gib ihm   When he comes, give him this
   diesen Brief !   letter!

wenn also = *whenever.*

Er klopfte immer zweimal,   He always used to knock twice
   wenn er einen Brief für   whenever he had a letter
   uns hatte.   for us.

(iii) With reference to past time, **als**.

Als ich ganz klein war, hatte ich einen Hund.	When I was quite small I had a dog.

NOTE.—**als** also means:

(i) *than* after a comparative.

Er ist kleiner als sein Bruder.	He is smaller than his brother.

(ii) *but* in the expression **nichts als**.

Er trinkt nichts als Wasser.	He drinks nothing but water.

(iii) *as* (= *in the capacity of*).

Als König würde er mir gar nicht gefallen.	I should not like him at all as a king.

(*c*) **da**.

(i) If it puts the verb to the end, **da** is a subordinating conjunction meaning *as* or *since*.

Da er das wußte, schwieg er.	Since he knew that, he kept silent.

(NOTE:

Seitdem er das gewußt hat, hat er nichts gesagt.	Since (the time that) he has known that, he has said nothing.
Seit seiner Ankunft.	Since his arrival.)

(ii) If it has the verb immediately after it, or if it occurs in the middle of a clause, it is an adverb, meaning *then* or *there*.

Da sah ich einen großen Thron.	Then I saw a great throne.
Er wollte nicht da bleiben.	He did not want to stay there.

(*d*) In the conjunctions **obgleich**, **obschon**, **obwohl**, the second constituent may be separated from the **ob**:

Ob er mich gleich kennt, grüßt er mich nie.	Although he knows me he never greets me.

(*e*) **ob** may introduce a question dependent on a verb which is understood from the wording or the sense of the preceding sentence. In translation into English some verb must be added.

Dies gilt nicht den Diplomaten und Regierungsleuten, sondern den Völkern. Ob doch nicht eines	This concerns, not the diplomats and government officials, but the peoples. (I wonder) whether one day

Tages die Völker erwachen
und ihre schwerhörigen
Führer zur Rechenschaft
ziehen werden?

the peoples will, after all,
awake and bring to judg-
ment their former leaders
who were so hard of hearing?

(*f*) Other Subordinating Conjunctions:

als wenn,
als ob,　}　as if
wie wenn,

wenn . . . nicht, unless

bis, until

wenn . . . auch noch so, if ever
so, though

je nachdem, according as

wie (+ adjective) auch, however

gleichwie, just as

ohne daß, without

so (adjective) auch, however

selbst wenn,

so sehr,　}　however much
so sehr auch,

wenn . . . auch,
wenn . . . gleich,　}　even if
wenn . . . schon,

zumal, especially as, considering that

Wie groß er auch sei.

However big he may be.

Die Menschen, die zu ihr
gehören, haben solche Bin-
dungen immer abgelehnt,
so sehr sie um klare religiöse
Erkenntnis gerungen haben.

Those who belong to it have
always refused such con-
nexions, however much they
may have striven for clear
religious conviction.

Immerhin müßte es daheim
zu einem knappen Siege
reichen, zumal der Hanauer
Sturm etwas höher ein-
zuschätzen ist als der des
Partners.

Yet there ought to be a narrow
victory at home, especially
as the Hanau attack may be
considered as somewhat better than that of the oppo-
nents.

(From some comments on Association football.)

(*g*) To translate the English 'lest.'

(i) After fürchten use daß + subordinate clause:

Ich fürchtete, daß er es
brechen könnte.

I feared lest he might break it.

(ii) Otherwise, aus Furcht daß or damit . . . nicht if the subject of the 'lest' clause is a different person from the subject of
the preceding verb on which the 'lest' clause depends, and aus
Furcht + zu + infinitive if the subject of both clauses is the same.

Wir banden ihm den Mund zu aus Furcht, daß er das Kind wecken könnte (damit er das Kind nicht wecken könnte).	We bound his mouth lest he should wake the child.
Er kroch leise umher, aus Furcht sie zu stören.	He crept about gently lest he should disturb her.

(*h*) In English a word may often be used for several different purposes. In translation into German care should be taken to realize what grammatical function such a word has.

Vor meiner Abreise.	Before my departure (preposition).
Bevor *or* Ehe er es las.	Before he read it (conjunction).
Ich habe ihn vorher nie gesehen.	I have never seen him before (adverb).

Similarly: nach, nachdem, nachher.

XX. PREPOSITIONS

PREPOSITIONS GOVERNING THE GENITIVE

216. Anstatt, statt, *instead of.*

Anstatt des Knaben erschien seine Schwester.	Instead of the boy his sister appeared.

Außerhalb, *outside, on the outside of.*

Er wohnt außerhalb der Stadt.	He lives outside the town.

(Do not confuse this with außer + dative, meaning *besides.*) (**218.**)

Innerhalb, *inside, within, on the inside of.*

Innerhalb einer Woche werden Sie es erhalten.	You will get it within a week.
Das Haus liegt innerhalb des Dorfes.	The house lies within the village.

(binnen + dative has the same meanings, but is rarely found with expressions of place.)

Oberhalb, *above, on the upper side of.*
Unterhalb, *below, on the lower side of.*
Diesseit(s), *on this side of.*

Wir haben ihn diesseits des
   Flusses gesehen.

We saw him on this side of the
river.

Jenseit(s), *on that side of, on the far side of.*

Jenseits der Grenze ist es
   verboten.

Beyond the frontier it is for-
bidden.

(*Cf.* Das Jenseits, 'the beyond,' 'the next life.')

Inmitten, *in the midst of, between.*

Inmitten des Waldes wurde
   ein Leichnam gefunden.

Right in the middle of the
wood a body was found.

Kraft, *by virtue of.*

Kraft seines Amtes durfte er
   die Sache so erledigen.

By virtue of his office he was
able to settle the matter thus.

Vermöge, *by virtue of, by means of, in consequence of.*

Vermöge des Verstandes bildet man Begriffe.

By means of the reason one
forms concepts.

   (Vermöge would seem to differ from kraft in that it refers
   to power natural to or inherent in the person or thing
   under consideration; kraft is more general in its use.)

Vermittels(t), mittels(t), *by means of.*

Vermittels des Radios wurde
   die Rede des Königs sogar
   in Indien gehört.

By means of the wireless the
King's speech was heard even
in India.

   (Used mostly in technical language to indicate power
   directly applied for a certain purpose.)

Längs, *along.*

Längs des Ufers angelten elf
   Knaben.

Along the bank eleven boys
were fishing.

Laut, *according to.* (Laut is also found governing the dative.)

Laut des Vertrages darf
   dieses Land ein stehendes
   Heer von hunderttausend
   Mann haben.

According to the treaty this
country may have a standing
army of 100,000 men.

   (Laut is used when referring to the contents of a document.
   Cf. lauten, to run.)

(*N.B.*—(i) Distinguish between this and the adverb lauter, the
adjective laut, and the adjective lauter (**107**, Note.)

(ii) Occasionally laut is found with a nominative, especially in
judicial language. Thus: Laut erster Punkt des Paragraphen.)

Trotz, *in spite of.*

(*Cf.* trotzen, to defy.)

Trotz des Sturmes hielt er den Kopf hoch.	In spite of the storm he kept his head high.

Um . . . willen, *for the sake of, on account of.*

Um Gottes willen, Mensch, laß ihn los !	For God's sake, man, let him go !

(*N.B.*—etwas um Gottes willen tun may also mean to do a thing without any hope of reward.)

Wegen, *on account of, with regard to.*

Wegen des schlechten Wetters muß er zu Hause bleiben.	By reason of the bad weather he has to stay at home.

(*N.B.*—meinetwegen : (i) for my sake ; (ii) for aught I care.

Machen Sie keine Umstände meinetwegen.	Don't make any fuss for me.
Meinetwegen darf er kommen.	He can come as far as I am concerned.)

Ungeachtet, *notwithstanding.*

(trotz is a much stronger word.)

Aller neulichen Anfälle ungeachtet macht er die Reise mit.	Notwithstanding all the recent attacks he too is making the journey.

Unweit, unfern, *not far from.*

Unweit des Dorfes bekam man ein schönes Tal zu sehen.	Not far from the village a beautiful valley was to be seen.

Während, *whilst, during.*

Während des Krieges mußten sie oft an Hunger leiden.	During the war they often had to suffer from hunger.

Infolge, *as a result of*; **zufolge,** *in consequence of.*

Infolge einer schlechten Ernte herrschte Hungersnot im Lande.	As a result of a bad harvest famine prevailed in the land.

NOTE.—ungeachtet usually follows the noun it governs.
　　　wegen may follow its noun.

If 𝔷ufolge follows its noun it governs the dative, *e.g.*, 𝔷ufolge des Beridjtes or dem Beridjte 𝔷ufolge.

Students may find in print or hear in conversation many of the above prepositions governing the accusative or the dative: as instances can be found in the work of authors of repute, it would be futile to say they are ungrammatical. Nevertheless, the foreigner lacking Spradjgefühl is advised to use them with the genitive only. In the following words their use with a case other than the genitive has become fixed:

> demzufolge, accordingly.
> trotzdem, in spite of that.
> demungeadjtet, notwithstanding (adverb).

217. The following prepositions also govern the genitive, but are not so frequently found as those above:

> abfdjläglidj, in part payment of.
> abfeits, away from, to one side of.
> abzüglidj, deducting.
> anbetreffs,⎫
> betreffs,　⎭concerning.
> anfangs, at the beginning of.
> angefidjts, in view of.
> anläßlidj, on the occasion of, brought into being by reason of.
> antwortlidj, in reply to.
> ausgangs, at the end of.
> ausfdjließlidj, exclusive of.
> einfdjließlidj, inclusive of.
> behufs,⎫
> 𝔷weds,　⎭for the purpose of, with a view to.
> bezüglidj, with reference to.
> gelegentlidj, à propos of.
> halb, halber, on account of.

Halb, halber (halben) usually follow the word they govern and are often written with it. Thus: meinethalb, meinethalben, on my account; franfheitshalber, on account of illness.

> hinfidjtlidj, with reference to.
> linfs, to the left of.
> redjts, to the right of.
> nördlidj, to the north of⎫
> öftlidj, to the east of　　⎪
> füdlidj, to the south of　　⎬ also followed by von + Dative.
> weftlidj, to the west of　　⎭

rittlings, astride, astraddle of.

unbeſchadet, with no detriment to.

rückſichtlich, with reference to, in respect of.

von ſeiten,
ſeitens, } on the part of, on behalf of.

zuſchläglich,
zuzüglich, } together with, with the addition of.

zu ſeiten, along the sides of.

zugunſten, in favour of.

(zugunſten takes the dative when it is placed after its noun; if used with pronouns it should be placed after the pronouns, which should, accordingly, be in the dative—mir zugunſten, more usually zu meinen Gunſten.)

This does not exhaust the number of prepositions governing the genitive; the number tends to increase, as many of these prepositions are formed from adverbs or noun phrases which would by their very nature and function require a genitive.

The genitive after jenſeits is easily explained when we think of the longer equivalent phrase, an jener Seite.

218.   PREPOSITIONS GOVERNING THE DATIVE ONLY

Aus, *from, of, out of.*

(a) Indicating movement from within.

Das Kind lief aus dem Haus.   The child ran out of the house.

(b) Indicating place of origin.

Er iſt aus Bayern.   He is from Bavaria.

(c) Indicating motive.

Das hat er aus Liebe getan.   He did it for love.

(d) Material.

Die Eingeborenen machten   The natives made their huts
ihre Hütten aus Zweigen.   out of branches.

Distinguish between aus and von:

(i) Indicating material of which something is made: von is used when the phrase in which it occurs is adjectival.

Damals beſaß ich eine Uhr   I used to have a gold watch
von Gold (eine goldene   then.
Uhr).

aus is used when the phrase is adverbial.

Der Bäcker macht Brot aus   The baker makes bread from
Mehl und Hefe.   flour and yeast.

(ii) Indicating motion from a place: if there is the idea of moving from *within* to some other place, **aus** is used; otherwise **von** is possible, as it indicates merely movement from the neighbourhood of a place.

Er nahm den Ring aus der Kiste.	He took the ring from the box.
Er nahm den Stuhl von der Wand weg.	He took the chair away from the wall.
Wie ein Blitz aus heiterem Himmel.	Like a bolt from the blue.

N.B.—**aus Versehen,** by mistake.

> **aus folgenden Gründen,** for the following reasons.
>
> **aus erster Hand,** at first hand.
>
> **aus dem Ausland,** from abroad.
>
> **aus der Rolle fallen,** not to play the part.
>
> **sich aus der Reichweite einer Sache begeben,** to put oneself beyond reach of something.
>
> **auswendig,** by heart.
>
> **durchaus nicht,** not at all.

Sein Buch besteht nur aus entlehntem Stoff.	His book consists only of borrowed material.
Was wird aus uns werden?	What will become of us?

Außer, *out of, besides, except.*

Außer sich sein.	To be out of one's senses, beside oneself.
Außer dem Gelde gab er dem Bettler auch Obst und Brot.	He gave the beggar fruit and bread besides the money.
Die Mitglieder des Vereins waren alle da außer Ihnen.	The members of the club were all there except you.
Außer Zweifel.	Beyond doubt.

Außer may also be found:

 (i) with the meaning of **außerhalb**

(ii) with the accusative on the analogy of prepositions which take the accusative with verbs of motion.

> (Students are advised not to imitate these uses.)

Bei.

(*a*) *By, near, at.* (Proximity.)

Weende, ein Dorf bei Göttingen.	Weende, a village near Göttingen.
Die Schlacht bei Waterloo.	The battle of Waterloo.

(b) At the house (shop) of. (Cf. French *chez.)*

Er war zu Besuch bei uns.	He was paying a visit at our house.
Das habe ich beim Buch=händler gekauft.	I bought that at the book-seller's.

(c) In the case of, with.

Bei den Franzosen kommt es häufiger vor.	It is of more frequent occurrence with the French.

(d) During.

Bei Tage, bei Nacht.	By day, by night.
Bei diesem Verfahren muß man sehr vorsichtig sein.	Whilst this process is going on one must be very careful.

(e) In the works of.

Diesen Ausdruck findet man nur selten bei Heine.	Only rarely does one find this expression in Heine's works.

N.B.—bei offnem Fenster schlafen, to sleep with the window open.

> bei seiner Rückkehr, on his return.
> beim Abschied, on departure.
> bei gutem Wetter, in good weather.
> bei der Arbeit, at work.
> bei der Hand, at hand.

Ich habe kein Geld bei mir.	I have no money on me.
Sind Sie bei Sinnen?	Are you in your right mind?
Es bleibt beim alten.	Things will remain as they were before.
Ich habe bei Müller gehört.	I have attended Müller's lectures.
Er ist bei weitem der beste Student.	He is by far the best student.
Sie nannten ihn beim Namen	They called him by his name.
Ich schwöre es bei meiner Ehre.	I swear it on my honour.
Bei Gott! Beim Himmel!	By God! By Heaven!
Er verharrt bei (or auf) seiner Meinung.	He persists in his opinion.
Nebenbei.	By the way.

Entgegen, *against, contrary to.*

> Meinen Erwartungen ent=
> gegen ist er doch gekommen.

Contrary to my expectations
he has come after all.

Entgegen will be found before and after its noun. Students
should carefully distinguish between the preposition **entgegen**
and the same word used as a separable prefix.

As a separable prefix it is found with verbs of motion with the
sense of: 'to go to meet' or 'to come to meet.' In a few expressions the preposition **entgegen** must stand before its noun in
order to avoid confusion with the separable prefix.

> Er kam, entgegen meinen
> Wünschen.

He came contrary to my
wishes.

> Er kam meinen Wünschen
> entgegen.

He met my wishes (*i.e.*, he
complied with them).

Gegenüber, *standing opposite to, over against.*

> Die Polizeiwache liegt dem
> Rathaus gegenüber.

The police station is opposite
the town hall.

(*Figuratively.*)

> Diesen Entdeckungen gegen=
> über kann ich es nicht mehr
> behaupten.

In view of these discoveries I
can no longer assert that.

(**gegenüber** usually follows its noun or pronoun, especially
when the word or words it governs have fewer syllables than
gegenüber.)

Gemäß, *in accordance with.*

> Ihrem Auftrage gemäß habe
> ich es beim Fürsten durch=
> gesetzt.

In accordance with your order
I got the prince to agree to it.

(**gemäß** may also precede its noun or pronoun.)

Mit, *with.*

> Er ist mit meinem Bruder
> nach Amerika gefahren.

He has gone with my brother
to America.

> *N.B.*—mit der Post, by post.
> mit umgehender Post, by return post.
> mit der Bahn, by rail.
> mit dem Dampfer, by steamer.
> mit der Zeit, in time, by and by.
> mit Fug und Recht, with full authority.

Haben Sie Mitleid mit mir !	Have pity on me !
Er verlobte sich mit Fräulein Else.	He has become engaged to Miss Elsie.
Er sprach mit mir	He was having a talk with me (*i.e.*, he and I were talking).

(sprechen zu, to speak to someone without there being any idea of reply or conversation; jemanden sprechen, to have an interview with someone.)

Der Hund wedelte mit dem Schwanz.	The dog wagged his tail.
Die Zahl der Toten wird mit 30 angegeben.	The number of dead is given as 30.
Er war mit meiner Schwester verheiratet.	He was married to my sister.
Mit ihm wagten wir keine Possen zu spielen.	We did not dare play pranks on him.
Damals beschäftigte er sich mit diesem Problem.	He was engaged on this problem at that time.

Nach, *after, towards, to.*

(*a*) *After*, with reference to time and space.

Nach der Pause mußten die Kinder in die Schule zurück.	After the interval the children had to go back to school.
Er schleppte den Sack nach sich.	He was dragging the sack behind him.

(*b*) Indicates direction *to*.

Der Lehrer sah nach der nächsten Klasse hinüber.	The master looked across at the next class.
Die Dampfer dieser Linie fahren von Hamburg nach Amerika.	The steamers of this line go from Hamburg to America.

(nach expresses movement towards a town, country, or any fair-sized place; zu is used of movement to a person or to a definite object;

but note—in die Schweiz, to Switzerland.
in die Türkei, to Turkey.)

(*c*) *According to.* (In this meaning it is sometimes found after the noun.)

Der Wettervorausjage nach haben wir morgen gutes Wetter.	According to the weather fore-cast we shall have fine weather to-morrow.
Meiner Meinung nach hat er recht.	In my opinion he is right.

Note.—(i) With the following verbs and nouns nach implies the idea of 'getting to,' 'attaining to':

Nach solchen nichtigen Ehren war er immer begierig.	He was always eager for such worthless honours.

> (begierig nach, eager to have.
> begierig auf, anxious to see, hear.)

Ich war immer gierig nach Büchern.	I was always greedy for books.
Es war klar, daß er nach diesen Ergebnissen nicht ge= forscht hatte.	It was clear that he had not sought these results.
Er fragte nach Herrn Schmidt.	He enquired about (*or* asked for) Mr Schmidt.
Der Künstler haschte nach einem romantischen Effekt.	The artist was straining after a romantic effect.
Das Kind hungerte nach Brot und schrie nach seiner Mut= ter.	The child was hungry for bread and was crying for its mother.
Er lief nach dem Arzt, weil seine Mutter in Ohnmacht lag.	He went to fetch the doctor as his mother had fainted.
Bei solchem Aufruhr mußte ich nach der Polizei schicken.	As there was such a riot I had to send for the police.
Er sehnte sich nach einer glück= licheren Zeit.	He longed for a happier time.
Die Soldaten schießen nach dem Flüchtling.	The soldiers are shooting at the fugitive.

(schießen auf is normal German for 'to shoot at' (**225**), but here nach is more forceful as it implies the idea of pursuit.)

Er schlug nach dem Hund mit seinem Rohr; der Hund aber schnappte nach seinen Waden.	He struck at the dog with his stick, but the dog snapped at his calves.
Er sah sich nach dem Ausgang um.	He was looking round for the exit.

Friedrich trachtete (strebte) nach dem Königstitel.	Frederick aspired to the title of king.
Tell zielte nach dem Apfel.	Tell aimed at the apple.

(ii) In the following phrases the fundamental meaning of nach seems to be *according to*.

Nach dem Alphabet.	In alphabetical order.
Man bezahlte uns nach der Stunde.	They paid us by the hour.
Dem Namen nach.	By name.
In solchen Sachen muß man nach Hunderten rechnen.	In such matters one has to reckon in hundreds.
Er richtete sich nach den Kräften seiner Studenten.	He adapted himself to the powers of his students.
Aller Wahrscheinlichkeit nach.	In all probability.
Er urteilte nach den Umständen.	He judged by the circumstances.
Jetzt müssen Sie nach meiner Pfeife tanzen.	Now you must dance to my tune.

N.B.—

Sie sind nach Berlin abgereist.	They have started for Berlin.
Dieses Gericht schmeckt nach Öl.	This dish tastes of oil.
Das Parfüm duftet nach Rosen.	The perfume smells of roses.
Er riecht nach Zwiebeln.	He smells of onions.

Seit, *since, for.*

seit + present tense describes the duration of a state or action which began in the past and continues into the present.

Thus:

Wir lernen Deutsch seit acht Jahren.	We have been learning German for eight years.

This implies that you began eight years ago and *are still going on* learning German.

seit + imperfect tense describes the same process at a later time when the former present time has become past time.

Damals lernten wir Deutsch seit acht Jahren.	At that time we had been learning German for eight years (*and were still doing so*). (**127** (*c*) Note.)

Von, *from, of, by.*

(*a*) Indicates motion, *from* a place.

Von Berlin nach Dresden reisen.	To travel from Berlin to Dresden.
Von der Universität aus gehen Sie geradeaus.	From the university go straight ahead.

(*b*) With verbs of speaking, *of, about.*

Er sprach von seiner Ankunft in Brasilien.	He spoke of (mentioned) his arrival in Brazil.
(Er sprach über seine Ankunft in Brasilien.	He discoursed upon his arrival in Brazil.)

(*c*) Expresses the agent with the Passive.

Er wurde von dem Lehrer gelobt.	He was praised by the teacher.

(*d*) Expresses the partitive idea.

Gib ihm von unserem Wein.	Give him some of our wine.

(*e*) von should be used in place of the Genitive:

 (i) where the case would not otherwise be shown.

Innerhalb von vierzehn Tagen.	Within a fortnight.

 (ii) to avoid an ugly double s sound.

Die Werke von Gryphius.	Gryphius' works.

 (iii) to indicate agency rather than ownership:

Eine Bildsäule von Epstein.	*i.e.*, Epstein has carved it.
Eine Bildsäule Epsteins.	*i.e.*, Either a statue which Epstein owns or one of which he is the subject.

(iv) when the genitive idea is separated from the word on which it is dependent:

Von allen seinen Freunden gehörte nur einer seiner Heimatstadt an.	Of all his friends only one belonged to his home town.

N.B.—

Dieses Wort ist die einzige Ausnahme von der Regel.	This word is the only exception to the rule.
Wir waren ganz entzückt von der Aufführung des Stückes	We were delighted with the performance of the play.

Das hängt von den Umständen ab.	That depends on the circumstances.
Ich kenne ihn nur vom Sehen.	I only know him by sight.
Er lebt von dem Gelde, das er vom Vater geerbt hat.	He lives on the money he inherited from his father.
Seine Haare waren naß von Gischt und seine Finger erstarrt vom Frost.	His hair was wet with spray and his fingers stiff with the frost.
Die Luft schwärmte von Maikäfern.	The air was swarming with cockchafers.
Ist er von Sinnen?	Is he out of his mind?
Das versteht sich von selbst.	That goes without saying.

Zu, *to, at.*

Wir waren zum Angriff bereit.	We were ready for the attack.
Zum Beispiel.	For example.
Er bildet sich zum Geistlichen aus.	He is training to be a clergyman.
Diese Truppen standen ihm zu Dienste (Gebot, Befehl).	These troops were at his service.
Das Haus diente ihm auch zu Bürozwecken.	The house also served as an office for him.
Wegen seiner Gutmütigkeit war er zu dieser Beschäftigung völlig geeignet.	By reason of his genial nature he was thoroughly suitable for this occupation.
Wir gratulieren der Universität zu ihrer Jahrhundertfeier.	We congratulate the University on its centenary.
Wir werden zu den Waffen greifen müssen.	We shall have to resort to arms.
Er schickte ihm die Karte zum Gruß.	He sent him the card in greeting.
Das kommt mir eben zugute.	That is just to my benefit.
Er wollte sie zur Frau haben.	He wanted her to be his wife. (*Cf.* the Biblical: to take to wife.)
Zu Hause.	At home.
Er schoß Rebhühner zu Hunderten.	He shot partridges by the hundred (*or* in hundreds).
Es ist zum Lachen.	It is enough to make one laugh.
Zu Lande und zu Wasser.	By land and water.

Fünf Marken zu 50 Pf.	Five 50 pf. stamps.
Mir ist nicht wohl zu Mute.	I feel uneasy.
Zu Ostern, Pfingsten, Weih= nachten.	At Easter, Whitsuntide, Christ- mas.
Sie paßte gar nicht zu einer solchen Stelle.	She was by no means suitable for such a post.
Zum Roten Löwen.	(At the sign of) The Red Lion.
Der Schlüssel zu dem Tore ist verloren.	The key for the gate is lost.
Eines Tages wird es mir wohl zustatten kommen.	I suppose it will come in handy some day.
Zu solchen Zwecken taugt das Buch gar nichts.	The book is no good for such a purpose.
Zum Teil.	Partly.
Was trinken Sie zu Ihrem Abendessen?	What do you drink with your dinner (supper)?
Er ist zu einem Weiberfeind geworden. (Also: Er ist ein Weiberfeind geworden.)	He has become a woman-hater.

But when professions, etc., are concerned, neither zu nor the definite article is used:

Er ist Schauspieler geworden.	He has become an actor.

219. The following govern the dative, but are not so frequently found as those above:

binnen, within (usually of time, but can also be used of place).
dank, thanks to.
nächst, ⎫ next to (of these two only nächst can be used
zunächst, ⎭ figuratively).
nebst, ⎫ together with.
benebst, ⎭
ob, above (archaic); on account of (also with genitive).
zufolge, in consequence of (in this sense it is also found with genitive); in accordance with (often follows its noun).
samt, ⎫ together with (a closer and more natural connexion
mitsamt, ⎭ than nebst).

Thus:

Einige Äste samt dem Obst wurden abgeschüttelt.	Some branches, together with the fruit, were shaken off.

But :

Er wird das Schloß nebst vier Häusern im Dorfe kaufen.	He will buy the castle, together with four houses in the village.

220.   Prepositions governing the Accusative only

Bis, *up to,* of time and place.

Er bleibt bei uns bis nächsten März.	He is staying with us until next March.
Ich begleitete ihn bis Hannover.	I accompanied him as far as Hanover.

bis can also be used before other prepositions; in this case the noun is governed by the preposition standing next to it.

Die Freundschaft dauerte bis zu seinem Tode.	The friendship lasted until his death.

N.B.—bis auf (i) *except.*

Ich habe alles bis auf die letzte Seite gelesen.	I have read everything except the last page.

(ii) *right up to* (and inclusive of).

Sie hatten das Gedicht bis auf das letzte Wort gelernt.	They had learnt the poem to the very last word.

Durch, *through.*

(*a*) Of place and time.

Er wanderte armselig durch den Saal.	He wandered wretchedly through the hall.
Durch das ganze Jahr. (Das ganze Jahr hindurch.)	The whole year through.

(*b*) Indicates instrument, cause, means: *by, by means of, owing to, as the result of.*

Durch große Anstrengungen.	By dint of great exertion.
Durch seine Verwandtschaft mit dem Minister hat er sich zu helfen gewußt.	Owing to his relationship with the minister he has managed to get on.
Durch einen Autounfall hat er drei Finger verloren.	He has lost three fingers as a result of a car accident.

N.B.—

Dividieren Sie 25 durch 5 !	Divide 25 by 5.
Durchaus nicht.	Not at all.
Durcheinander.	In confusion.
Durch und durch.	Thoroughly, utterly.

Für, *for.*

Ist dieser Brief für meinen Vater?	Is this letter for my father?

N.B.—

An und für sich ist das Buch gar nicht schlecht.	In itself the book is not at all bad.
Für diesen Fehler wird er immer blind sein.	He will always be blind to this fault.
(*Cf.* Er ist blind auf einem Auge.	He is blind in one eye.)
Für den Vater wäre das ganz anstößig.	That would be quite offensive to the father.
Der Ausschuß entschied sich für Herrn Dr. Braun.	The committee decided in favour of Dr Braun.
Sie erkannten das Gesetz für ungerecht.	They recognized the law to be unjust.
Ich möchte für 10 Pf. Schokolade (haben).	I want 10 pf. worth of chocolate.
Diese Behauptung erklärten wir für die Wahrheit.	We declared this assertion to be the truth.
Schritt für Schritt folgten sie ihm hierher.	They advanced, following him step by step.
Klopstock wurde von dem Hainbund für ein Genie gehalten.	Klopstock was considered to be a genius by the Hainbund.
Er interessiert sich sehr für Musik.	He takes a great interest in music.
Für die Schüler ist ein solches Verfahren ganz vorteilhaft; für die Schülerinnen aber wird es nachteilig sein.	Such a process is quite advantageous to schoolboys; but it will be detrimental to schoolgirls.

Wider, *against* (usually in a figurative sense and only where opposition is indicated).

Er hat es wider meinen Willen getan.	He has done it against my will.

o

Gegen (sometimes abbreviated to **gen**), *towards*.

(*a*) Of time.

Gegen Ende des Jahres kehrte er zurück.	He returned towards the end of the year.

(*b*) Of place (in this sense always abbreviated to **gen**).

(i) Poetical.

Wir fuhren gen Schweden.	We advanced against Sweden.

(ii) With points of the compass.

Er flog gen Norden.	He flew northwards.

(*c*) Expressing a friendly or hostile attitude.

Seine Pflichten gegen die Eltern hat er immer getan.	He has always done his duty to his parents.
Wir haben gegen die Russen gekämpft.	We have fought against the Russians.

(*d*) (*In exchange*) *for*.

Er wollte seine Stelle gegen diejenige seines Bruders austauschen.	He wanted to exchange his position for his brother's.

N.B.—

Er ist argwöhnisch gegen seinen Nachbar und miß- trauisch gegen seinen eige- nen Sohn.	He is suspicious of his neigh- bour and mistrustful of his own son.
Friedrich führte Krieg gegen Österreich.	Frederick was waging war on Austria.
Haben Sie ein Mittel gegen Kopfschmerzen?	Have you a cure for headaches?
Wegen dieses einzigen Fehlers war er zornig gegen ihn.	He was angry with him for this single mistake.

Many English adjectives are used with the preposition 'to' where the German equivalents have **gegen**. The commonest are:

> empfindlich gegen, sensitive to.
> falsch (treulos) gegen, disloyal to.
> frech gegen, insolent to.
> (un)freundlich gegen, (un)friendly to.
> (un)gerecht gegen, (un)just to.
> gleichgültig gegen, indifferent to.

grauſam gegen, cruel to.
großmütig gegen, magnanimous to.
gut gegen, good to.
gütig gegen, kind to.
hart gegen, hard to (severe with).
(un)höflich gegen, (im)polite to.
leutſelig gegen, affable to (with).
liebevoll gegen, affectionate to.
mild gegen, gentle to.
mitleidig gegen, compassionate to (with).
nachſichtig gegen, indulgent to (with).
ſtreng gegen, severe to (with).

Ohne, *without, but for.*

Ohne Brille kann er nicht leſen.	He cannot read without spectacles.
Ohne den Matroſen wäre ſie ertrunken.	But for the sailor she would have been drowned.
Ohne mich war er ein Mann des Todes.	But for me he would have been a dead man.

Sonder, *without* (poetical or in archaic style, and even then only in fixed phrases).

Der Ritter war ſonder Furcht und Tadel.	The knight was 'sans peur et sans reproche.'

Um.

(*a*) *around, about:* of place (position and motion).

Die Bauern ließen ſich um das Schloß herum nieder.	The peasants settled down around the castle.
Beim Glockenſchlag flogen die Vögel um den Turm.	As the bells sounded the birds flew around the tower.

(*b*) *at* (time of day).

Dieſer Zug fährt um neun Uhr ab.	This train leaves at nine o'clock.

N.B.—Many idiomatic uses of um:

(i) In expressions having the basic idea of *request for* something.

Er mußte um Brot betteln.	He had to beg for bread.
Wir baten um Erlaubnis, die Handſchrift anzuſehen.	We asked for permission to see the manuscript.

(With **bitten um** compare **fragen nach,** which means to inquire for or about.)

Er bewarb ſich um eine Stelle in einer Bank.	He applied for a position in a bank.

(Also **nachſuchen um,** to apply for.)

Er wollte um die Hand des Mädchens werben.	He intended to sue for the girl's hand.

(Also **anhalten um,** to sue for.)

(ii) In expressions having the basic idea of *exertion to obtain* something.

Die Knaben balgten ſich um den Ball.	The boys grappled for the ball.
Die Höflinge bemühten ſich um den Schutz des Kardinals.	The courtiers strove to obtain the Cardinal's protection.
Der Kampf ums Daſein.	The struggle for existence.
Sie ſtritten ſich um die Frau.	They quarrelled about the woman.
Die Brüder zankten ſich um das Gut.	The brothers quarrelled about the estate.

(iii) In expressions having the basic idea of sorrow for or anxiety about.

Man ſollte ſich nicht um einen ſolchen Menſchen bekümmern.	One ought not to be concerned about such a fellow.

(Similarly: **bekümmert um,** worried about.
                  beſorgt um, anxious about.
                  Sorge um, Beſorgnis um, anxiety about.)

Es tut mir leid um den Kerl.	I am sorry for the fellow.
Das ganze Volk trauerte um den Tod der Königin.	The whole nation mourned the death of the queen.

(iv) Further idioms with um.

Ich beneide Sie um Ihre Beherrſchung der Sprache.	I envy you your mastery of the language.
Der Tod ſeiner Tochter brachte ihn um ſeinen Verſtand.	His daughter's death bereft him of his reason.
Es dreht ſich alles um dieſe einzige Bedingung.	Everything hinges upon this one condition.

Es ist um ihn geschehen.	It is all over with him.
Der Vater ist um einen Kopf größer als sein Sohn.	The father is taller by a head than his son.
Es handelt sich um das Vorwort zu diesem Buch.	It is a question of the preface to this book.
Es ist eine schöne Sache um die Freiheit.	Freedom is a fine thing.

(Compare the French idiom: *C'est une belle chose que la liberté*.)

Um diesen Preis wäre es zu teuer.	At this price it would be too dear.
Sie hatte sich um das Volk verdient gemacht.	She had deserved well of the people.
Der Buchhändler hatte sich um 50 Pf. verrechnet.	The bookseller had miscalculated to the extent of 50 pf.
Sie schießen um die Wette.	They are shooting in competition with one another.
Sie schrieen um die Wette.	Each shouted his loudest.

221. PREPOSITIONS GOVERNING THE ACCUSATIVE OR THE DATIVE

General Remarks as to their use.

(*a*) If they are used to form **adverbial expressions of place**:

(i) They govern the dative to render the idea of *place in which*; this idea expresses either *rest in that place*, as in

Der Großvater sitzt im Garten.	Grandfather is sitting in the garden.

Or *motion in that place*, as in:

Der Hund lief im Garten herum.	The dog was running about in the garden.

(ii) They govern the accusative to render the idea of *motion towards or into a place*.

Ich ging auf ihn zu.	I went up to him.
Die Soldaten kamen in das Dorf.	The soldiers came into the village.

The above remarks do not cover all cases where such prepositions are used to form adverbial expressions of place; with certain verbs there seems to be some inconsistency. Thus one says:

Der Postwagen kam in das Dorf.	The mail-coach came into the village.

But Der Poſtwagen kam in dem   The mail-coach arrived at the
    Dorf an.   village.
  Er kehrte in die Stadt zurück.   He returned to the town.
But Wir kehrten damals in der   At that time we put up at the
    Jugendherberge ein.   Youth Hostel.

A thoroughly logical explanation of this is not forthcoming,
but it might be suggested that, in the second and fourth sentences, the addition of the prefixes has restricted the idea of
motion inherent in the verb.

(*b*) If they are used to form **adverbial expressions** of time:
(i) They govern the accusative in answer to the question
How long?

Ich gehe auf vierzehn Tage   I am going to Germany for a
    nach Deutſchland.   fortnight.

(ii) They govern the dative in answer to the question *When?*

Die Begegnung fand am   The meeting took place on
    Montag ſtatt.   Monday.

(*c*) The greatest difficulty arises when we come to expressions
in which the prepositions are used **with a figurative or abstract
meaning.**

Sometimes the analogy of the physical meaning will help.

Sie wälzten ihren Haß auf   They transferred their hatred
    ihn.   to him.
Von hier aus hat man einen   From this point one has a good
    guten Blick auf den Berg.   view of the mountain.

The accusative **den Berg** is used because the idea is that of
motion of sight from one place to another.

Der Lehrer ſchrieb den Satz   The master wrote the sentence
    an die Tafel.   on the blackboard.

The accusative **die Tafel** is used because the idea represented
by **Satz** is transferred from one medium, the mind, to another,
the blackboard. This analogy with the physical is, however, by
no means infallible.

In his *Grammar of the German Language* (revised edition, 1922),
Curme gives a rule which is decidedly helpful. It is that:

    where manner, cause, or means are expressed,

        an, in, unter, vor take the dative,
        auf and **über** take the **accusative.**

In accordance with this rule are the expressions:

Jn dieſer Weiſe.⎫ Auf dieſe Weiſe.⎭	In this way.
Sie ſang aufs ſchönſte.	She sang most beautifully (Absolute Superlative).
Unter allen Mitgliedern ſang ſie am ſchönſten.	Of all the members she sang most beautifully (Relative Superlative).
Wir freuen uns auf die Gelegenheit.	We are looking forward to the opportunity.
Er freut ſich an der Ausſicht.	He rejoices at the prospect.

It is obvious that this rule, however helpful, does not cover all the uses of these prepositions in abstract or figurative meanings. It does not help one to decide whether to put accusative or dative after **glauben an,** to believe in. One is, unfortunately, driven to the conclusion that the decision can only be made after learning of, or reference to, the following lists:

222. An.

1. With the dative.

(*a*) *On* (situation at).

Frankfurt an der Oder.	Frankfort on the Oder.

(*b*) *On* (contact with a side surface).

Das Bild hing an der Wand.	The picture was hanging on the wall.

(*c*) *On* (with days of the week and in dates).

Am Mittwoch.	On Wednesday.
Am 11. November kam der Waffenſtillſtand.	On the 11th of November came the Armistice.
Am Morgen.	In the morning.

(*d*) *In the matter of.*

Für die deutſche Bühne war zunächſt aber maßgebend, was ſie tatſächlich an feſten Schauſpielbeſuchern erreicht hatte.	What was of primary significance, however, to the German stage was what had been achieved in the matter of regular theatre patrons.

NOTE.— an with the dative in :

abnehmen an

Der Schmerz nimmt an Heftigkeit ab. (also zunehmen an.)	The pain is decreasing in violence. (to increase in.)

anpochen an

Pochen Sie an der nächsten Tür an.	Knock at the next door.

Anstoß nehmen an

Man hat an seinem Benehmen Anstoß genommen.	People have taken offence at his conduct.

Anteil nehmen (haben) an

Ich nehme Anteil an Ihrem Leid.	I sympathize with you in your trouble.
Ihr gütiger Anteil an meinem Ergehen . .	Your kind interest in my welfare . . .

arbeiten an

Er hat lange an dem Gedanken gearbeitet.	He worked at the idea a long time.

sich ärgern an (also über + accusative)

Sie ärgerte sich an seiner Faulheit.	She was annoyed at his laziness.

arm an (also reich an)

Er ist arm am nötigen Gelde, aber reich an guten Eigenschaften.	He lacks the necessary money, but is rich in good qualities.

aufbieten an

Er bietet all seine Kraft an dem neuen Werke auf.	He is putting all his strength into his new work.

sich begeistern an

Er begeistert sich an ihrer Reinheit.	He is inspired by her purity.

sich beteiligen an

Ich beteilige mich an dem Fest.	I am taking part in the festivities.

dicht an

> Das Jägerhaus lag dicht am Walde.

The keeper's lodge was close by the wood.

sich (er)freuen an

> Ich (er)freue mich an seiner Kunst.

I delight in his art.

ergiebig an

> Dieses Bergwerk ist sehr ergiebig an guten Kohlen.

This mine is very rich in good coal.

sich ergötzen an

> Sie hat sich an dem Kleid ergötzt.

She was extremely delighted with the dress.

erkennen an

> Am Ton erkennt man den Meister.

One can recognize the master by the tone.

erkranken an

> Sie ist am gelben Fieber erkrankt.

She has fallen ill with yellow fever.

erlahmen an

> Sie erlahmt an der Eintönigkeit ihrer Tagesarbeit.

She is growing weary of the monotony of her daily work.

fehlen an (also other verbs indicating 'lack,' *e.g.*, gebrechen, mangeln)

> Es fehlt ihm an gesundem Menschenverstand.

He lacks common sense.

> Es gebricht diesem Lande an Geldmitteln.

This country lacks money.

> Aus Mangel an gründlicher Kenntnis.

For lack of reliable information.

> Es mangelt mir an guten Freunden.

I lack good friends.

festhalten an

> Er hält an den alten Gebräuchen fest.

He sticks to old customs.

fressen an (also nagen an)

> Sein Verbrechen frißt an seinem Seelenfrieden.

His crime preys on his peace of mind.

fruchtbar an

    Dieses kleine Land war sehr fruchtbar an guten Staatsmännern.   This little country was prolific in good statesmen.

Gefallen finden an

    Ich finde Gefallen an der neueren Dichtung.   I take pleasure in modern poetry.

Geschmack haben an

    Er hat Geschmack an guter Musik.   He has a taste for good music.

gesund an

    Ich bin gesund an Leib und Lunge.   I am sound in wind and limb.

gewinnen an

    Das Stück gewinnt dadurch an dramatischem Interesse.   By this the play gains in dramatic interest.

gleich an

    An Stärke ist er seinem Vater gleich.   He is equal to his father in strength.

halten an

    An diesem Grundgedanken müssen wir festhalten.   We must hold to this basic thought.

hängen an

    Er hängt an seiner Mutter   He is very much attached to his mother.

handeln an

    Sie handeln immer gut an ihren Arbeitern.   They always do well by their workmen.

hinaufsehen an

    Sie sah an ihm hinauf.   She looked up at him.

(ver)hindern einen an

    Wir müssen Sie nicht an Ihrer Arbeit (ver)hindern.   We must not keep you from your work.

Interesse zeigen (nehmen) an

Er zeigt großes Interesse an der Sache.

He shows great interest in the matter.

(Also: Interesse haben für etwas.)

jung an

Er war damals sehr jung an Jahren.

At that time he was very young in years.

kleben an

Das Plakat klebt an der Anschlagsäule.

The poster is stuck on the hoarding.

krank (erkranken, kränkeln) an

Arm am Beutel, krank am Herzen,
Schleppt' ich meine langen Tage.

Poor of purse and sick at heart, I dragged out the long days.

Er ist an der Cholera erkrankt.

He has fallen ill with cholera.

lahm an

An dem linken Bein ist er ganz lahm.

He is quite lame in the left leg.

leiden an

Er litt an keiner ansteckenden Krankheit.

He was not suffering from any infectious disease.

(leiden unter, to suffer by consequence of

Wir litten unter der großen Hitze.

We suffered from the great heat.)

liegen an

Es liegt an seiner Frau, daß es ihm mißlungen ist.

It is his wife's fault that he has failed.

Lust haben an

Ich habe Lust an der Dichtung.

I like poetry.

sich rächen an (Rache nehmen an)

Wir werden uns an ihnen rächen.

We will take revenge on them.

reich an

> Die Bibliothek war sehr reich an literarischen Schätzen.

The library was very rich in literary treasures.

sich reiben an

> Das Schwein rieb sich an dem Baum.

The pig was rubbing itself against the tree.

schuld an

> Ich bin schuld an seinem Un-glück.

I am to blame for his misfortune.

unschuldig an

> Ich wenigstens bin unschuldig an ihrem Unglück.

At any rate I am not to blame for her misfortune.

schwach an

> Er ist sehr schwach am Leibe.
> (*But:* schwach im Kopfe.)

He is physically very weak.

Spaß haben an

> Ich habe viel Spaß an ihm.

He causes me much amusement.

sterben an

> Er starb an einer schweren Krankheit.

He died of a serious illness.

(*N.B.*—sterben vor, of emotions:

> Ich starb beinahe vor Angst.

I almost died of fright.)

teilnehmen an (also Anteil haben an)

> Ich nahm an dem Fest teil.

I took part in the festivities.

> (Teilnahme an ihrem Leid.

Sympathy with her sorrow.)

tragen an

> Wir tragen alle an demselben Schicksal.

We all share the same fate.

Überfluß haben an

> Wir haben Überfluß an gutem Wein.

We have a superabundance of good wine.

übertreffen an

Er übertrifft mich an musika= | He surpasses me in musical
lischer Begabung. | talent.

sich vergehen an

Er hat sich tätlich an ihm ver= | He has assaulted him.
gangen.

ein Vergehen an

Es war ein Vergehen an | It was a neglect of sacred
heiligen Pflichten. | duties.

Vergnügen an

Er findet Vergnügen am | He finds much pleasure in
Schwimmen | swimming.

verlieren an

An Glanz hat der Stoff viel | The material has lost much of
verloren. | its sheen.
An ihm habe ich einen guten | I have lost a good friend in him.
Freund verloren.

(*But:* verlieren etwas an jemanden

Er hatte fünfzig Pfund an | He had lost £50 to his neigh-
seinen Nachbar verloren. | bour.)

vermehren an

Sie vermehren sich stark an | They are greatly increasing in
Zahl. | number.

sich versuchen an

Er versuchte sich an der Dich= | He tried his hand at poetry.
tung.

sich versündigen an

Er hat sich an Gott und an | He has sinned against God and
dem Gesetz versündigt. | against the law.

verzweifeln an

Sie verzweifelt an ihrem | She despairs of her fate.
Schicksal.

Vorrat an

Sie hat immer einen guten | She always has a good stock of
Vorrat an Lebensmitteln. | provisions.

zugrunde gehen an

Ich gehe an diesem zerrütteten Leben zugrunde.	I am being ruined by this dissolute life.

zweifeln an

Ich zweifle an seiner Treue.	I have doubts about his fidelity.

Note also:

Lehrer an einer Schule.	Teacher at a school.
Professor an einer Universität.	Professor at a university.
Prediger an einer Kirche.	Preacher at a church.

223. An.

2. With the accusative.

(a) *On to* (approach to or contact with the side surface of something).

Wir hängen die Karte an die Wand.	We hang the map on the wall.
Das Wasser kam bis an die Mauer	The water came right up to the edge of the wall.

(b) *About* (with numbers).

An die 400 Personen verhaftet.	About 400 people arrested.

NOTE.—an with the accusative in:

sich (an)klammern an

Sie klammert sich an mich an.	She clings to me.

anknüpfen an

Er knüpft an frühere Begebenheiten ihres Lebens an.	He refers back to earlier events in her life.

sich anschließen an

Er schloß sich an seine Freunde an.	He joined his friends.

sich begeben an

Er begab sich an die Arbeit.	He set to work.

binden an

Sie ist zu sehr an den Haushalt gebunden.	She is too much tied to housework.

denken an

Wir hatten eben an Sie gedacht.	We had just been thinking of you.

erinnern an

Sie erinnert sich an ihre Mutter.	She remembers her mother.
Ich erinnere sie an die Tatsache.	I remind her of the fact.

(er)mahnen an

Ich (er)mahne Sie an Ihre Pflicht.	I remind you of your duty.

fallen an

Dieses Land ist an den Staat gefallen	This land has become public property.

fesseln an

Du kannst mich nicht an deine Idee fesseln.	You cannot win me over to your idea.

gelangen an

Er gelangte an die Grenze von Deutschland.	He reached the frontier of Germany.

sich gewöhnen an

Sie gewöhnt sich an das neue System.	She is growing accustomed to the new system.

gehören an

Efeu gehört an alte Mauern.	Ivy is in its right place on old walls.

glauben an

Napoleon glaubte an seinen Stern.	Napoleon believed in his star.

greifen an

Das greift mir an die Ehre.	That touches my honour.

grenzen an

Das grenzt an die Unmöglichkeit.	That borders on the impossible.

sich halten an

Ich halte mich an die alten Regeln.	I keep to the old rules.

sich knüpfen an

Keine Erinnerungen an die Vergangenheit knüpfen sich an seine Person.	No memories of the past are bound up with him.

klopfen an

Wer klopft an die Tür?	Who is knocking at the door?

richten an

Richten Sie diese Frage an mich!	Address this question to me.

rühren an

Das rührt an meine Ehre.	That reflects on my honour.

schreiben an

Vor kurzem habe ich einen Brief an Sie geschrieben.	A short time ago I wrote a letter to you.

an den Tag legen

In den letzten Spielen hat er eine aufsteigende Form an den Tag gelegt.	In recent games he has shown improvement in form.

treten an

Der Angestellte tritt an die Stelle seines Chefs.	The clerk took over his chief's position.

sich verkaufen an (more commonly **sich verkaufen** + dative.)

Er hat sich an den Teufel verkauft	He has sold himself to the devil.

vermählen an (more commonly **vermählen** + dative)

Herr Schmidt hat keine Eile, seine Tochter an einen Nichtswürdigen zu vermählen.	Mr S. is in no hurry to marry his daughter to a worthless fellow.

verraten an

Ich verriet ihn an den Feind.	I betrayed him to the enemy.

verſchwenden an

| Sie verſchwendet viel Geld an ſchöne Kleider. | She spends a great deal of money on fine clothes. |

verſetzen an (also **verſetzen nach** + dative, and **verſetzen in** + accusative)

| Der Profeſſor wurde an einen anderen Ort verſetzt. | The professor was transferred to another place. |

N.B.—Use **verlegen an** to translate 'transfer to' if referring to *things*.

verteilen an (also **verteilen unter** + accusative)

| Sie verteilten den Schatz an die Armen. | They distributed the treasure to the poor. |

ſich wegwerfen an

| An ſo einen Mann hätte ſie ſich nicht wegwerfen ſollen. | She ought not to have thrown herself away on such a man. |

weiſen an

| Ich wies ihn an einen Advokaten. | I directed him to a barrister. |

ſich wenden an

| Man wende ſich an den Hausmeiſter ! | Apply to the caretaker. |

224. **Auf.**

1. With the dative.

(*a*) *On, upon.*

(*b*) *In* (often used where the idea is that of being on top of something or in something situated on a high level):

> auf der Straße, in the street.
> auf dem Lande, in the country.
> auf dem Schloß, in the castle.
> auf meinem Zimmer, in my room.
> auf der Kanzel, in the pulpit.

(*c*) *At*, in a few expressions:

> auf dem Markt, at the market.
> auf dem Bahnhof, at the railway station.
> auf dem Ball, at the dance.
> auf der Jagd, at the hunt.
> auf der Konferenz, at the conference.

Note.—auf with the dative in:

anlangen auf

Er ist auf dem Gipfel angelangt.	He has reached the summit.

ansetzen auf

Er hat es auf der Rechnung angesetzt.	He has put it down on the bill.

beharren auf

Ich beharre auf meinem Entschluß.	I adhere to my decision.

beruhen auf

Das beruht auf einer bewiesenen Tatsache	That is based upon a proved fact.

bestehen auf

Ich muß auf meinem Recht bestehen.	I must insist on my rights.
Er besteht auf seinem Kopf.	He stubbornly adheres to his opinion.

blind auf

Auf dem linken Auge ist er ganz blind.	He is quite blind in the left eye.

> *N.B.*—blind für, blind to someone or something you are unable to see.
>
> blind gegen, blind to someone or something you are unwilling to see.

ertappen auf frischer Tat

Ich habe den Knaben auf frischer Tat ertappt.	I caught the boy in the very act.

folgen auf den Fersen

Der Schutzmann ist ihm auf den Fersen gefolgt.	The policeman followed close on his heels.

gründen auf (also with accusative)

Ich möchte mein ganzes Dasein auf diesem Gedanken gründen.	I should like to form my whole life on this thought.

auf der Hut fein

> Sie follten vorfichtig und auf   You ought to be careful and on
> der Hut fein.   your guard.

fich niederlaffen auf (*also with accusative*)

> Er ließ fich auf einem Stuhl   He sat down on a chair.
> nieder.

(*But* fich fetzen auf einen Stuhl !)

taub auf

> Der Greis war auf beiden   The old man was deaf in both
> Ohren taub.   ears.

auf der Univerfität

> Die Studenten ftudieren auf   The students study at the uni-
> der Univerfität.   versity.

N.B.—In der Univerfität, in the university buildings.

(There is the same distinction between auf der Schule and in der
Schule :

> Als ich auf der Schule war,   When I was at school I did not
> hatte ich kein Griechifch.   take Greek.
> Wo ift Hans? In der Schule.   Where is Hans? At school.)

> Die Profefforen lehren an der   The professors teach at the uni-
> Univerfität.   versity.

225. Auf.

2. With the accusative.

(*a*) *On to* (or towards the upper surface of) :

> Wir legten das Buch auf das   We placed the book on the
> Pult.   desk.

(*b*) *For*, with reference to time in the future :

> Almanach auf das Jahr 1934.   Almanack for the year 1934.
> Er wird auf vorübergehende   He will stay with us for a short
> Zeit bei uns bleiben.   time.
> Er hat mich auf (*or* für)   He has invited me for to-
> morgen abend eingeladen.   morrow evening.
> Er hat die Zeitung auf ein   He has ordered the newspaper
> Jahr beftellt.   for a year.

Note.—auf with the accusative in :

abonnieren auf

Wir müssen auf die D.A.Z. abonnieren.	We must take (subscribe to) the D.A.Z. (*Deutsche Allgemeine Zeitung*).

(abonnieren + Acc., without auf, is also found.)

absehen auf

Er hat es auf mich abgesehen.	He meant it for me.

achten auf (achtgeben auf, achtlos, achtsam, auf)

Ich habe nicht auf ihn geachtet.	I paid no attention to him.

ankommen auf

Es kommt bloß auf den Zufall an.	It is merely a matter of chance.
Es kommt darauf an.	It depends.
Es kommt mir nicht auf ein paar Taler an.	I am not particular to a dollar or so.
Da können Sie sehen, daß es mir auf die Sache und nicht auf die Person ankommt.	There you see that I am concerned with the principle of the thing and not with the individual.

anspielen auf

Der Schriftsteller spielte auf das moderne Drama an.	The author was alluding to modern drama.

Anspruch auf

Er erhob Anspruch auf sein Recht.	He laid claim to his right.

antworten auf

Ich bin bereit, auf alle Fragen zu antworten.	I am ready to answer all the questions.

(eine Antwort auf, an answer to.)

anwendbar auf

Das Prinzip ist auch auf die bildende Kunst anwendbar.	The principle is also applicable to plastic art.

Appetit auf

Ich habe heute keinen Appetit auf Fleisch.

I have no appetite for meat to-day.

aufmerksam auf

Ich möchte Sie auf diese Seite seines Lebens aufmerksam machen.

I should like to draw your attention to this side of his life.

aufpassen auf

Passen Sie mal auf seine Worte auf.

Just take notice of his words.

ausdehnen auf

So eine Idee kann man nicht auf den Film ausdehnen.

One cannot extend such an idea to make it apply to the film.

Aussicht auf

Dieses Fenster gewährt Aussicht auf den Garten.

This window gives one a view of the garden.

Auf feste Anstellung hatte ich keine Aussicht.

I had no prospect of permanent appointment.

bauen auf

Ich baue auf Ihre Hilfe.

I am relying on your help.

bedacht auf

Er war ganz auf ihren Erfolg bedacht.

He was quite intent on her success.

sich belaufen auf (also betragen auf)

Die Kosten belaufen sich auf eine große Summe.

The costs amount to a great deal.

berechnet auf

Die Anspielung war auf die Gräfin berechnet.

The allusion was intended for the countess.

sich berufen auf

Ich berufe mich auf sein Gerechtigkeitsgefühl.

I appeal to his sense of justice.

beſchränken auf

Sein Wiſſen iſt auf das Prak=
tiſche beſchränkt.

His knowledge is limited, to
practical things.

ſich beſinnen auf

Ich muß mich auf das Wort
beſinnen.

I must try to think of the word.

ſich beziehen auf

Dieſe Bemerkung bezieht ſich
auf mich.

This remark refers to me.

(Also in Beziehung auf, mit
bezug auf.

With reference to, with regard
to.)

blicken auf

Sie blickte ſchnell auf den
Platz und kehrte ſich um.

She cast a quick glance at the
square and turned round.

böſe auf

Ich bin böſe auf Sie.

I am angry with you.

(*N.B.*—böſe über etwas, angry about something.)

bringen auf

Ich brachte ſie auf dieſe Idee.

I suggested this idea to her.

(ſich) einbilden auf

Sie bildet ſich viel auf die
Ihrigen ein.

She thinks a lot of her own
people.

Er iſt auf ſeine Schlagfertig=
keit eingebildet.

He is conceited about his quick-
ness at repartee.

eiferſüchtig auf

Kain war eiferſüchtig auf
ſeinen Bruder Abel.

Cain was jealous of his brother
Abel.

Einfluß auf

Sein Einfluß auf dieſen
Mann wird oft überſchätzt.

His influence on this man is
often exaggerated.

eingehen auf

Er ging auf meinen Plan ein.

He agreed to my plan.

Er ging eifrig auf die Sache
ein.

He took up the matter **warmly**.

ſich einlaſſen auf (also in + accusative).

| Der Feldherr ließ ſich auf eine Schlacht ein. | The general engaged in battle. |

einſtellen auf

| Der Aſtronom ſtellt das Fernglas auf den Mond ein. | The astronomer is focussing the telescope on the moon. |

eitel auf

| Sie iſt ſehr eitel auf ihr braunes Haar, obſchon es nicht waſchecht iſt. | She is very vain about her brown hair although the colour is not genuine. |

endigen auf

| Das Wort endigt auf einen Konſonanten. | The word ends in a consonant. |

erkennen auf

| Der Richter erkannte auf Todesſtrafe. | The judge pronounced the death sentence. |

erpicht auf

| In keiner Weiſe iſt er auf allgemeine Anerkennung erpicht. | He is in no way intent on general recognition. |

ſich erſtrecken auf

| Dieſe Idee erſtreckt ſich auf ein großes Gebiet. | This idea applies to a wide sphere. |

erwidern auf

| Er erwiderte nicht auf meine Frage | He made no reply to my question. |

auf eigne Fauſt (auf eigne Hand)

| Ich unternahm es auf eigne Fauſt. | I undertook it on my own initiative (off my own bat). |

fahnden auf (also fahnden nach)

| Sie fahnden auf einen Mann, der Engliſch kann. | They are on the look out for a man who can speak English. |

feuern auf (Feuer geben auf)

| Die Truppen gaben Feuer auf den Feind. | The troops fired on the enemy. |

folgen auf (to follow in a time sequence)

Auf den Großen Kurfürsten folgte Friedrich der Erste.	Frederick I succeeded the Elector.

(To follow in a space sequence, folgen with the dative.)

sich freuen auf

Ich freue mich auf sein Kommen.	I am looking forward to his visit.

(sich (er)freuen an, to take delight in; sich (er)freuen über, to be pleased about something.)

ein Gedicht auf

Er schrieb ein Gedicht auf den Tod seines Kindes.	He wrote a poem on the death of his child.

geeicht auf

Die Wage ist auf ein Milligramm geeicht.	The balance is adjusted to a milligram.

gefaßt auf

Ich bin auf das Schlimmste gefaßt	I am prepared for the worst.

gehen auf

Es geht mir auf die Nerven.	It gets on my nerves.

aufs Haar

Ich habe es aufs Haar geprüft.	I have examined it to the smallest detail.

halten auf

Er hält sehr viel auf diesen Ring.	He attaches great value to this ring.

herauskommen auf

Das kommt auf dasselbe heraus.	That amounts to the **same** thing.

hinlenken auf

Er lenkte auf dieses Problem hin.	He turned to a discussion of this problem.

hinweisen auf

Er wies auf neue Probleme hin	He indicated new problems.

hoffen auf

Wir hoffen auf gutes Wetter | We are hoping for good weather.

Also: Hoffnung auf . . . | Hope of . . .

hören (also horchen) auf

Hören Sie nicht auf meinen Mann, er folgt wie gewöhnlich einer ganz falschen Methode. | Don't listen to my husband. As usual he is following an entirely wrong method.

sich legen auf

Legen Sie sich auf das Deutschlernen. | Apply yourself to learning German.

sich auf den Weg machen (begeben)

Mache dich schnell auf den Weg, sonst kommst du zu spät. | Off you go or you will be late

merken auf

Merken Sie auf das, was er sagt. | Pay attention to what he says.

neidisch auf

Auf solche Eigenschaften kann man nicht umhin neidisch zu sein. | One can't help being envious of such qualities.

neugierig auf

Seine Wirtin war sehr neugierig auf sein früheres Leben. | His landlady was very curious about his earlier life.

raten auf

Sie riet oft auf seinen ehemaligen Beruf. | She often made guesses as to his former profession.

rechnen auf

Auf meine Diskretion dürfen Sie rechnen. | You can rely on my discretion.

reimen auf

Alle Verse reimen auf =eben. | All the lines rhyme in =eben.

richten auf

  Er hat seine Augen auf ein höheres Ideal gerichtet. — He has fixed his eyes on a higher ideal.

Rücksicht nehmen auf

  Wir müssen auf sein Alter Rücksicht nehmen. — We must take his age into consideration.

  (Also mit Rücksicht auf + accusative — With a view to.)

schätzen auf

  Ich schätze die Strecke auf eine Meile. — I estimate the distance to be a mile.

schielen auf

  In der Zwischenzeit schielte die Alte auf sein Gewehr. — In the meantime the old woman cast furtive glances at his rifle.

schießen auf

  Auf meine Wiener soll man nicht schießen! — Let there be no shooting at my Viennese.

schimpfen (schelten) auf

  Er schimpfte auf den Wirt wegen seines schlechten Weines. — He railed at the landlord for his bad wine.

  (schelten über, to grumble about something.)

schwören auf

  Sie können auf ihn schwören — You can have implicit faith in him.

  Der Soldat schwört auf die Fahne. — The soldier takes an oath on the flag.

  (*But:* schwören bei Gott, bei den Heiligen. — To swear by God, by the saints.)

sinnen auf

  Die Verbrecher sinnen auf Böses. — The criminals are plotting mischief.

sticheln auf

  Die Menge stichelte auf den Heiligen. — The crowd jeered at the saint.

stolz auf

Er ist stolz auf seine Gelehrsamkeit.

He is proud of his learning.

stoßen auf

Bei diesen Leuten stößt er auf viele Vorurteile.

He meets with many prejudices among these people.

studieren auf

Er studierte auf den Doktor hin.

He was studying for the degree of doctor.

sich stützen auf

Ich habe mich auf die schlagendsten Gründe gestützt.

I have had the most cogent reasons to support me.

taufen auf (see also 193)

Er taufte ihn auf den Namen Hans.

He baptized him with the name Hans.

trinken auf

Wir trinken auf Ihre Gesundheit.

We drink to your health.

Auf Ihr Wohl!

Here's to you!

übertragen auf

Die Kosten wurden auf meine Rechnung übertragen.

The expenses were transferred to my account.

verfallen auf

Sie verfiel plötzlich auf die Idee, nach Hamburg zu gehen.

She suddenly hit upon the idea of going to Hamburg.

verklagen auf

Er verklagte die Bank auf Zahlung seines Guthabens.

He sued the bank for payment of his balance.

sich verlassen auf

Ich verlasse mich auf Sie.

I am relying on you.

sich verlegen auf

Der Feind verlegt sich auf die heimlichen Überfälle.

The enemy is devoting his attention to the secret attacks

verseſſen auf

    Er iſt ganz verſeſſen auf das   He is obsessed with the girl.
    Mädel.

verſchieben auf

    Die Trauung wurde auf   The marriage ceremony was
    März verſchoben.   postponed until March.

vertagen auf

    Die Sitzung wurde auf die   The meeting was adjourned
    nächſte Woche vertagt.   until the following week.

ſich verſtehen auf

    Sie verſtehen ſich auf das   You are an expert at cooking.
    Kochen ſehr gut.

vertrauen auf

    Die Amerikaner vertrauen   The Americans have confidence
    auf ihren Präſidenten.   in their president.
    (Also Vertrauen haben in + acc. *or* zu + dat.)

verweiſen auf

    Ich verweiſe den Leſer auf   I refer the reader to this
    dieſes grundlegende Werk.   authoritative work.

verzichten auf

    Sie müſſen auf meinen Bei=   You must do without my sup-
    ſtand verzichten.   port.

ſich vorbereiten auf

    Wir haben uns auf ihre An=   We are prepared for her arrival.
    kunft vorbereitet.

warten auf

    Seit 6 Uhr warten wir auf   We have been waiting for him
    ihn.   since 6 o'clock.

Wert legen auf

    Er legt großen Wert auf alles,   He attaches great importance
    was er tut.   to everything he does.

wirken auf

    Ich gehe, um es auf mich   I am going in order to let it
    wirken zu laſſen.   have its effect on me.

aufs Wort glauben

Natürlich glaube ich aufs Wort.	Of course I believe every word of it.

zählen auf

Jedenfalls können Sie auf ihn zählen.	In any case you can count on him.

jemandem auf den Zahn fühlen

Wir wollen ihm noch einmal auf den Zahn fühlen.	Once more we will put him **to** the test.

zeigen auf

Der Zeuge zeigte auf mich.	The witness pointed to me.

ziehen auf

Sie dürfen auf mein Konto ziehen.	You may draw on my (banking) account.

zielen auf

Zielen Sie auf die Pferde!	Aim at the horses.

zugehen auf

Er ging sofort auf ihn zu.	He immediately went up to him.

zürnen auf (zornig sein auf)

Der Vater zürnte auf seinen Sohn.	The father was angry with his son.

Also: zürnen mit jemandem ⎫
　　　zürnen jemandem ⎭ to be angry with someone.

But: zürnen über etwas, to be angry about something.

zurückführen auf

Alles war auf die Mißhandlungen des Vaters zurückzuführen.	Everything could be traced back to the father's bad treatment.

Note also: auf jeden Fall, in any case.
　　　　　auf alle Fälle, at all events.
　　　　　auf die Dauer, in the long run.
　　　　　auf Wunsch, by request.
　　　　　aufs Geratewohl, at random.
　　　　　auf sein Geheiß, at his bidding.
　　　　　auf Befehl, at your command, at your service.

auf jede Gefahr hin, at any risk.
aufs Land gehen, to go into the country.
auf diese (Art und) Weise, in this way.

226. Hinter.

1. **With the dative.**

Indicates position *behind*.

Hinter dem Hause lag der Wald.	Behind the house lay the forest.
N.B.—Hinter seiner Geschichte ist etwas.	There is something at the bottom of his story.
Hinter dem Ofen sitzen (hocken).	To sit (crouch) by the fire.

2. **With the accusative.**

Indicates movement *towards a position behind* something.

Ich rückte den Stuhl hinter das Pult.	I moved the chair to behind the desk.
N.B.—Die Pferde hinter den Wagen spannen.	To put the cart before the horse.
Hinter die Schule gehen.	To play truant.
Jemanden hinters Licht führen.	To deceive someone.
(*Cf.* hintergehen, to deceive.)	

227. In.

1. **With the dative.**

(*a*) Position *at*, *in*, or *within*.

Der Wein ist in der Flasche.	The wine is in the bottle.

(*b*) Movement *within* a restricted area.

Das Pferd trabt im Stall umher.	The horse is trotting round in the stable.

(*c*) Movement *within* a medium.

Der Fisch schwimmt im Wasser.	The fish is swimming in the water.

(Movement from one area into another, from one medium into another is, of course, rendered by in with the accusative.

Die Ente schwamm im Wasser; plötzlich flog sie in die Luft.	The duck was swimming in the water; suddenly it flew into the air.)

Note.—in with the dative in:

ankommen in

Er ist erst heute morgen in der Stadt angekommen.	He arrived in the town only this morning.

aufgehen in

Er geht ganz in der Sache auf	He is quite absorbed in the matter.
5 geht nicht in 12 auf.	12 cannot be divided by 5 without a remainder.

bestehen in

Sein Hauptvorzug besteht in großer Klarheit des Stils.	His chief merit is his great clarity of style.

einkehren in

Wir kehrten im ersten Wirtshaus ein.	We put up at the first inn.

geschickt in

Im Schachspiel ist er sehr geschickt.	He is very clever at chess.

unwissend in

In solchen Angelegenheiten bin ich sehr unwissend.	I am very ignorant of such matters.

verschwinden in

Das Schiff verschwand im Nebel.	The ship disappeared into the mist.

Also:

Sie liegen einander immer in den Haaren.	They are always at one another's throats.
Da war kein Zweifel, daß er die schlimmsten Sachen im Schilde führte.	There was no doubt that he had the worst intentions.

in Schach (Respekt) halten, to hold at bay.
in Geschäften, on business.
im großen und ganzen, on the whole.
im Gegenteil, on the contrary.
im Durchschnitt, on the average.

228. **In.**

2. **With the accusative.**

Indicates motion *into*, either physical:

Wir gingen in den Wald hinein.	We went into the wood.

or where the idea is abstract. Many of the expressions listed below have in with the accusative because of the inherent idea of motion.

sich auflösen in

Das Schluchzen des Kindes löste sich in leises Weinen auf.	The child's sobs subsided into quiet weeping.

aufnehmen in

Wir nehmen ihn in unsern Kreis auf.	We are admitting him into our circle.

ausarten in

Seine Begeisterung artet in bloße Schwärmerei aus.	His enthusiasm is degenerating into mere fanaticism.

bannen in

Was in Mörike groß ist, bleibt in seine Lyrik gebannt.	The secret of Mörike's greatness lies hidden in his lyric poems.

sich denken in

Denken Sie sich in meine Lage.	Imagine yourself in my place.

eingreifen in (sich Eingriffe erlauben in)

Er erlaubt sich Eingriffe in mein Gebiet.	He is encroaching upon my province.

sich einlassen in

Ich lasse mich in diese Sache nicht ein.	I am not having anything to do with this business.

sich einmischen in

Mischen Sie sich in meine Privatangelegenheiten nicht ein!	Don't interfere with my private affairs.

einreihen in

    Er reiht den Dichter in diese Gruppe ein.   He places the poet in this group.

Einsicht in

    Er hat mir bereits die Einsicht in die Handschrift gewährt.   He has already allowed me to have a look at the manuscript.

einteilen in

    Er teilt alle Dichter in drei große Gruppen ein.   He divides all poets into three large groups.

einweihen in

    Er will mich nicht in das Geheimnis einweihen.   He does not want to let me into the secret.

(ein)willigen in

    Ich willigte in seine Pläne ein.   I agreed to his plans.

Ergebenheit in

    Sie zeigt eine große Ergebenheit in ihr Schicksal.   She shows herself to be quite resigned to her fate.

sich finden in

    Sie werden sich schwer in diese Sache finden.   You will find it difficult to get your bearings in this matter.

sich fügen in

    Er fügte sich in diese Zucht.   He submitted to this discipline.

gehören in

    Sie gehören in diese Gruppe.   They belong to this group.

    (gehören with the dative indicates possession:

    Das Gut gehört meinem Vater.   The estate belongs to my father (*i.e.*, he owns it).

sich ins Fäustchen lachen

    Sie lachte sich ins Fäustchen.   She was laughing up her sleeve.

passen in

    Er paßt schlecht in diesen Kreis.   He is out of place in that circle.

Q

sich retten in

Er rettete sich in die Vergangenheit. | He took refuge in the past.

sich schicken in

Sie schickte sich in diese Umstände. | She adapted herself to these circumstances.

schlagen in

Die Reiterei schlug den Feind in die Flucht. | The cavalry put the enemy to flight.

stechen in

Das sticht ins Komische. | There is a touch of the comic about that.

Der Rock hat einen Stich ins Grüne. | The coat has a tinge of green about it.

übersetzen in

Übersetzen Sie das in gutes Deutsch. | Translate that into good German.

(ver)hüllen in

Der Vertrag blieb in vollkommenes Schweigen gehüllt. | The pact remained shrouded in complete silence.

verlegen in

Das Büro ist in das nächste Haus verlegt. | The office is transferred to the next house.

sich verlieben in (verliebt sein in)

Der Prinz verliebte sich in das Gänsemädchen. | The prince fell in love with the goose-girl.

Sie ist noch in ihn verliebt. | She is still in love with him.

vernarrt sein in

Die Tante war in das Kind vernarrt. | The aunt was 'crazy about' the child (*i.e.*, infatuated with it).

sich versenken in

Er versenkte sich in die Philosophie. | He immersed himself in philosophy.

vertiefen in

　　Er ist in die Arbeit vertieft.　　He is immersed in work.

verwandeln in

　　Der Zauberer verwandelte sich in einen Bettler.　　The magician changed himself into a beggar.

verweisen in

　　Er verwies ihn in die Verbannung.　　He banished him.

verwickeln in

　　Er ist in schwierige Angelegenheiten verwickelt.　　He is involved in a difficult situation.

zerfallen in

　　Sein Leben zerfällt in zwei Teile.　　His life falls into two divisions.

zerlegen in

　　Er zerlegte das Gedicht in verschiedene Teile.　　He divided the poem into different sections.

sich zurückziehen in

　　Er zog sich in seine amtliche Tätigkeit zurück.　　He withdrew to his official duties.

229. Neben.

1. With the dative.

(a) *Near, beside, alongside,* position at rest:

Der Hund lag neben meinem Stuhl.　　The dog was lying beside my chair.

(b) Occasionally means *as well as* (*cf.* the more usual word nebst):

Neben meinem Gehalt habe ich auch andere Einkünfte.　　I have other sources of income as well as my salary.

2. With the accusative.

Motion *near* to a position alongside:

Stellen Sie das Tischlein neben das Sofa.　　Put the little table beside the sofa.

230. Über.

1. With the dative.

Over, above (not touching)
either literally:

Der Vogel schwebt über der Stadt.	The bird is hovering over the town.

or figuratively:

Seine Satiren stehen über denen von Juvenal.	His satires are better than Juvenal's.
Er hat das Eine über dem Anderen vergessen.	In remembering one thing he has forgotten another.

2. With the accusative.

(*a*) *Over,* motion *to* a place above or beyond.

Das Luftschiff flog über den Berg.	The airship flew over the mountain.
Wir sind noch nicht über den Berg (probably gekommen is understood).	We are not out of the wood yet.

(*b*) *After,* in phrases of repetition (the basic idea being that of piling one event on top of another):

Er hatte ein Verbrechen über das andere getan.	He had committed one crime after another.

(*c*) *More than* (*cf.* English 'over'):

Der Anfall dauerte über zehn Minuten.	The attack lasted more than ten minutes.
Es waren über fünfzig Leute da.	There were more than fifty people there.
Er steckt bis über die Ohren in Schulden.	He is up to his neck in debt.

(*d*) Motion *over* a surface followed by contact with it:

Das Wasser rollte über die Ebene.	The water rolled over the plain.

(*e*) *Through, via:*

Der Zug fuhr über Aachen, eine sehr alte Stadt.	The train went via Aix-la-Chapelle, a very old town.

When the idea is abstract, the uses of über with the accusative fall into three main groups:

(i) *In the matter of, on the subject of, about:*

sich beratschlagen über

Wir haben uns über Ihren Plan beratschlagt.	We have deliberated on your plan.

berichten über (Bericht erstatten über)

Er berichtete über seine Reise.	He reported on his journey.

sich entscheiden über

Ich kann mich über diesen Punkt nicht entscheiden.	I cannot make up my mind on this point.

nachdenken über

Er denkt mit Freuden über den Erfolg seiner Oper nach.	He reflects on the success of his opera with a great deal of pleasure.

nachgrübeln über

Der Gefangene grübelte über sein Schicksal nach.	The prisoner pondered on his fate.

nachsinnen über

Er sann lange über das Wort nach.	He meditated on the word for a long time.

reden über (eine Rede halten über)

Er redete über die Musik von Schönberg.	He was speaking about Schönberg's music.

scherzen über

Wir scherzten über sein Aussehen.	We joked about his appearance.

sprechen über

Ich sollte über Bach sprechen. (sprechen über sprechen von	I was to speak about Bach. to hold a discourse about. to speak of, whilst possibly discussing other things.)

streiten über

Sie stritten über den Vorrang.	They disputed about precedence.

tröſten über

> Ich werde mich über den Ver= | I shall know how to solace
> luſt zu tröſten wiſſen. | myself for this loss.

übereinkommen über

> Ich komme mit Ihnen über | I don't agree with you about
> dieſe Schwierigkeit nicht | this difficulty.
> überein.

im Ungewiſſen über

> Über die Einzelheiten bin ich | I am very uncertain as to
> ſehr im Ungewiſſen. | details.

ſich unterhalten über

> Sie haben ſich über ſeine zu= | They have had a talk about his
> künftige Laufbahn unter= | future career.
> halten.

urteilen über

> Ich will über ſeine Verant= | I don't want to judge as to his
> wortlichkeit nicht urteilen. | responsibility.

(ii) *By reason of, because of, about*, usually after an expression indicating emotion:

aufgebracht über

> Sie war über ſeine Frechheit | She was greatly incensed at his
> ſehr aufgebracht. | impudence.

ſich beklagen über

> Sie beklagt ſich über mich. | She is complaining about me.

erröten über

> Sie errötete über das Lob. | She blushed at the praise.

erſtaunt über

> Ich war über ihren Stolz | I was surprised at her pride.
> erſtaunt.

ſich freuen über

> Ich freue mich ſehr über | I am very pleased at your
> Ihren Erfolg. | success.

(Also **frohlocken über**, to exult at.)

ſich grämen über

> Er grämt ſich über meine | He is vexed at my departure.
> Abreiſe.

lachen über

Über die Sprachfehler eines Ausländers sollte man nicht lachen.	One ought not to laugh at a foreigner's linguistic mistakes.

murren über

Sein Vater murrte über seine Faulheit.	His father grumbled about his laziness.

schelten über

Er schilt über ihr Benehmen.	He grumbles at her behaviour.

spotten über

Wir spotteten über ihre veralteten Ansichten.	We mocked at her antiquated opinions.

trauern über

Sie trauert über den Verlust ihres Sohnes.	She is mourning the loss of her son.

(Also trauern um, **220**.)

verdrießlich über

Ich bin verdrießlich über das schlechte Wetter.	I am vexed about the bad weather.

sich wundern über

Ich wundere mich oft über seine schlechte Laune.	I am often astonished at his ill-humour.

(iii) After certain expressions implying domination over, control of:

herrschen über

Der Kaiser herrschte über viele Staaten.	The emperor was lord of many states.

ein Recht ausüben über

Er übte nur selten sein Recht über dieses Volk aus.	Only rarely did he exercise his right over this nation.

siegen über

Endlich siegten die Römer über diesen Stamm.	At last the Romans were victorious over this tribe.

verfügen über

Er verfügt über viel Geld.	He has a lot of money at his disposal.

N.B.—Also:

Ich warf alle Regeln über den Haufen.	I threw all the rules to the winds.
Der Feind fiel über die Stadt her.	The enemy assailed the town.
Diese Arbeit ist mir über den Kopf gewachsen.	This work has become too much for me.

übermorgen, the day after to-morrow.
heute über acht Tage, a week to-day.

231. Unter.

1. With the dative *under, below, beneath.*

Unter meinem Fenster wächst ein Mandelbaum.	An almond tree is growing below my window.

among:

Unter den Gefangenen befand sich ein Spion.	Among the prisoners was a spy.

N.B.—

Unter vier Augen.	Tête-à-tête.
Unter diesen Bedingungen.	On these conditions.
Was verstehen Sie unter diesem Ausdruck?	What do you understand by this expression?

2. With the accusative, indicates movement *to* a place *below* or *among.*

Wir zählen Sie unter unsere Bekannten.	We count you among our friends.
Er verteilte die Summen unter die Armen.	He distributed the sums of money among the poor.

232. Vor.

1. With the dative.

(a) Place *before, in front of:*

Der Hund lag vor der Tür und ich konnte nicht vorbei.	The dog lay before the door and I could not get past.

vor allem, above all
vor Anker liegen, to lie at anchor
vor den Schranken stehen, to stand at the bar of judgment

(*b*) Time, *before, ago*:

Vor meiner Ankunft haben Sie das nicht tun können.	You could not do that before I came.
Vor zwanzig Jahren lag die Stadt in Trümmern.	Twenty years ago the town lay in ruins.

(*c*) In expressions implying *fear of*:

Er fürchtete sich vor dem Tod.	He was afraid of death.
Sie zeigte eine große Furcht (Angst) vor Pferden.	She showed a great fear of horses.
Die meisten Frauen haben Ekel vor Mäusen.	Most women have an aversion from mice.
Nehmen Sie sich in Acht vor ihm!	Beware of him!

(*d*) Protection *against*:

Er schützte sich vor dem Glanz der Sonne mit einem Augenschirm.	He protected himself against the glare of the sun by an eyeshade.
Ich möchte Sie vor der dringenden Gefahr warnen.	I should like to warn you of the imminent danger.
Da ist man sicher vor jedem Anfall.	There one is safe against every attack.
Er rettete sie vor einem jähen Tod.	He saved her from sudden death.

(*e*) Occasionally *by reason of, for*:

Sie weinte vor Freude.	She was weeping for joy.
Ich starb beinahe vor Angst.	I almost died of fear.
Er war rot vor Zorn und zitterte vor den Folgen seiner Tat.	He was red with anger and trembled at the consequences of his deed.
Der Greis war vor Alter gebückt.[1]	The old man was bent with age.

233. Vor.

2. With the accusative, movement *to* a position *in front of*:

Der Wagen fuhr vor das Haus.	The carriage drove up before the house.
Er trat vor den General hin.	He stepped up to the general.

[1] More usual: Der Greis war vor Alter gebeugt.

Die Polizei brachte den Verbrecher vor Gericht.	The police brought the criminal to trial.
Er wurde vor den Richter geladen.	He was summoned to appear before the judge.

N.B. also:

Er sprach vor sich hin.	He was speaking to himself.

234. Zwischen.

1. With the dative.

(a) Position *between*:

Das Haus zwischen den zwei Pappeln ist zu verkaufen.	The house between the two poplars is for sale.

(b) Movement *in* an area lying *between*:

Die Schildwache ging zwischen den Mauern auf und ab.	The sentry was walking up and down between the walls.

2. **With the accusative,** movement to a place *between*:

Setzen Sie sich zwischen die beiden Knaben.	Sit between the two boys.

235. Strengthening prepositional phrases by addition of other words.

Words, chiefly those otherwise used as separable prefixes (195–96), may be added to a prepositional phrase in order to bring out the meaning of the prepositional phrase.

. . . dessen schöpferische religiöse Kraft durch mehr als ein Jahrtausend hindurch bis heute lebendig geblieben ist.	. . . whose creative religious vigour has remained, for more than a thousand years, active until to-day.
Diese Art Politik war ihnen von jeher verhaßt.	From time immemorial they had detested politics of this kind.
Diese Männer mit ihrem Blick über das Mittelmeer hin. . .	These men with their eyes directed beyond the Mediterranean . . .
Zusammen wollen wir unsrer Stadt aus unseren tiefsten Kräften heraus dienen.	Together we intend to serve our town with our utmost power.
. . ins Blaue hinein.	. . . at random.

XXI. WORD ORDER

236. 1. The inflected verb is the first word in a clause:

(*a*) In simple direct questions:

Iſt Herr Braun zu ſprechen? May I speak to Mr Brown?

(*b*) In direct commands of the first and second persons:

Gib es mir ! Give it to me.

Reichen Sie mir, bitte, die Please pass me the newspaper.
  Zeitung !

Gehen wir ſchnell ! Let us go quickly.

(*But:* Gott bewahre ! God forbid !)(3rd person
  Gott ſei Dank ! Thank God !/imperatives.)

(*c*) In the optative subjunctive (**202**):

O ! wäre ich zu Hauſe Oh! would that I had stayed
  geblieben ! at home!

(*d*) In the rendering of a conditional clause without **wenn**:

Wäre ich König, würde ich If I were king, I would not
  das nicht erlauben. allow that.

NOTE.—Ob or wenn can be omitted from als ob, als wenn with a
similar result:

Er benimmt ſich, als wäre er He is behaving as if he were at
  zu Hauſe. home.

2. In statements which are main clauses the inflected verb is
the second grammatical idea.

The first idea may be:

(*a*) A simple subject. 1 2

  Karl geht ſpazieren.

(*b*) A subject and its attributes.

  Der alte Mann geht ſpazieren.

Der junge Mann, den wir
  jeden Morgen ſehen, geht ſpazieren.

(*c*) An adverb.

  Abends geht er ſpazieren.

(*d*) A phrase.

  Durch die Felder rannten die Kinder

(*e*) The object, direct or indirect.

1　　　　2

Mir　　werden sie nichts geben.

Diesen Menschen　werde ich nie lieben können.

(*f*) A subordinate clause or clauses.

Wenn es nicht regnet

und wenn er Zeit hat,　geht er spazieren.

NOTE.—(i) After a subordinate wenn clause the word so is often inserted before the main clause verb.

Wenn er da gewesen wäre, so hätte er es gewiß getan.

(ii) Aber, nämlich and jedoch may separate subject and verb.

Die Nachtigall jedoch singt in der Nacht.

3. Putting a direct or indirect object before the verb has the effect of **emphasizing** it. This and questions of euphony and sentence balance should be borne in mind when considering word order in German.

4. The **inflected verb** is placed at the **end of subordinate clauses.**

Als er aus dem Zimmer gehen wollte, rief ich ihm zu.	When he was about to go out of the room I called to him.

NOTE.—This rule is broken when the inflected verb is the auxiliary of a modal verb which has a dependent infinitive.

Wir schlugen mit dem Korb hart auf den Strand, nach= dem wir vorher die Ventile hatten aufreißen können.	We struck the shore heavily with our gondola after we had managed to tear open the valves.

But:

Wenn ich gekonnt hätte . . .	If I had been able . . .

The hätte is in a normal position because the modal has no dependent infinitive.

237. The end of the clause. (Rule (4) above overrules any following statements which may seem to conflict with it.)

(*a*) The past participle in a compound tense usually stands at the end of its own clause.

Ich habe ihn nur zweimal gesehen.	I have only seen him twice.

Note.—Poetry and modern usage do not always follow this rule:

Die junge Frau war voraus=gegangen ins Haus.	The young woman had preceded us into the house.

(The student is advised to follow the rule.)

(*b*) The infinitive stands at the end of its clause.

Er wird die Schubertlieder singen.	He will sing the Schubert songs.
Wir haben uns entschlossen, gleich hinzugehen.	We have decided to go at once.

(*c*) Auxiliary infinitives stand after the past participles.

Er wird es gesehen haben.	He will have seen it.
Es wird getötet worden sein.	It will have been killed.
Wir werden gelobt werden.	We shall be praised.

But the modal infinitive or the modal past participle will be last in any case.

Er wird es tun können.	He will be able to do it.
Er hat es bauen wollen.	He has wanted to build it.

(*d*) Of two past participles worden will stand last.

Er ist geliebt worden.	He has been loved.

(*e*) In the simple tenses of a separable verb in main clauses the separable prefix goes to the end of its own clause.

Er sah sie lange an, und ging dann zur nächsten über.	He looked at her for a long time, and then moved on to the next.
(*But:* Er hatte sie lange angesehen.	He had looked at her for a long time.)

238. 5. **Order of objects** after a verb or in a subordinate clause. If two objects, one direct, the other indirect, come together after a verb or in a subordinate clause, the order is determined as follows:

(*a*) If both are nouns: dative before accusative. Er gab dem Kind ein Messer.

(*b*) If one is a pronoun and the other a noun: pronoun before noun. Er gab es dem Kind.

(*c*) If they are both pronouns: accusative before dative. Er gab es ihm.

239. 6. **Order of adverbs.**

If adverbs stand together the order is usually: Time, Place, Manner, Cause, Purpose.

Ich habe heute in der Schule eine Aufführung mit meiner Klasse.	At school to-day I am having a performance of a play by my form.

But here, as elsewhere, normal order may be upset for purposes of **emphasis**; the emphatic positions in a German clause are the beginning and the end.

Another tendency is to have a shorter adverb first despite the order given above:

Er ging schnell ins Rathaus hinein.	He went quickly into the town hall.

240. 7. Position of the **Reflexive Pronoun.**

As this is relatively an unimportant word, in main clauses it usually comes after the inflected verb, and in subordinate clauses after the subject or even before it.

Er hat sich der Burg genähert.	He has approached the castle.
Das Gericht konnte sich nicht zur Auslieferung entschließen.	The court could not decide in favour of extradition.
Er behauptet, er habe gesehen, wie sich der Dieb gebückt habe, um seinen Hut aufzuheben.	He maintains that he saw the thief bending down to pick up his hat.

241. 8. When, in a main clause, the subject follows the verb, a short **object pronoun** may be found standing between verb and subject. The principle seems to be that the longer element seeks the later place.

Mit leuchtenden Augen sah ihm die junge Frau entgegen.	With gleaming eyes the young woman looked towards him.

242. 9. (*a*) zu stands immediately next to the infinitive it controls.

Er war fest entschlossen, sie noch einmal zu sehen.	He had firmly resolved to see her once more.

(b) um in an um . . . zu + infinitive expression stands first.

Ich bin gekommen, um den Armen Hilfe zu bringen.	I have come to bring help to the poor.

243. 10. In reported discourse daß may be omitted; normal order is then observed. (**199** (d). Note ii.)

Er sagt, daß er morgen kommen werde, *or:* Er sagt, er werde morgen kommen.	He says (that) he will come to-morrow.
Wir müßten vorgeben, wir seien zu Fuß gekommen, *or:* daß wir zu Fuß gekommen seien.	We should have to pretend (that) we had come on foot.

INDEX

THE NUMBERS REFER TO SECTIONS, NOT TO PAGES
EXCEPT WHERE OTHERWISE INDICATED

NOTE

1. References to English grammatical terms have the initial letter **capital**, and are in italic; *e.g.*, *Indirect Object*.
2. Many English words and phrases are given where it is felt that translation into German involves idiomatic usage. Such words and phrases are **printed** with the initial letter small; *e.g.*, "warn of."
3. The references to main parts of strong verbs are not given in this index; these main parts will be found arranged alphabetically under 168.

ABBREVIATIONS USED IN THE INDEX

Acc., Accusative Case	*Indef. Art.*, Indefinite Article
Adj., Adjective	*Infin.*, Infinitive
Adv., Adverb	*Part.*, Participle
Dat., Dative Case	*Plur.*, Plural
Decl., Declension, or Declined	*Prep.*, Preposition
Def. Art., Definite Article	*Pres.*, Present
Engl., English	*Sing.*, Singular
Fem., Feminine	*Subj.*, Subjunctive
Gen., Genitive Case	*Vbs.*, Verbs